The Blue Waterfall

When moving forward means acknowledging the past.

Written by CJ Bralt

Copyright Page

The Blue Waterfall © Copyright <<2020>> CJ Bralt

It is not legal to reproduce, duplicate, or transmit any part of this document in either electronic means or printed format. Recording of this publication is strictly prohibited.

Dedication Page

This book is dedicated to my best friend and love of my life, C.M., who supported me through it all.

Also want to thank a wonderful teacher and supporter of my writing, M.S.

Some names and identifying details have been changed to protect the privacy of individuals.

In memory of everyone who passed away but had a lasting impact on my life.

Chapter One

My dad was born in the summer of 1942 in small town Iowa, the first child of his parents. His dad was in the Navy and worked at the local factory. My dad's brother, Donny, was born two years later in 1944. Donny passed away from pneumonia when he was six months old. Shortly thereafter my dad's parents divorced. This was the start to my dad's rough childhood. He moved around to different homes. My understanding is his dad received full legal custody because he had remarried, and they had money. What was never spoken about is why his mother never had any sort of custody and was not allowed to be a part of my dad's life. My dad did not get along very well with his stepmother and stepsister, so he was sent to live with his paternal grandparents who had several children that were right around my dad's age. For a reason that I am unaware of, he did not stay there. He lived with his maternal grandparents as well, who also had children his age. It is my understanding that my dad continued to move back and forth between these three homes. I do not believe my dad was a problem child. Since this was post World War II, I believe the families were all having economic hardships and my dad just got the raw end of the deal. Since he grew up around his aunts and uncles, he was closer to them than he was his own siblings. His dad and stepmom had two more children, a girl and a boy. His mom remarried and had two more children, also a girl and a boy. He was never raised around his mom's other children and was not close to them. My dad had been closest to his sister from his dad. She passed away from injuries sustained from an auto accident in 1968 at the age of nineteen. I was named after her.

My dad had some childhood memories that haunted him. He had memories of being locked in a closet, being threatened with objects, and of brushing a woman's hair. These memories were somewhat blurred. He did not like to talk about them. It was not until the early 1990s, after his motorcycle accident, that these memories became clearer. He changed after that.

My mother was born in the winter of 1944 in Texas. She had two older brothers and a younger sister. Her dad passed away from a heart attack in 1957 after they moved to California. He worked construction and I was told he built several churches in Texas, Washington and California. The last church he built was in Wenatchee, Washington. He was twenty-seven years my grandmother's senior and he had four other children from a previous marriage. My mother and her siblings were not close to, nor did they know, their father's other children until decades after their father passed away. The other children were close in age to my grandmother. After he passed, my grandma Berta took a job in a factory where she later lost a finger from operating machinery. My grandma

Berta never remarried. Her children were sixteen, fifteen, twelve and ten when their father died. Both of my mother's brothers had to get jobs and my mother took babysitting jobs to help my grandma with bills and groceries. My mother was also a majorette for her high school. Last I knew she still had her baton and uniform, including her white boots that we were never allowed to touch. My mother had family all up and down the West Coast and Texas. Along the West Coast is where all my mother's living relatives still reside. My mother did not get along with her mother, her younger sister or one of her brothers. She always boasted about her father though.

My dad went into the Navy in 1959 after getting kicked out of high school. When he was stationed in San Diego, California, and while on one of his furloughs in 1960, he visited relatives that lived out there which is how he met my mother. My mother was babysitting for a family that lived next door to my dad's cousins. My parents became pen pals, which continued for the three years that he was doing his basic training and on the USS Hornet. They were married in the summer of 1963 in California, two months after she graduated from high school. She was eighteen years old; he was twenty-one. Their honeymoon was driving back to Iowa to make a home in my dad's hometown. When they arrived back in his hometown, my dad started working fulltime as an engineer for a large local corporation. His father and a few other relatives also worked in the factory department of this corporation. With the Navy he was able to get his degree in engineering. While on the USS

Hornet, my dad was both a mechanic for the airplanes and a cook in the mess hall.

My parents bought a little two-bedroom post-war Levittown style house in a cookie cutter neighborhood that was less than ten years old. That is where both my older sisters were born. Sue was born in the spring of 1965. Tracy was born in the spring of 1967. There were lots of stories about how Tracy, even though she was younger, picked on and somewhat tortured Sue. Tracy was good at doing something wrong so Sue would be the one to get blamed. That caused tension between them that is continued through to this day. At the same time though, I also heard that Tracy threw huge temper tantrums. I believe she is the only one of us kids that ever did.

Sometime after the flood in 1969, my parents bought their second and current home. An older late 1800s two-story home on a quiet street lined with big spruce trees. Sometime before they purchased it, the house had been updated turning the back porch into a kitchen, bathroom, and main floor bedroom. It was built in the days of out-houses, so it did not have an original bathroom. It had three bedrooms on the second floor. This home is where I would spend my childhood.

My mom did not work outside, or inside, the home for that matter. Since my dad was a Navy Reservist, he went one weekend a month to Chicago to the naval base for training and usually spent two weeks every year in Hawaii for training. When he was not working or doing his Navy training, he was usually out in the garage working on either one of his own vehicles or one of his friend's vehicles. The neighbors and his co-workers were always bringing their vehicles over to be worked on or at least have my dad diagnose the problem. My dad had an extended, double car, heated, attached garage with more tools than most mechanic shops. I believe he inherited tools from his late grandparents because some of the tools looked ancient. The neighbors and co-workers would usually pay him with a case or two of beer, which my mother did not like. The vehicle owners and the neighbors would stay in the garage to drink with my dad while he worked on the vehicles. My dad was a very social person and seemed to have a lot of friends, even though later he states that he was not a people person. It was my mother that did not seem to have any friends, and no one ever came over to visit with her like they did my dad. I was told my dad used to be a smoker until after Tracy was born, then Mother made him quit. Mother tried for years to get him to quit drinking and attend church services with her. Neither of those happened until my late teen years when my dad quit drinking due to a head injury, he sustained from a motorcycle accident.

Another pastime of my dad's that I remember is him sitting in his recliner reading a thick war novel while watching football, a war related television show or a movie. I could never figure out how he could pay attention to the television and read his novels at the same time. My dad also enjoyed motorcycle riding. He would take us for rides quite a bit. Sometimes it was just down the alley and back since Mother did not really approve of that either.

My mother's pastimes? Let's see, she did not cook other than liver and onions which, thank goodness, she only made for her and my dad. Those were the nights that us kids had to 'fend for ourselves' which was perfectly fine with me. She did not clean. Her story was that she cleaned all the time and kept the house spotless until the flood of 1969 devastated their first home. She said after that she did not see the point of keeping a meticulous house when it could all be taken away in the blink of an eye. They did fix the damage done and it has been their rental house since they moved into their current home. Mother did attend church on a regular basis and read her Bible every day. I do not have a lot to say about my mother's hobbies or likes. I do not recall anything else my mother did.

For most of my early years, the story was that there was a miscarriage between Tracy and me. That was why there were six years between us. It was when I was pregnant with my third child that the story turned into two miscarriages between Tracy and me. My mother had mentioned how my pregnancies were like hers and let me know that a miscarriage was a possibility. My dad is the one that piped up stating that she had two miscarriages instead of one. That has always kind of bothered me. I do not know if the miscarriages affected my dad more than my mother or if there was more going on.

In early 1973, I was the third child born to my parents. My sisters were six and eight years older than me. I spent a lot of my childhood in the doctor's office. I was told that I was a very sick baby born with all kinds of health issues. Apparently, I had allergies to almost everything and was colicky. I have been told that my dad was the only one that could ever calm me down. He says he used to walk the floor with me at all hours of the night because I would not calm down for anyone else, not even my mother. I was told that I was allergic to breast milk and formula, so I was placed on 'special' milk until I was twelve years old. The stories were that I was born with deformities with no known causes. My parents said that my brain was tilted to one side of my head which caused my neck muscles to be underdeveloped. The stories were that I could not hold my head up until I was about three years of age. Since I could not hold my head up it caused balance issues so I could not crawl or walk until close to three years of age. I can only go by what I have heard because I have never seen photos of myself prior to the age of four. For whatever reason my parents stated that the doctors did not believe that I would live past the age of three either. I also had hearing loss due to a deformity in both of my inner ears.

Three years after I was born, near the end of 1976, came their first and only son. The stories that I remember hearing were that my parents only wanted three children. It was said that when they found out that I was sick and was not supposed to live past the age of three, they decided to have my brother. He was born exactly six months after my third birthday. At the least, my mother and Tracy were not happy when I continued to live. My dad, at least for the first few years, did seem happy that I was still alive.

Tracy was not a nice sister. Even though she hated me and made that quite clear, I still for some reason looked up to her.

As an adult I wonder if it could possibly be that I feared her more than anything else. I know that she was angry about me being a girl. The story that I heard was that when my mother was pregnant, Tracy told her kindergarten teacher that her mom was pregnant with a baby brother. The story is that she got into trouble with that teacher for lying. My mother did not look pregnant which is part of the reason the teacher did not believe my sister. Once I was born, though, the teacher refused to apologize to my sister because she was still incorrect about me being a little brother. Those were back in the days when teachers and principals could use yard sticks on their students for punishment. My sister continued to blame me for decades for her getting into trouble.

My paternal great-grandma Ivy moved a half a block to the north of our house just before my brother was born. My dad's birth mother, Vera, lived a block and a half to the south. My great-grandma Ivy took care of us kids until I was eight years old. She did the cooking and gardening, she walked with us to the corner market, and she played kick-the-can, among other games, with all the neighborhood kids. If it were not for her I would probably have never met my dad's mother. Even though she lived close, my dad did not visit his own mother or talk to her. Great-grandma Ivy would walk us down the alley to visit my grandma Vera. Sometimes my dad would help my grandma Ivy in the garden and sometimes he would cook dinner. He usually cooked big pots of chili, goulash, or stew since he was used to cooking for the Navy crew when he was on the

USS Hornet. We would visit some extended family and sometimes they would come to visit us. My favorite place to go was to visit my great-great-aunt Vesta, my great-grandmother Ivy's sister, in the nursing home. When my great-uncle Vern and his family would come up from Arizona, we would put tents up in our yard. Great-uncle Vern's kids were a few years older than me, so they hung out more with my sisters. I became close with my dad's cousin who was my age. Matt was the son of my great-aunt Virginia. Great-uncle Vern and Aunt Virginia were my dad's maternal uncle and aunt. They were all around the same age, though, and were raised together on the farm. My great-grandparents lived and worked on a farm outside of town until Great Grandpa passed away when I was three. That is when Great-grandma Ivy moved to the apartment down the street to the north of us.

We traveled a lot. Dad had made many friends while in the Navy and they were scattered around the United States. We also visited some of my mother's family. I remember visiting a family in Ohio who had two daughters that were my sisters' ages. There was a family in Arizona with a daughter that was a little older than me. I do remember her being a little mean even though I do not remember any details to back up my feelings. We went once a year down to Texas to visit with a few of my mother's relatives. We always stayed at my mom's aunt and uncle's where we would play in their leaves, push wheel barrels, and lay on the ground watching the jets fly overhead. One year we drove out to the East Coast to visit my mother's aunt. These trips were good times. Everyone seemed to get along and we seemed to be a family. It was on these trips that I kind of became mesmerized by the semi-trucks that we passed. My dad taught my brother and me that if we put our arm up and moved our arms like we were pulling a horn that the drivers would blow their horns for us. We also went out to California to visit relatives of my dad's that lived out there as well as Mother's family. It seemed like we went on these trips quite often in my younger years, then slowly became less often. The last trip we went on as a family was probably when I was thirteen or fourteen years old, but Sue was not with us. Not sure why they slowed down and then eventually discontinued.

There are all kinds of stories of how my mother treated my siblings. I will tell a few just to set the stage a little for my own experiences with her. Tracy was known for her many temper tantrums as mentioned earlier; Mother would throw hot water on her to get her to stop. Obviously, it was not boiling since she did not have burn scars and Mother was never charged but I heard it was more than room temperature. I believe it was when she was in middle school, that a teacher noticed marks on Tracy. Believing that they were from the hands of our father, the school called Mother in to discuss their concerns. Tracy told me that she was more scared of our mother than the school, so when Mother was in the office with her, she did not let the school know how she really got the marks. Instead, Mother made an excuse of Tracy falling. My oldest sister, Sue, got pregnant at seventeen so my parents sent her away until she had the baby and she gave him up for adoption. It was more about how it made my mother look rather than what was best for Sue and the baby. I remember how depressed Sue was when she came back. She was not herself anymore.

We three girls did all the house cleaning with help from Great-Grandma Ivy when she was at our house. My mother spent a lot of time at the table with mounds of papers in front of her. She always said she was either writing letters or paying bills. I did not think anything of it when I was a kid, but as an adult it does not make sense. I cannot figure out how it took her several hours a day, every day of the year to pay bills. I take about an hour a month to pay mine. She spent the rest of her days in bed. Usually stating that she was not feeling well. Again, as a kid, I did not think twice about it. As an adult, though, especially after getting my Psychology degree, I would guess that she was depressed and or going through a mid-life crisis.

For as long as I can remember, my mother has continuously reminded me that my head is crooked, and my ears stick out. One time she even explained to me that my whole body was not symmetrical, that it was like I was two people combined into one. No matter how old I was, she was always fixing my hair to cover my ears. If I tucked my hair behind my ears, she would reach over to pull it back out and fluff it over my ears. If I put my hair up in a ponytail, she would take it down and tell me that I should not wear ponytails because of my crooked head and big ears. This continued into my adult years after I, myself, became a parent.

I do remember that I was quite sick and on dozens of daily medications which I cannot name. I have no idea what medications my mother administered to me each day. I have since tried to find out. My sisters have no idea what the medications were; they just remember me being sick and a lot of changes were made around the house to accommodate. The family friends and other older relatives do not recall what medications, just that I was very sick. I continued to have health problems until close to my teenage years. I missed more school than I attended and was at the doctor's office more than I was in school. My mother was always the one at these appointments with me. She told the doctors my 'symptoms' and they talked to her about the concerns instead of me. One of the doctors had such a heavy Asian accent that, combined with my hearing loss, I could never understand him anyway. I had thought that was the reasoning for him always speaking to my mother instead of me.

Since I was sick a lot, I did not get to go outside much. I would sit on the steps that lead to the house from the garage to watch my dad tinker with cars or whatever he was fixing. I would watch my siblings playing with the neighbor kids through the front porch windows. When I was able to go outside, I usually played with the youngest two Erickson boys from across the street and the granddaughter of the family two doors to the south. The Erickson's had five children. Age wise, I was right between the third and fourth children, but was always closest to the fourth child, Michael. Michael was my first ever best friend and am still friends with him today. I do have a lot of memories of being outside or playing, but they were not as often as it may seem. They were the best days of my childhood, so they seem to stand out more. Sometimes I would pretend to feel well, so I could go play and sometimes even just to go to school. Since becoming an adult, I have noticed a pattern to my illnesses. I seem to have been the sickest when I had the most contact with my mother.

Chapter Two

My first ever memory was when I was about three years old, being scared and locked in a small bathroom. My memory is of a small room with dark pink walls, a sink that came to the top of my head, and a sliding wooden door that retracted into the wall. I do not remember crying or what I may have been saying, but I do remember trying to get help. Once the door became unlocked, all I see is my mother standing in the doorway, very angry, a look of hatred on her face. A look that still haunts me to this day. Her hair was straight black and a little longer than shoulder length. She did not have eyeglasses on her face. Other than this specific memory, I do not recall ever seeing her hair that straight and long or her without eyeglasses. I do not remember what she said to me, but I do know that I was in huge trouble for locking myself in my grandmother's bathroom. I also know that this was probably one of the first times I realized that I was scared to death of this woman. My fear of being trapped in this little bathroom was nothing compared to the fear I felt of her.

The best memory that I have of my mother is ironically a devastating circumstance that forced me to learn about mortality. I had just turned eight years old a couple weeks prior. My mother called my brother and me into the kitchen. She knelt on one knee so that she was somewhat eye level with us, told us that our great-grandmother Ivy had passed away, and gave us a quick hug. This was the same great-grandmother that lived five houses north of us on the same street. She had been very involved with us pretty much daily, so we took it quite hard. She was very active for being in her 80's so that was also a shock.

My mother had been going with my dad on his Chicago weekends while we stayed with Great-Grandma Ivy, but that all ended when she passed away. My brother and I started going on the weekend trips to Chicago, usually during the summer or when there was no school on a Friday. We always stayed in the same hotel, which had an attached restaurant. My brother and I would get the same thing to eat every time, so the waiter got to know our 'usuals'. Our usuals were pancakes and chocolate milk. My brother always had the chocolate chip pancakes though. I always felt good on the trips, so I do not think Mother gave me my medicines while in the hotel. There was also an outside pool that we could swim in. My brother and I would play tag or Marco polo. When we did not get to go to Chicago, we would spend the weekend with one of two church families. They both had children that were a few years older than me, but we had fun at these homes. These are some of the other experiences where I was able to witness a different kind of family dynamic than what my family had. One of the families lived in the country with lots of animals. I loved riding their horses, playing with the dogs and chasing the cats. I was told that I was riding these horses before I could even walk. I usually wanted to play with the cats, but they were wild farm cats who were not used to being held. I was one of those kiddos that would try to force the kitties to let me hold them like babies. The other family was on a lake, so during the spring and summer we would swim there. In the winter we would ice skate on that same lake. That home also had lots of jars full of candy around the house and the mom loved to bake a lot of goodies. This home is where I learned about soft rock music. The daughter would play records of Air Supply and Chicago in her bedroom. I have loved these bands ever since.

    My mother was the Girl Scout leader at my elementary school. She had been the leader since my older sisters were involved. I remember selling Girl Scout Cookies and how much I enjoyed being outside interacting with the neighbors. I also loved every summer that I was able to go to Girl Scout Camp. I was never sick at Camp and I met many amazing people. I am still in contact with a girl that I met my first summer there. After that first summer, Sarah and I planned every other summer so that we were at the same camp at the same time sharing the same tent or cabin. Her family accepted me into theirs quickly. I felt so much love in that family. I had never experienced that with my own family. I saw something close to it with extended family, but it felt very different. My mother was voted out as Girl Scout leader a couple years after I joined. I knew a lot of the girls did not like my mother, but there was something that had apparently happened. I was told by one of the girls a few years later that even some of their mothers had an issue with my mother. Anyway, once she was no longer the Girl Scout leader, she became the Boy Scout leader for a year or two while my brother was a scout.

I spent a lot of my early childhood years close to my father. He always took me fishing and called me his good luck charm. He took me on a lot of motorcycle rides. My mother drove a motorcycle also, but I never rode with her, my brother always did. My dad and I did projects together. He had pneumonia for about six months when I was about four. I was told that I did not like it after he got better because he went back to work. I was also told that I never left his side while he was home sick.

My dad's two weeks in Hawaii for his Navy duties was usually in March, which is my birth month. For most of my childhood years, since he was away, I would receive a postcard from him for my birthday. My dad also tried to play with us kids by tickling us in a wrestling form on the floor. He would tickle us until we could not breathe from laughing so hard. He had long thick fingernails, but I do not remember it hurting or any of us getting scratched. It was fun, it was a bonding we all shared with our dad. I do remember my mother always yelling at him to stop. I never remember my mother ever playing with us. I never saw her dance. I do not even remember her ever being happy. She always seemed angry about something or everything. The only time that I ever heard my mother sing was to the hymns at church. She acted totally different out in public than she did at home. At church, she would smile and seemed like she enjoyed people. She was even nice to us kids. Once we would leave the church though, the smile would go away, and she would complain about everyone at church. I felt like she thought she was better than everyone else and that she could do no wrong.

From as early as I can remember all the way through my teen years, I remember my dad consistently trying to give affection to my mother. My dad would pat her on the rear or rub her back or shoulders. If she was standing, he would go up behind her and put his arms around her like a hug. He would kiss her on the forehead or cheeks. It was always quick, not a lingering 'petting' like he was wanting something in return. My mother's reaction was always getting mad at him and yelling that all he ever wanted from her was sex. I do not remember any conversation, per se, but it was ingrained in me, for life, that sex was bad.

We switched around to several different churches. Any time Mother either disagreed with someone or the pastor, we would start attending a new church. She would read and highlight passages in her Bible, but whenever she was volunteering to be a Sunday School teacher, she always asked my dad where to find such and such in the Bible. That was the funny thing, I have never seen my dad even touch a Bible, but he had the whole book memorized. Anyone could read him a passage and he would tell them which book, chapter and verse that it was. Anyone could give him a book, chapter, and verse and he would recite it as if it were in front of him. Whereas, like I said, my mother had her face in the Bible on a regular basis but could not recite by memory like my dad could.

Since I missed a lot of school, I did not have a lot of friends. I was made fun of for the clothes I wore because my hand-me-downs were not always the 'in' thing. I was teased for being the only girl in my class without her ears pierced. I was quiet, shy, and kept to myself. I followed every rule to a T because for some reason I was always afraid of getting into trouble. I was probably more scared of my mother if she found out than whatever the actual consequence would have been. Though, I have continued to be that way through my adult years as well and I still cannot please my mother. For a period of time, I tried to learn to pee standing up. In my child brain I thought that it would somehow turn me into a boy so that my mother would love me. It was not until decades later that I realized nothing I ever did was ever going to be good enough nor was she ever going to love me.

When I was eight or nine years old, I found a pearl-looking necklace on the playground at school. I gave it to the teacher on recess duty. This teacher told me that she would put it in the lost and found. I do not remember if it was a couple of weeks or a couple of months later, but this same teacher called me to the office to tell me that the necklace was never claimed so I could keep it. I was so excited that I wore it home and could not wait to tell my family. Instead of being happy for me, my mother accused me of stealing the necklace from her jewelry box. I remember telling her to call Mrs. Hunt at the school to verify my story, but I do not think that she ever did. When my dad came home, she proceeded to tell him that I stole it out of her jewelry box, so I was punished a second time for something that I did not do. This was the first time I ever even heard about her having a jewelry box and have still to this day never seen her jewelry box. I am assuming that she either never called the school or just decided not to give it back or apologize to me. I never heard about or saw that necklace again.

One evening, all of us kids were called to the living room. I do not remember what was said or what we were getting in trouble for, but I do clearly remember that something had happened. Mother was on one of her angry rampages. No one was admitting the blame for whatever is was, so we were all punished except for my brother. My sisters and I were lined up against the wall, facing the wall, while my brother was sitting on the floor behind me. My mother took my dad's belt and whipped all three of us girls at the same time. Now remember the fact that my sisters are much older than I, their bottoms were about even with the middle of my back. My back is where that belt hit me. I still to this day do not know what we got in trouble for or who was the real culprit. That is one of the things that I made sure never to do to my own children.

When any of us wanted something, like to walk up to the corner store, or to go play with friends, etc., we would always ask Mother because we knew she was the boss of the household. She would always tell us to go ask Dad, then he would send us back to her to ask again. This would continue for several times before my dad would finally give in and say yes. He always said yes. Then he would get the third degree from Mother for not saying no. Since I was hardly let out of the house, most of these situations were what I witnessed with my sisters. Mother would wait until after my sisters had already gone before she would start yelling at Dad. I remember her saying something about him always making her the bad guy and him needing to learn to say no. I always remember him saying something about if she wanted the answer to be no then she should just tell us kids no instead of sending us back and forth.

My dad would sometimes watch shows like *Dukes of Hazard*, *Smoky and the Bandit*, and *Every Which Way but Loose*. They all showed how friendly and helpful truck drivers were. During my teen years, I was trying to figure out what I wanted to be when I grew up. I thought being a truck driver would be cool. I could travel, help people, and honk my horn for kiddos in passing cars. I do not remember how or why the conversation came up, but I do remember my mother telling me that I could not be a truck driver because I was too small. I also threw around the idea of being a teacher. I remember seeing houses that looked abandoned or neglected while we traveled. Even at ten years old I would imagine what those houses looked like and how I would fix them up. That was before I knew that flipping houses was an actual job. I would kind of do the same thing in the doctor's office. I would imagine how I would turn the doctor's office into a bunch of apartments for the homeless or low-income families.

Things kind of went downhill from the time Great-grandma Ivy passed on. First was her passing away. She was pretty much our primary caretaker. Then my oldest sister moved out of the house. Sue and I were not close, but dealings with mother were less buffered with one less child in the house. The Erickson's moved to Minnesota, which was almost as devastating as losing Great-grandma Ivy. At the age of ten, I made my last craft project with my dad. We made a four-legged wooden stool. There is at least one picture of us in the process of staining it. I was wearing a yellow sweatshirt. I still have this stool and cherish it. Around the age of twelve, I overheard a conversation in the kitchen between my mother and dad. She told him that I was getting to the age where he could get into trouble for spending too much time with me. At the time I did not understand. Now as an adult, I can only assume. The tension in the house became hard to live with and it was very lonely. I felt like my brother was all I had left and that was only sometimes. The motorcycle rides stopped, the fishing trips stopped, the tickling from my dad stopped, and he just seemed to stay away from me. He seemed to stay away from everyone. Our relationship became just me watching him, from a distance, while he worked on cars in the garage.

    Tracy was now old enough to watch my brother and me while our parents went to Chicago, so our trips also slowed down. Whether my parents were home or not we always had to go wherever my sister was going. There were times she took us to work with her and we would be busboys clearing all the tables. We tagged along when she hung out with her friends, when she went shopping, when she went to football games, and when she went to work. I do remember her being upset that she had to be the parent to her younger siblings. Tracy always treated my brother better than she did me though. Whenever I had to go with her or wanted to go wherever she was going, Tracy would make me change my clothes and fix my hair how she wanted it done. She was very judgmental and critical of everything that pertained to me.

Since Tracy was so much older than me, she was able to get a job and drive a car. I remember her buying Kellogg's Froot Loops cereal, red licorice, and many other goodies. My mother did not buy these foods, so Tracy kept these in her bedroom and did not share. She also bought herself a lot of her own clothes. Being the third girl, all my clothes were hand-me-downs from my sisters and my cousins. I was always intrigued with what Tracy bought and would sit in the doorway to her bedroom while she went through her most recent shopping purchases. One day she purchased these dark beige, single-strapped, open toed, open back, wooden high heels that I just adored. They were better than candy in my eyes. While she was out of her room, I snuck into her room to try on those high heels to experience how it felt to wear them. She walked in and scolded me to high heavens, barred me from her room, and told me how ridiculous I looked in high heels. Now being a ten or eleven-year-old girl, I probably did look a little silly being in high heels that were several sizes too big, but even in my adult years, she continued to remind me that I "could not pull off high heels."

Every little girl has a dream of finding true love in a prince charming and living happily ever after. Me? Even at ten years of age, I just dreamt of being loved, having a big family, and being an old lady surrounded by tons of kids and grandkids. I wanted fifteen of my own kids. Marriage and having a husband were not in my dreams. At the time, I did not know that sex was required to make children. I did not want to get married and did not want any part of sex. Extended family had always been important to me. As a child I kept in contact with my paternal grandmother who was estranged from my father. I was very close to my maternal aunt who had a strained relationship with my mother. Learning my genealogy was also a pastime that I shared with my paternal great aunt. I enjoyed any time that I had with any relative; whether it be a sibling, my dad, grandparent, aunt, uncle, or cousin.

My entire childhood was sheltered. I had allergies to everything. My parents had to special order food from Oregon that looked and tasted like plastic. I was on dozens of daily pills. I had iron and calcium deficiencies as well as other issues. My mother said I was allergic to animal dander. This included cats, dogs, horses, etc. She said that was why my legs would break out after riding a horse, or why my eyes watered from being around the cat and dog. I grew up around animals. My parents always had cats and dogs. I am not complaining. I love animals and am glad that I grew up with them, but people always ask if I was allergic, then why did we have pets. I have never been able to answer that question.

I was also born with significant hearing loss due to a birth deformity. There are three bones that everyone is supposed to have in order to hear properly; they are the Incus, Stapes, and Malleus. I was born with only one and a half of those bones in each ear. I did not have the Incus at all in either ear. That is the middle bone that connects the other two. I was born with only part of the Stapes bone, which is the most inner bone. I did, however, have the entire Malleus in both ears, which is the outer bone. I had two surgeries on my right ear when I was eleven and then again at age twelve to insert a prosthesis to mirror the functions of my missing bones. Neither of these procedures were successful. I continued to have several ear infections a year through to my adult years and was told that I would be completely deaf by the time I was twenty-five years old. Even though my hearing has deteriorated, I do still have some hearing and received hearing aids for the first time when I was forty-one years old. Now I am finally trying to learn sign language. To my knowledge no one ever offered or discussed the possibility of my family needing to learn sign language, even though the continued increase in deafness was inevitable.

I had my first ear surgery around Thanksgiving of my sixth-grade year. It was inserting a prosthesis into my ear that represented my missing bones. I was in band and played the clarinet. When I returned to school, I was in the band room. I do not remember if it was class time or if I was in there to ask what to work on since I had been gone a few days. I remember a specific girl was in the room. There was some sort of altercation between her and me to where she ended up hitting me in the head with my clarinet case just as our band instructor walked into the room. The jolt from getting hit knocked my prosthesis out of place.

The following year, again right around Thanksgiving, I had my second surgery to do the same thing. The doctor took the previous one out since it had been sitting in the bottom of my ear canal for a year. He put in a new prosthesis that was a hair bigger so that maybe it would not loosen. When I returned to school, my PE class was doing swimming in class. I had a note from my doctor that I was not to participate in swimming due to just having surgery. I did not dress in my PE clothes and sat on the bleachers of the pool area so that I was still able to watch and listen to the teacher. My PE teacher was mad that I did not dress out and lectured me in front of the entire class before she threw me into the pool fully clothed. I was then sent to the principal's office.

I sat in the principal's office dripping wet until my mother came in. She was in the office with the principal, so I do not know what all was said or how my mother handled the situation. When she came out, she just said to me "let's go" and we left the school. I do not know if it was a few days or weeks, but there was a meeting at the superintendent's office with both my parents and the school board. All I remember is that I was transferred to another school while that PE teacher continued to teach until she retired, which was at least two more decades after this incident.

Around twelve-thirteen years old, while in sixth grade, a classmate was wanting to taste my 'special milk' so I tasted her 2% milk that the school provided. She liked my special milk and I liked the regular milk. I did not have a reaction to it, so this became our new daily lunch ritual. Since I was not reacting to the regular milk, I started rebelling against my medicines and about being confined inside the house as well. I did not feel comfortable or like being around my mother. She did not work outside the home, which made it quite unbearable to never have time away from her. I remember a few times, not feeling well, but I tried to act like I was fine so that I could go to school anyway. I remember my mother telling me that she knew I did not feel good because my complexion was a pale grayish color. Sometimes I went to school anyway. I started hiding my medicine instead of taking them. I would put them in the couch cushions, in the heater vents, down the toilet, and anywhere else that I could stash them. After a few months of not taking my medicines, I started to feel 'normal'. I was not sick and felt the best that I had ever felt. Instead of being happy and relieved that I was not sick anymore and no longer needing these medications, my mother became very angry with me. According to my mother, the doctor stated that sometimes this happens due to the hormonal changes of puberty, but that the allergies and illnesses would eventually reappear. I am in my late forties now and have yet to see them return. As an adult with a little more education under my belt, I have often wondered if my mother suffers from Munchausen Syndrome by proxy.

Chapter Three

My mom found a pack of red Marlboro brand cigarettes somewhere in the house. While standing in the middle of the kitchen she berated me on my smoking, then walked me into the bathroom that was just off the kitchen to make me watch while she broke and flushed them down the toilet. Mother did not believe me that they were not mine. I was about eleven years old at the time and really did not know whose cigarettes they were until I got yelled at by Tracy for Mother finding her cigarettes. Since she accused me of already being a smoker, I decided to ask one of Tracy's friends to teach me how to smoke. My mindset was if I am going to get accused of smoking, I might as well see what the fuss is about. I continued to smoke for the next fourteen years.

Now I was not always an innocent child. I did more than just rebel against my daily medicines and start smoking. I wanted to learn how to drive so that I could find a way to leave home. My parents were in Chicago, so Tracy was watching my brother and me. She was not paying attention, so I went outside and got into my mother's brown Pontiac. I started the car, put it into gear and started moving. The problem was that I did not know which pedal was the gas pedal and which was the brake, so I did not press either but was still moving in the driveway. When I got close to the garage, I switched into reverse and then when I got close to the alley at the end of the driveway, I would put it back in drive. Tracy came out of the house screaming at me about being an idiot and told me which pedal the brake was, but not before I dented the garage door. She supposedly covered for me and told our parents that she accidentally dented the garage door, but Mom was angry at me for the dent once they got home.

    Since I stopped taking my medications and started to become healthy, the tension between my mother and me grew severely intense. My brother could watch whatever he wanted on television and play outside or with friends whenever he wanted. I had the household chores to do as well as my homework. By this time, both of my sisters had moved out of the home. My mother spent most of her time in her bedroom. To my knowledge, she was always napping. Again, with educating myself as an adult, I now wonder if she was depressed. My father was still employed full time at his engineering job. When he was home, he was either in his chair watching television and reading his novels or in the garage working on cars. There was not much interaction with anyone. My mother still did not cook, so my brother and I usually did the fend-for-ourselves kind of thing. This was great for me since I was finally able to eat the foods that I once could not eat due to alleged allergies. I was not allowed to leave the house except to go to school and church though. When I wanted to go for a walk or take the dog for a walk, my brother was always instructed to go with me IF my mother gave in and let me venture.

My favorite television shows were *The Brady Bunch*, *Eight is Enough*, and *The Walton's*. I think I liked them because they showed loving, helpful families that kind of filled a little bit of the hole I felt. Everyone always said that was just make-believe, they were just shows for Hollywood. I still did not really know that my family was not normal. I do believe these shows helped me to be the mom that I became. I tried the best I could to raise my kiddos like those shows had taught me. I did not have a motherly role model other than these shows and the church families we spent time with. Where I failed as a parent was not keeping toxic people out of the lives of my children and myself. I also did not choose good fathers for my children. I married according to what I saw with my parents, not what I saw on television. I also married to please my mother, not because I wanted to be married.

My mother was very judgmental and critical of everything and everyone. I am sure that is where Tracy learned her behavior. My mother claimed to be a Christian lady, raised in a Southern Baptist home, but she was a huge gossiper, backstabber, and liar. She behaved one way in public and totally opposite behind closed doors. I never heard her say a kind word about anyone other than her deceased father. She seemed to be full of hate. She complained about our neighbors, everyone who attended our church, all her relatives, all my father's relatives, my father, and all of us kids.

One day as we were driving past a tennis court (I was in my early teens), my mother told me that it was our (my father and us kids') fault that she never was able to pursue her dream of being a professional tennis player. As a child I did not think anything of it, but I realize that in all my forty-seven years, I have never once known of anytime that she has ever played tennis or even held a racquet. Somewhere around this same time, a brother of one of her high school friends was going through a divorce. I remember she looked sad like she felt bad for the guy, but she also made the comment that he was the one she should have married. I have never said anything about that because there was never anything to say. I just never forgot it.

The older I got the more I seemed to notice things. I always knew that my mother was two different people around our town, one way in public and another behind closed doors. I did not quite understand why she acted the way she did, but I did know that I felt like she was fake. I knew right away that I did not want to be like her, so I have tried very hard my entire life to be the opposite of her. I noticed that around our town she would dress almost like she was homeless. My dad made good money for that time period so there was no reason she needed to dress like that. She would also go to the free clothing drives to get her clothes. Those are the places that are usually church volunteers who drive for clothes to be donated to help the poor. This one church had free clothing for people trying to get jobs but could not afford decent clothes to go to an interview in. My mother would shop there. She did not work, was not going to find work, and my dad made plenty of money for her to buy clothes if she needed. She also admitted to dumpster diving for clothes and food. Besides, a few of us have caught her digging through the neighbor's garbage. She had a few nice clothes in her closet that she hardly ever wore. In my teen years I noticed that these nice clothes are the ones she takes on vacations, especially to visit her relatives. I felt like she wanted everyone in our hometown to think we were needy and poor when we were not and that she wanted her family to think we were well off, maybe more so than we actually were. I am not sure though since I have never talked to her about this strange behavior. I just know that no matter how much money troubles I was having, I tried not to let others know, and I have always worn decent clothes all the time. I still get many hand-me-downs from friends, but they are nice clothes.

In my early teens, my hair was so long that it reached the back of my knees. In school, when I was sitting at a desk, kids would walk on my hair and they would try to tie pencils and pens in it. I would find spitballs in it. I was a teenager whose Mom had to help wash my hair. My mother did not allow me to get my hair cut. I asked many times for at least a year with no success in getting her to change her mind. So, when I was in ninth grade, I took a pair of scissors into the girls' restroom at school and chopped my hair off at just about shoulder length. When I got home from school and she saw what I had done, she was livid. She called me the devil child and when she started to use curse words, she blamed it on my behaviors.

When I was about fourteen, I was sitting at the dining room table doing my homework. My mom yelled at me for not getting the dishes done. I do remember stating that I was trying to get my homework done first, but do not remember anything else about a conversation. My mom yanked me out of the chair and started swinging at me. I put my arms up to block her swings, but she would not stop. She then shoved me into the wall so hard that it took my breath away and I slid down the wall until I was in a sitting position on the floor. Later, I realized that when I hit the wall, the light switch hit the middle of my back leaving an imprint. I was wearing the shirt that my maternal grandmother Berta bought me for my birthday. It was new just for me, instead of my usual hand-me-downs, it was a navy-blue sweatshirt with black and white designs, white ribbing around the neck, sleeves and waistband, and it had three-quarter sleeves. When I was finally able to stand up, I realized the seam on my right shoulder was ripped. I was more upset about my shirt getting ripped than the physical altercation itself. I did not report or talk about this to anyone due to embarrassment. Besides, since this was normal behavior in our house, I assumed this was how it was in everyone's homes.

For as long as I can remember, I never felt like I belonged in this family. All I ever felt from my mother and Tracy was hatred. I felt inadequate and worthless. I felt like I had lost my only parent, my dad, when I was twelve. Even though he was still around and was still married to my mother, he kept his distance like he was not allowed to love me. I felt somewhat close to my brother, but he never saved me from the wrath of my mother. My brother was younger than me. I do not think he quite understood either. Eventually years later, once all of us girls were out of the home, he had his own experiences with the physical violence from our mother.

In my teens, I lied to classmates about who I was. I was looking for acceptance anywhere that I could get it. I told people that I was adopted and that this was my foster family. I told people that I had a twin and my real family lived in California. I know that was not the right way to deal with things and I greatly wish I had handled that differently. I was a teenager just wanting to be loved and belong somewhere. I had no one to talk to, I did not even know that my home life was that different from anyone else's, but I also did not know how others handled their unbearable home lives. The problem was most of these classmates had known me for most of my life and they knew I looked like my sisters. This ended up giving me a not-so-good reputation at school.

The summer between ninth and tenth grade, I ran away from home on two separate occasions. I already felt unwanted at home and the physical altercation with my mother just made it that much clearer that I was not wanted. Then I made it difficult and awkward at school, which had been my safe haven for most of my life. The first attempt, I snuck out in the middle of the night, lugging about half my bedroom and heading west. I took so many belongings that I would carry some of it about a half a block or so and go back to get the rest. I would walk that load about a half block past my first load, set it down and go back for the first load. Needless to say, it took me twice as long to get anywhere. I was almost to the edge of town when a police officer pulled up next to me. He took me to the police station since I was refusing to tell him where I lived. Anyway, my parents came to pick me up and the officers sent me home with them. I obviously had to change my course of action. The next time I ran away was still in the middle of the night but without luggage. We lived a half block from the cemetery, so I walked down to the cemetery, slept for a few hours and then walked myself up to the police station. I told them that I did not want to live with my mother and that if they sent me back home, I would just run away again.

They finally decided to listen and put me in a shelter. I loved it there! The first time ever that I felt like I really belonged somewhere. I felt free and felt like someone did care about me. While at the shelter, I pierced my own ears with a tack and some ice cubes. I had been asking my parents since third grade to pierce my ears without success. After two months in the shelter, though, they returned me to my parents since they really did not have any reason to keep me. Shelters were for kiddos with either behavioral issues or home lives where the parents were in legal trouble. At that time, I did not fit either criteria. By the time I was returned to my parents, tenth grade had started, and I did not want to run away during the school year. I still loved school.

My mother was just as livid over my ears being pierced as she was when I had cut my hair. She decided to put me in individual therapy with a Christian counselor. He had a Doctor title and shared the same family name as my mother's maiden name so I think she thought they could have been distant relatives. I remember him explaining the confidentiality of therapy, that legally he could not tell my parents anything that we talked about. I do not remember much that I may or may not have told him. The only thing I do remember is that we talked about my lack of a relationship with my mother and the conversation that I overheard between my parents when I was about twelve. I remember his response clearly because it is something that has been repeated by several of my other counselors over the years. He said that when people have traumatic childhood experiences usually later on in life certain things can trigger the memories, behaviors or feelings. He continued saying that he was not my mother's counselor, therefore could not explain why she handled things this way or that way but did say that he could see some parallels. My mother was the third of four children, I was the third of four children. From stories that I heard, she was close to her father, and I had been close to mine. She lost her father when she was twelve, she put a wedge between my father and me when I was twelve. I remember him saying that it could be a variety of reasons: my turning twelve could have brought her feelings of loss to the surface, something more traumatic could have happened to her around her father's death, the possibility of her father being accused of being inappropriate towards her, or someone else had been inappropriate with her after or around his death.

During tenth grade I got a school boyfriend, Dave. Since my parents' rules were no dating until age sixteen, I could only see him at school. He was what I thought would be the opposite of what my mother would approve of. Dave was tall, skinny, brown haired, brown-eyed, smoked cigarettes, had a full beard, had prison looking tattoos, piercings, wore holey jeans, used more curse words than I had ever heard before, and the list went on. My mother did see him one day when she picked me up from school. She made the comment that he was no good and that I should stay clear of him. Obviously, that fueled my desire to continue to be with him. I turned sixteen before the end of tenth grade but was still not allowed to date. Before school was out, Dave gave me this turquoise unicorn ring as a promise ring and told me not to forget him over the summer. He also asked if I would marry him in August before my eleventh-grade year and move to South Dakota with him and his father's side of the family.

My first school boyfriend was James. He was my first crush. He had sandy-blonde shaggy hair, brown eyes and a dark tan. He reminded me of what the television shows portrayed California surfers to look like. We had gone to school together since elementary school. He was my school boyfriend from about age ten through fourteen. I was his girlfriend when he did not have another girlfriend. He would break up with me to date someone else. Then come back to me when they broke up. He was very sexual with the other girls. He had tried with me, but I always refused and that seemed to be about the time he would break up to get a new girlfriend even though it was short lived.

In the spring of 1989, Sue's live-in boyfriend's little brother needed a date for prom. I did have a boyfriend, Dave, but my family did not know about him. For some reason my parents allowed me to attend this event. I did not really know the boy and did not really feel comfortable with him. Though, to get out of the house and do something that a normal teen would do was exciting. I dressed in the maid of honor dress that I wore for Tracy's wedding the month before. The boy picked me up, seemed friendly with my mother and then we headed off. Within a block, he lit up a cigarette and took out a big bottle of beer wrapped in a paper bag. He was drinking and driving which really made me nervous. We stopped off to pick up a few of his male friends, who all were drinking and smoking as well. Once at the school where the prom was located, this boy touched my leg and tried to move his hand up my dress. I immediately jumped up and told him that I would like to dance. He did not want to dance, so one of his friends decided to dance with me. I did not have a good time like I initially thought that I would, so after a couple of hours I asked him to take me home. He was not happy about that but did take me home. Then the next day my mother yelled at me about being rude to the boy and wanted me to apologize for not enjoying my night out. When I tried to tell her about his wandering hand, his smoking and drinking, she acted as if I was lying and that I was in the wrong.

  In the summer of 1989, a longtime family friend came over to chat with my mother. He was about Sue's age and his family used to attend church with my family. He had joined the Army a few years earlier, had been drinking while on a furlough, fell out of a third story building, and became paralyzed from the waist down. He was discharged from the Army due to the accident. He came over in his wheelchair of course. After chatting with my mother, he asked if I could walk down to the cemetery with him. My mother agreed. I had known him my whole life, so I did feel comfortable around him, just thought it was odd that he wanted to spend one on one time with me. In the cemetery he asked me how life, school, and church were going. I was not completely honest due to that fact that I did not know how much he would repeat to my mother. I pretty much acted as if everything was normal and talked about subjects I was taking in school. We talked for a bit and then he asked me to sit on his lap. I hesitantly agreed, hoping it was some sort of big brotherly gesture. He asked if I had my first kiss yet and if I was interested in sex. I had kissed James and Dave, but I was not going to give this guy more information than he needed. When I said no to both, he leaned in to kiss me. I jumped up saying that I was ready to go home. He asked why and wanted to know if he could be my first sexual encounter. I said no. I told him that I would not tell my mother, but that I would rather him not hang out with me anymore. He then said, "I guess all the rumors are true, there is only one Manning girl that will put out." I looked at him in confusion when he added that he had tried this with both my sisters before and only one of them allowed him to continue into sexual relations. I knew it was Tracy. More than just because of her reputation, there had been a few times that Tracy went over to this guy's house and made my brother and me stay in the car while she went inside. She would come out with messy hair and fixing her clothes. This was not the first time that I heard it said that there was only one of us girls that was easy. Different people just used different names for the fact that Tracy would have sex with just about anyone. James admitted that he was using me to get to Tracy because he wanted to have sex, which became the reason we broke up for good. He was already told that she would have sex with just about anyone.

One night during the summer, the neighbor lady, Susan, asked my mom if I could babysit for her. My mom was hesitant, but I did get to go. Susan allowed me to go up to the town loop, so I could see Dave before she went out on her date. As I came around the corner of a building, I saw Dave hanging all over this red-headed girl. As he is just about to kiss her, he sees me and jumps backwards about three feet. He acknowledges that he did not expect to see me knowing how my parents never let me out of the house. This was the second time that I knew about him cheating on me. The first time was while we were still in school. His other girlfriend (who was older and had dropped out of school) showed up to school wearing his jean jacket. We had almost broken up at that time when instead he promised that I was the one for him and he would break it off with her. Anyway, on the town loop, I threw the turquoise unicorn ring at him and walked back to babysit Susan's kids.

Shortly after this incident, I ran away from home again. I no longer had a boyfriend, things at home were not improving and my hope of getting away from my mom by marriage faded away. They sent me to the same shelter. This time there was also another girl from my hometown. We were in different circles. Angie was in the popular group while I was somewhere between the nerd and nobody circles. Angie and I became close though. She said that we would stay friends even after we went back home. Again, I was only there for about two months. This time, however, they decided to send me to a group home, an hour away from my parents, to live until I turned eighteen. And again, I loved it there, even more so than the shelter. I was sixteen years old and never again lived under my parents' roof. Now not everything in this group home was perfect or great, but it was the best two years of my life. I did keep in touch with Angie while I was at the group home though. She returned to her parents in our hometown.

You may be thinking it sounds like *The Breakfast Club*. That is because John Hughes wrote the truth about teenage issues, it was not just another Hollywood fantasy movie. That is why so many people of so many generations can relate to this movie. If you cannot relate to this movie or think that it is make believe, then count yourself lucky and rare.

Chapter Four

I did not know that I suffered from childhood abuse at this time. I thought what happened with my mother was normal, I just could not take the emotional pain any longer. While in the group home it is mandatory that all residents be treated by a therapist. I talked to my therapist regularly about everything. During the two years that I was in this group home, I only remember seeing my parents one time and that was within my first month there. They were supposed to come for a family therapy session, but my mom refused to participate. She thought that I was the only one with a problem and that this group home was not helping me.

It was a campus of several houses that housed hundreds of kiddos. Each house had a different set of ages. One of the houses even had kiddos as young as infants. These were not just kids that had been in trouble with the law. Most of the kids were placed here because their parents were in trouble with the law or other legal issues. The teenager home was located about a block away from the homes for the younger kids. We would still go over to the main campus quite a bit for various reasons. One of the main buildings had the therapist's offices, the kitchen that cooked the food for all the buildings, and there was also a big gym so we could go play and exercise. In the home where I was placed, there were beds for fifteen teenagers. It only housed teenagers. I believe the youngest was thirteen or fourteen and up through eighteen. This house was co-ed.

This house had eleven bedrooms with four of them being double bunked. There were six resident bathrooms that were in between rooms for only those living in attached bedrooms to use. At the most we had three teens sharing one bathroom. The staff had their own bathroom in the front hall. There was an area we called the pit where we watched television and there was an area for reading or playing board games. We had a dining room, kitchen, walk-in pantry, laundry room, and a recreational room with a piano and pool table.

My first roommate was Katrina. She got along great with her parents and did not want to be there. She was placed in the home due to her parents getting caught with marijuana. Katrina was a great roommate and eventually great friend. We listened to music, she tried to teach me to dance, and we just had fun. I have a picture of Katrina and me dressed up for Halloween. I was a dead football player and she was the vampire that bit me. My first Christmas there, Katrina was upset that she was not allowed to go on a home visit. She missed her parents, so her plan was to run away to go see them. I ended up going with her, so she did not go alone. We spent a couple nights at her parents' home and then went back to the group home. That is when I found out that there was a two-week period that residents can be on the run and not lose their spot at this house. It's a good thing that we were only gone a few days because I really liked it there and did not want to lose my spot.

Katrina was eventually sent back home to her parents which caused room changes throughout the home. I was given a room to myself for a while, but I had what we called hallmates with which I shared a bathroom. The other girls in the house taught me about make-up, jewelry, hairspray, curling irons and styling my hair. These are things that my sisters nor my mother ever used so I was never shown.

I became quite close with most of the residents. We all became like siblings, watching out for each other and helping each other with homework or chores. We did activities as a group. Sometimes we went to the movie theaters, bowling alleys, or skating rinks. Sometimes we stayed at the house to do something fun like have mud fights in the yard or shaving cream wars indoors. There were a couple of the boys that would allow us girls to do their hair and makeup and dress them up in our clothes. We each had mandatory daily chores as well as extra chores that were available to volunteer for to earn extra allowance. We were given weekly allowance for doing our daily chores, extra chores, and keeping our rooms clean/ beds made. We also were all required to do our own laundry so there was a laundry schedule posted.

Besides a weekly allowance that we could spend on snacks or drinks when we were out and about, we each had a monthly clothing allowance. For the first time in my life I was able to shop for myself to buy new clothes. It was difficult for me because I did not know what I liked or what my style was. So, the staff that took us shopping and the other female residents helped me pick out clothes that looked good on me. I still have and wear some of the clothes that I bought while in the group home which has been over thirty years ago. I take very good care of my belongings so no one can tell that my clothes are that old.

Do not get me wrong, it was not always rainbows and sunshine. There were fifteen teenagers, boys and girls, in one house. There was drama, fights, snarls, bickering, etc. Compared to the home I came from, though, to me this was perfect. In this home, I knew what was expected, I knew the rewards, the consequences, and everyone was treated the same. We had to work up a level system in order to earn privileges. Even on level one, I had more freedom there than I had my entire life living with my parents. I was not sick here and could eat everything that everyone else ate. I ate foods that I did not even know existed. This is where I learned to cook. The main campus prepared and supplied meals for the weekdays, but on the weekends, at least for our house, the staff and residents cooked the meals.

This campus was established about twenty plus years before I was placed there. I reached the highest level during my time there. I was the first one to ever reach the highest level. I watched so many kids come and go. Most kiddos were there less than a year. I was there for two years. I was there the longest, so in the last year I was also the oldest in the house. Most of the kids referred to me as their big sister. A lot of them would ask me for advice or come to me instead of staff. I kept their confidentiality at the same time making sure my advice was like what the staff would say.

My second roommate was Heather. She was placed in the home due to her parents going through a very nasty divorce. Since her parents could not agree on anything, including who should get the kids, Heather and her sister were placed in this group home. Heather's sister was placed in one of the other houses though. We were goofy girls when we were together. We wanted to arrange our room into a maze. One day we moved one of the beds to where it was near the door. It was far enough away that we could still open the door, but we had to climb over the bed to get to the door. One of the staff came in catching us jumping on our beds, shook her head, explained why both the jumping and the position of the bed were unsafe, and instructed us to move the beds back.

I do not remember the exact details of the level system. I do remember that it was not too difficult to climb. Basically, follow rules, go to counseling, respect the staff and residents, do your chores, work on the goals you set with your counselor, etc. You start out not being allowed to go anywhere without a staff member. Some activities are for once you get up to a certain level. I want to say that there were ten levels. You had to work on things for so long before moving up. I think it took me about a year to reach the highest level. The top level allowed me to get a job, go out with friends, and pretty much go on walks wherever within reason. When I would leave, there was a sign in/out sheet near the front door. I would write what time I was leaving, where I planned on going and who I would be with, if anyone. When returning I would write in my return time. I had a city bus pass to get to school, work, and anywhere further than walking distance. Dating was one of the privileges I earned but could not use. That was a privilege that the home still had to get permission from my parents to allow me to use. Of course, my parents refused to sign saying I could date.

I was constantly asking for extra chores to earn extra allowance. I remember at least one time where they cut me off to give other residents a chance to do some of the extra chores. I was building up a savings with just my weekly allowances. I was excited to finally be able to get a job. I put almost all my checks into the savings account. I got a job at a day care center. I worked from noon to five, Monday through Friday. I was only going to school a half day so I would ride the city bus from school, to work, then to the home. Once I was done with high school, I switched to another day care center working eight to five, Monday through Friday. It was a Montessori preschool. I had taken a Child Development class my senior year which helped. My Child Development class had an assignment that I do not remember the exact details of, but I do remember that one of the staff members allowed me to take his three-year-old son to class for this assignment. I believe this staff stayed in the classroom while his son was with me. This class and my jobs aided in me realizing how much I love working with kids.

Since I was free, learning and doing stuff that I had never done or experienced before, I realized I was accident prone. I enjoyed all of it though. I would do it all again if I had the chance. Within about a twelve-month period I had some unique injuries that I love to tell people about. The first incident was when we all went to the beach. Some of us decided to play volleyball. It was so much fun; I think it was my first time playing. Somehow though, I literally got sand in my eyeball. One of the staff took me to the emergency room where the doctors used something like tweezers to remove a sand-sized rock from my eyeball and I had to wear a patch for a couple of weeks.

The second incident happened when we all went over to the main campus gym to play Dodgeball. I had played this game before in PE during my earlier school days. Again, I thought it was fun even though I seemed to be an easy target. One of the boys threw the ball just right and it caught my lower jaw. I remember it stinging but not much pain, per se. I also remember that I could not talk and ended up having to walk over to a staff, pointing at my face. The staff rushed me to the emergency room again. I know that four hands of two male doctors could not fit in my mouth at the same time, but it sure felt like that is what they were doing. The Dodgeball had knocked my lower jaw loose, so the two doctors had to put it back in place and wire it shut. I had to eat everything through a straw for six weeks.

The third incident was just after my senior year started. A few of us residents were piling into a staff car so we could ride up to the main campus. It was a two-door Pontiac. As I was climbing into the car, I had put my right hand on the top of the door frame. They thought I was in and closed the door. . . on my hand. There were some kids and staff standing on the porch to the house who could see my fingers poking out the top. They were yelling to open the door while the staff came running to help. I was calmly telling them to open the door because my hand was shut in the door. My hand had jammed the door, so it took them a few minutes to get it open. Two people were on the outside of the car while at least one from the inside fought to get the door open. It did not hurt. I could not really feel anything. Once they got the door open, I jumped out of the car and my hand was throbbing like no other. Still no real pain, just throbbing and swelling. I had all my fingers spread as far as they would go but they were still touching each other. My fingers had the little round indentions from the holes in the door frame that holds on the seal. Again, staff took me to the emergency room. They put a brace on my hand. I went to laser therapy about three times per week for about three months. I lucked out. They said that the laser therapy kept my hand from becoming permanently paralyzed. One of my classes was a typing class, with typewriters since computers were still somewhat rare. My school had computers, but there were only a few in the library. I learned to type with one hand. I still got an A in the class, for effort I suppose.

My second Christmas there, I was the only resident that did not go home for a holiday home visit. It was okay with me though; I had a blast playing games and watching movies with the staff. Within the first month here, there was a meeting with three counselors, my parents, and myself. I remember the counselors mentioning something about family therapy and my mother got up and walked out. That was pretty much the last time I saw my parents. One therapist was supposed to be my individual counselor, the second one was supposed to be for family therapy and the third was the head of the counseling department, which ended up becoming my therapist for my entire two years. When I was forty-one years old, I went to get copies of my discharge papers. In these discharge papers, it stated that they did not suggest a reconciliation with my parents due to the psychological abuse caused by my parents. It also stated medical neglect by my parents since the group home had tried to get my parents' permission to take me to a specialist for my ears.

Since I was in the home when I took drivers education, the staff had to teach me and drive with me so I could get practice. One of the maintenance cars was a Chevy Corsica. I grew to love that car, but never did buy one for myself. Since the house had to have certain staff-to-resident ratio, my counselor set up for one of the maintenance men to take me out to practice in the maintenance car. He was an older gentleman who did not seem to be scared to teach me. I am guessing he had already done this with his own children and possible grandchildren.

I attended the high school near the group home for my eleventh and twelfth grade years. I made a few friends there. It was a big school, probably twice the size of the high school from my hometown. Since I had earned privileges through the level system, I was able to hang out with friends and go to school functions. I went to one of the football games with a couple girls, Belle and Holly, who lived with her grandmother.

They had been best friends since elementary school. Another gal was of Hispanic background. She invited me to a family party where I had a blast, even though I did not understand much. I had taken two years of Spanish at my hometown high school, but it did not help me here. She explained that the school teaches the formal language, that they speak slang, and depending on which part of South America they are from, the slang is different for each area. Plus, they spoke so fast, combined with my hearing loss, I could not understand. Shay was another gal I hung out with occasionally that lived near the group home so we would walk together to and from the bus stop. I had a couple male friends that I hung out with as well. One of them lived a few blocks away also. The other one grew up to be a famous lead singer in a hard rock band just like he said he would. I have his school picture where he signed the back "to my biggest fan."

I graduated early at mid-term. I was seventeen when I graduated. I had my graduation party at the group home. My parents did not come, neither did any other family members. Some of the former residents came and several friends from school. Some of my teachers also attended. My friend, Sarah from Girl Scout camp, attended bringing her little sister also. One of the staff helped me make the mints and all the residents helped decorate the house, inside and out.

While I was in the group home, I regularly corresponded by written letters with my grandma Berta and Aunt Lorraine, my mother's sister. Grandma Berta never went into detail about the difficulties with my mother, but she did understand my issues with my mother. She was also not surprised about the behaviors of my mother. Grandma apologized to me for what I had dealt with. My aunt Lorraine, on the other hand, did let me know that most of what I had encountered with my mother, she had also experienced. It started out being an ear to lean on, someone other than my therapist to vent to. My therapist was wonderful, I felt lucky to have her. It just felt different talking to someone who knew my mother. I think I was wanting someone to tell me that I was not alone, that I was not her only victim. I found out that my mother treated my aunt the same way she treated me and caused severe anxiety for my aunt as well. In those letters my aunt suggested that I think about moving out to California after I was released from the group home. She said she would be able to help me get a job and maybe attend college.

When I turned eighteen, I had to move out of the group home. I moved in with my friend, Shay, and her family just two blocks from the group home. I turned eighteen two months after my graduation party. There was a waiting list for kids needing a bed. I did not want to leave, but I aged out, which is what they call it. I understood. It was just still very hard. The group home helped me set up a savings account, so I did have money set aside. They also helped me collect things for my hope chest. They did a pretty good job preparing me for being on my own.

I do not recall any conversation about continuing services for me after I aged out. I guess there were services for me to continue individual and group counseling as well as them helping me get into an apartment. In my discharged papers it mentioned these services and that I did not accept them. After eighteen, I guess they could not force me. I wish I would have accepted the continued services or even took my aunt up on her offer. I am not sure why I did not. I think my life would have turned out a lot differently either way. Maybe for the better, but there is no way to know. If my life had turned out differently, though, I would not have a book to write.

Chapter Five

While at this high school, I met Charlie, who became my best friend for life. Charlie was several inches taller than me; the top of my head came just short of the top of his shoulder. He had a full head of soft curly blonde hair and blue eyes. He was scrawny. . . skin and bones. He was baby faced, not yet growing facial hair. I never saw him in shorts, even during nice weather, because he said he had chicken legs. He also wore a lot of long sleeve shirts because he had these large strong looking hands, but his arms were twigs. He was the most polite and sweet guy that I had ever met, though, and that is what drew me to him. Charlie and I met in driver's education class. This is back when driver's education was a class elective during school instead of outsourced through other companies for out-of-school hours. Charlie sat behind me in class and we were two of four students put into the same car for driving practice. I was the only girl in our car.

One of the other guys gave me the creeps because he made very inappropriate gestures towards me. The creepy guy sat behind Charlie in class. Our first interaction was that I had asked Charlie to sit so he could block the creepy guy from being in my view. Charlie started out being my protector from the creepy guy, more than just during class. When in the car, Charlie would sit between the creepy guy and me. When Charlie was driving, he talked the third guy into sitting between the creepy guy and me in the back seat. Charlie and I started hanging out at school, in between classes, which grew into hanging out outside of school. While I was in the group home, I worked up on the level system to earn privileges, so I had a lot of freedom considering where I lived. Charlie and I walked everywhere just talking. He was the boy who lived a few blocks from the group home. We laughed a lot and enjoyed each other's company. We would usually walk to the gas station to get pop and some snacks before hanging out at a nearby park. I did most of the talking; he just listened. I talked to him about literally everything.

Since Charlie lived a few blocks from the group home, we sometimes would hang out at his house. A few times we hung out at the group home and we would play pool in the rec room. Charlie could do impressions very well. He could always make me laugh. He did cartoon impressions like Donald Duck, Marvin the Martian, Hugo the Abominable Snowman, Foghorn Leghorn, Kermit the Frog, and many more. Charlie and I hung out a lot, but I never knew or met any of his other friends. He met some of mine a few times. I was still seventeen when I finished high school so even though I was in the group home I got a full-time job. By the time I graduated, Charlie and I spent almost every day together. While he was in school, I was at my job, so we still had evenings and weekends to hang out.

Charlie did have a part time job though so there were evenings that I would hang out with other friends. Holly had a car.

Sometimes I would hang out with Holly and Belle when Charlie was working. I remember us driving through the drive-thru of Taco Bell just to see or talk to Charlie. Belle liked the food there anyway so she would order something, so we did not get Charlie into trouble. Riding around with Holly and Belle is when I first heard the song "Ice Ice Baby" by Vanilla Ice. It was Holly's favorite song.

When I moved out of the group home, Shay borrowed her mom's car. I did not have a lot of belongings, but more than what we wanted to carry the two blocks to her house. Shay and Charlie both helped me pack my stuff into the car and unload everything at Shay's house. She was excited to have a sister-like roommate. Even though she was still in high school, we spent some nights staying up late talking. She had a boyfriend that was a few years older that she talked a lot about. Shay said it was like having a sleepover every night.

Charlie and I hung out even more often, especially after I was able to buy a car. I bought a 1986 Pontiac T1000. It was a cream-colored car with light tan interior. It was five years old. I paid $2600 for it. We would drive over to the airport a lot. Back then there was a small parking lot outside the fence where we could park to watch the airplanes take off. We would sit in this parking lot and talk for hours while watching the planes. I remember Charlie would turn around in the passenger seat so that his back rested against the glovebox and his knees rested on the edge of the seat. We both loved feeling the vibrations from the jets through our bodies. It reminded me of my childhood vacations to Texas. For him, it was different. He also loved the bass vibrations from listening to loud music or a loud action movie for the same reason as the vibrations from the jets.

Sometimes we would just drive around with no specific destination. I would drive all over town, not really going any certain place. Sometimes it would just be through town, other times we took the highway or interstates. Sometimes we would still hang out at different parks just to get out of the car. We would just talk for hours. No matter which activity we chose to do, there was always the gas station pit stops for a fountain pop and cigarettes. We would always fill the biggest cup mixing all the fountain pop flavors together. We also were both smokers which was another reason we stopped at the gas station. Back then I could fill up my gas tank, buy a carton of brand name cigarettes, and a bottle of pop for twenty dollars.

One day we were at a park playing on the equipment when Charlie asked me if he could kiss me. I thought he was joking so I laughed and said no. He joked around a lot making me laugh so I initially thought that was what he was doing. We were just friends, so I did not take him seriously. He had a look of disappointment on his face though. He was one of few guys that I think had respect enough to ask instead of lean in to take a kiss. We did not talk about this incident until decades later. We continued our friendship as usual, but the look of disappointment on Charlie's face haunted me for years.

Now that I had my own car, I ended up taking on two more jobs. With my one full-time job and two part-time jobs, plus Charlie working part time at Taco Bell while still attending high school, our hang-out times lessened. Our hangouts continued to be almost a daily occurrence though. I was still working eight to five at the preschool, one of the part-time jobs was working in a pizza parlor, and the second one was cleaning houses. The pizza parlor was near a major university, so I usually worked from about five-thirty to two in the morning. I cleaned houses when I had the evening off from the pizza parlor, plus the weekends, since I did not work at the preschool.

Shay's mom did not like the hours I was working so she did not want me to stay at their home anymore. I understood. I shared a room with Shay who was still in high school. She also had a younger brother. I loaded up my car and lived out of it for the next couple of months. Sometimes I would stay at a friend's house or sometimes I would sleep in this abandoned house near the group home. I ended up living off about two to four hours of sleep a day, sometimes taking naps at Charlie's house. He lived with his mom and two sisters. One sister was one year younger than Charlie and his other sister was just two years old. Sometimes he would have to babysit his two-year-old sister, so I would nap in the top bunk of the bunk beds he shared with the teen sister, Aimee. Most of the time I had trouble falling asleep, so Charlie would spoon me and hold me until I fell asleep. I remember one time; I was mostly asleep but was aware that he was getting out of the bed. Hanging onto the railing of the top bunk he leaned over to kiss my forehead. For many years I thought that kiss on my head was just a dream, but he confirmed it to be true about twenty-five years later.

There was a late evening, I cannot recall how late it was, just that it was dark and hardly any vehicles were on the interstate. Charlie and I were just driving around and talking like usual. I was not paying attention to the fuel gauge, so we ended up running out of gas on the interstate. While we were deciding on if we thought we could walk to the nearest exit, an older red pickup pulled over in front of us. First, I said that I would ride in the truck to get gas while Charlie stayed with my car. He said no way, the guy could be a serial killer. Then I said I would stay with the car and he can go with the guy in the truck. Again, Charlie said no way. He did not think either of those were safe options. We locked up my car and both of us got into the truck with the elderly gentleman. He drove us to the gas station just off the nearest exit, we got some gas, and the kind gentleman took us back to my car. The container we used only carried about two gallons of gas, so we did go back to the gas station to fill up my tank before we continued our drive. That was the first time of running out of gas for both of us. He says because of that incident he has ALWAYS made sure whatever vehicle he was driving or riding in, had plenty of gas. Me? Running out of gas continued to be a bad habit of mine for the next two decades.

Since most of the former residents were younger than me, they were able to move back home with their parents. Considering that I felt closer to some of them than I did my own family, I tried to visit at least one of them per week. They were like my brothers and sisters, so I wanted to see them and make sure they were doing okay. I tried to be the big sister that I wish I would have had. Besides becoming like a big sister to most of the residents, some of their parents also befriended me. One of the kiddos, Eric, was an only child. He left the group home shortly after I did. He continued to get into trouble though so his mom, Patti, would call on me to go do my "big sister" thing. He had been placed in a shelter and his mom wrote me down as his sister along with being an approved visitor. Patti is also the one who got me the job cleaning houses. I slept on her couch a few times as well.

During my junior and senior years, I was dating a guy named Sam. I hardly saw Sam, though, since I spent most of my free time with Charlie. I thought I was in love with Sam. We talked about marriage, kids, and careers. I do not know if it was the fact that I spent so much time with Charlie or if I really did not truly know Sam, but it caught me off guard when I caught him cheating on me. The only place I knew to go was to Charlie's.

I ended up in a car accident that totaled my car while I was en route to Charlie's house. It was dark, I was driving, crying, and smoking. Just as I was coming up to a stop light, I tossed my cigarette out the window. I had the green light, heading west across the intersection, when a car coming from the north failed to stop at her red light. We crashed; my car spun. When my car came to a rest, I was facing south, and partially onto the median. My devastation from Sam turned into shock and confusion at what just happened. I tried to get out of my car, but the door was jammed so I climbed out the window. A female officer was already on scene. When I got out, I walked around my car to look at the damage to my car and saw fluids just leaking out all over the ground. I started heading over to the lady who hit me when I got dizzy and weak. The officer saw me and helped me to sit down on the curb. She explained to me that she witnessed the entire accident. She had been following me to issue ME a ticket. Apparently, it was against the law to toss a cigarette out the window instead of in the ashtray of the car. I usually did use my ashtray, not sure why I had not this time. She also explained that she was no longer going to give me that ticket because it was her belief that it would have blown me up if I would have put the cigarette out in my car. All the fluids leaking out of my car mixed with a cigarette that would most likely still be lit, she believed would have caused a fire. The final result was that I did not get any tickets. The other lady received many tickets... running a red light, speeding, having no insurance, failure to maintain control, etc. My car was towed away so the officer drove me to Charlie's house. When I did finally get to Charlie's, I cried on his shoulder about both the car accident and catching Sam with another girl.

The most impressionable memory that stayed with me for many years was a day that I was hanging out at Charlie's house. He made us a peanut butter sandwich to split. His mom left to go to her second job and Aimee was out with friends, so he was watching the two-year-old. Charlie asked me if I would lay on the couch with him. He then asked if he could hold me without our shirts on, bare chest to bare chest. I hesitated, but I felt completely safe with him, so I agreed. A feeling that I had never felt before and would eventually find out that I would never experience that safe comfortable feeling with anyone else. I made him promise not to peek at my naked breasts though. He of course promised and did not peek. He was literally the sweetest person that I knew. We cuddled, bare chest to bare chest, under a blanket on the couch, for a good chunk of time. It was a pure moment, the purest that I would ever encounter. He did not try to seduce me; our hearts were beating together, and I could feel the beating all through my body. It was a connection that I have only felt with Charlie. It was a deep intimate connection, like we were talking without talking. It was not sexual; it was a unique bonding of our hearts and souls. Too bad I was too young to realize what that moment really meant. I was ignorant in the area of what makes a good relationship and what love really was. That was the first time I saw his bare chest. The warmth of his skin next to mine was soothingly comforting and I never forgot how it felt.

He asked me to be his girlfriend. I said no because I thought it would ruin our friendship. The other two reasons that I gave myself were that he was younger than me by fifteen months and he was blonde with blue eyes. He had a full head of soft naturally curly blonde hair. I am not sure why I thought the man should be older than the woman, but I let it bother me for decades. I was blonde haired, blue eyed and always felt ugly. That mainly came from the criticism I received from my mother. I did not want my future children to look like me. I thought the only way to make sure that I did not have children who looked like me was to have kids with a brown haired, brown eyed man. Now those seem like the worst reasons ever not to date my best friend, but at the time those were very important reasons to me.

One summer evening, Charlie had to work, I did not. None of my other friends were available to hang out, so I decided that I would hang out with Aimee until he got off work. She was bored and wanted to go on a road trip. I loved to drive so I was not opposed to the idea. My auto insurance had gotten me a rental car while the accident was being processed. The only place I knew to go was back to the town my parents lived in. I had not been there for over two years. We drove an hour, decided to drive the loop to see if I knew anyone up there. Lo and behold, we ran into Dave. He had been hanging out on the loop with his sister's boyfriend. He was riding a bicycle since he did not have a driver's license. We followed him back to his mom's house where he lived in the basement. This is the guy I caught on the loop two years earlier with the red headed girl. We talked about getting back together, we made out, he gave me a hickey and I spent the night. I would later regret this decision. I learned that this was one of the biggest mistakes that I would ever make.

The next day, I took Aimee back home. Charlie was there and not very happy with me at all. I had never seen him upset before. He was lecturing me like he was my parent. He saw the hickey and continued to lecture me. He reminded me that this is the same guy who cheated on me more than once. He went on to say that chances are Dave had not changed and would never change. Me being an eighteen-year-old know-it-all girl, thought I knew better. I was older than Charlie for goodness sake. I got mad at Charlie, got in the rental car to leave, he threw a glass pop bottle at the car in frustration, and what I saw in my rear-view mirror was another memory that haunted me for years. The look on his face was not anger, but pain and disappointment. I did not understand what I was walking away from and he did not know how to make me understand. He knew he loved me and that I was his true love, his soulmate. Years later I found out from Aimee that he wanted to die that day, stood in the middle of a busy street trying to get hit. I had broken his heart.

Since I had gotten my car, I had been looking at this cute little house to buy on the same side of town as Charlie lived. The siding was blue, it had a single car garage and was two-bedroom, one bathroom. It was going to need a little love, but it was livable. No one was residing in it at the time. The realtor thought the process would go quickly since the owners were needing it sold as soon as possible. I had also applied to get into the local community college. I had been accepted and was scheduled for orientation to sign up for classes about a month later. For some reason I walked away from all of that as well. I was a dumb kid who was going to learn the hard way. I look back still trying to figure out what my younger self was thinking.

Chapter Six

I had quite a bit of savings, so I got an apartment for Dave and myself to live in back in our hometown. His sister, Jane, her boyfriend and her two-year-old son all moved in with us as well. Dave did not have a job and I was having trouble finding one. We did not have a vehicle, so we walked everywhere that we needed to go. Since the lady who hit me did not have insurance, my insurance had to pay for the accident. My car was totaled. The insurance only gave me enough to pay off my loan, not enough to get another car. I was not wanting to get pregnant for many different reasons. I went to the doctor to get on birth control. It was making me extremely sick. I could not keep anything down and within two weeks I had dropped from ninety-five pounds to eighty-two pounds. I then went to the OB/GYN and after some tests they discovered that I was allergic to the main chemical in birth control. They said I was very fertile as well and their best suggestion for me was either abstinence or religiously use condoms. Dave was not thrilled with this news, but I told him either condoms, no sex, or we end the relationship. He agreed to the condoms.

After about a month, his dad and stepmom from South Dakota told us that there were plenty of jobs out where they lived. So, like we had planned two years prior, we moved to South Dakota. I was excited about a change of scenery. I had not reconciled with my parents, so I was a little nervous about running into them now that I was living back in my hometown.

More so my mother than my father, but I was just not ready to deal with that whole reunion yet. We moved in with his parents. Dave got a security job at the local lumber mill. His stepmom got me a job at the nursing home where she worked. She was in housekeeping, but they were hiring for nursing assistants willing to take classes to become certified. So that is what I did. I took the classes to become a Certified Nurses Aid (CNA). When I was not working, I was helping Dave's three younger stepsiblings with chores. This is where I learned to play the Nintendo. Dr. Mario was my favorite and only game I ever played on a home game system. Dave's dad had an extra pickup that they allowed me to drive. They lived in the country, so nothing was walking distance to get to. Dave did not have his license, so I was the only one that was able to drive.

It took us about two months to save up enough money to get our own apartment. We went through my savings quickly living in my hometown with no jobs. Since we both had full-time jobs now, we were able to get a one-bedroom apartment above an arcade. Now that we were in town, we were within walking distance of both our jobs and the grocery store. It was a small town so we could literally walk the whole town in probably less than an hour. Sometimes our landlord needed us to work the arcade downstairs which was nice. It was fun, plus the extra money was needed. We also got to play the games for free while we were working in there. My game of choice was Pac-Man.

About a month later, I was pregnant with my first child. I still made Dave wear condoms every time, but the box says they are not one hundred percent effective. Since Dave worked overnight and I worked day shift, we hardly saw much of each other. We had a neighbor that lived across the hall. Her family lived on a farm and the family cat had kittens. She asked if we wanted a kitten since they had just turned five weeks old. I thought it would help me to have some company in the apartment at night, so I was excited. We picked out a black furry male. I named him Blacky. He was so friendly and cuddly, but he meowed a lot as he wandered the apartment like he was looking for a four-legged friend. A couple days later, we decided to get a second kitten so Blacky could have someone to play with while Dave and I were gone or asleep. We got his black furry sister, which I named Midnight. She was extremely smart, but stubborn and not very friendly.

For the first two weeks of having Midnight, she sat in the kitchen window all the time. The window was a tall narrow window that stretched from about six inches from the ceiling to about six inches from the floor. She would hiss at us every time we walked by her. She would not let us pet her and she made it quite clear that she did not want us talking to her either. She would not eat while we were in the room. I think she waited until either we were asleep, or both gone. Same scenario when it came to her litter box as well. One evening Dave was at work and I was sitting on the couch crocheting. Midnight slowly stretched to the floor from the window, slowly walked over to me, sniffed my leg, used her claws to climb my pant leg, sniffed my hands, and then made herself a bed right on top of my yarn, crochet hook, and hands. Since she was finally warming up, I did not want to disturb her, so I just let her lay there. She eventually moved up to my shoulder. She was small enough that she could lay on just my right shoulder without falling off. That became her spot anytime that I was sitting on the couch. She also started cuddling with me while sleeping, sitting on my lap while in the bathroom and sitting on the side of the tub or toilet while I bathed or showered. She became my baby before I had my baby. Midnight was easy to litter-train whereas Blacky was not. I would put him in the bathroom and shut the door while no one was home. We quickly realized that Midnight knew how to jump and use her claws to turn the knob to let him out.

Six months later, Dave lost his job, and I found out that he was not good with money. I never saw his checks. I would ask him for his half of all the bills. What he did with the rest of his checks, I do not know. When he lost his job, he was broke. He had not saved any of his money. I was setting some aside in savings after I was paying my half of the bills. My mother never worked, but she had complete control over all my father's money. I refused to be that way with any man that I was in a relationship with, so Dave's money was his money after he paid his portion of the bills. One night we needed some items from the grocery store. I gave Dave cash along with my list to go to the store. When he came back, I compared the receipt to the amount I gave him and the change he handed me. He was short twenty dollars. He nonchalantly said that it must have fallen out of his pocket on the walk back to the apartment. We both got our coats on and retraced his steps. We did not find the missing money.

About a month after he lost his job, I lost mine. My obstetrician put me on light duty at work. My boss was not happy with this news as we were short staffed in the nursing department. I was put on part-time duty to come in only to help during feeding at mealtimes. The schedule was put out every two weeks. I was only on the schedule for two or three days per week. I was eventually taken off the schedule completely with no explanation. The last time I went in to check the schedule, it had been about five days since I had worked. My name was not on the schedule, so I went to talk to the Director of Nursing (DON). There was a new lady in there who had just started. She told me that the other DON was no longer employed there, and she had no records of me. She told me that I would have to reapply, but that in my condition she most likely would not hire me. She also did not have my certificate that was supposed to be put on file for me after I passed the Certified Nurses Aid classes. I ran into one of my favorite resident's daughter in the store after this. She told me that her mother had passed away suddenly. She also informed me that close to fourteen residents had passed away in the couple weeks after I left. She was talking about filing a complaint with the state about treatment of the residents. She had also told me that I was her mother's favorite nurse there and did not like anyone else in her room.

For money we continued to work in the arcade. I also took on several babysitting jobs, including babysitting for Dave's aunt and uncle. I became close with his oldest stepsister who liked to come hang out with me while I was babysitting. Dave did not seem interested at all in applying for any new jobs, not that there were a lot in this small town, but he was making no effort. We did not have a vehicle to drive to another town, so this town was pretty much where we needed to find work. Besides, since he did not have a license, I would have to drive him everywhere if we did have a vehicle. I applied at a few places, but no one would hire me while I was pregnant. I was not real big so no one could really tell that I was pregnant, but it was a small town where everyone knew everything. Dave's parents literally knew everyone, which did not help with the news getting around.

We were constantly fighting these days. Dave wanted to move back to our hometown, but I did not. Dave was telling everyone that I cheated on him because he was sterile, therefore could not conceive a child. It was causing a lot of stress for both of us. About this time, I was really missing my best friend, Charlie. It was at this time that I realized Charlie WAS truly my best friend and I needed him. At one point, I took a walk late at night to think about my situation. I found myself at the edge of town. A semi was in the distance coming in my direction. I walked into the street and stared at the headlights as they drew closer. It was sort of mesmerizing. I had hoped there would be no way I would live through getting hit by a semi-truck. I looked down at my swollen belly and rubbed my hands across in a circular motion. That's when I thought of my unborn child. I thought that this was not his fault. I had made a mess of things and none of this was fair to him. I decided I needed to live for my baby. At least until I could figure out a better plan for him.

    We started selling off everything that we could; the couch, table, television, end table, our bed, Atari with games, our dishes, etc. We were able to sell enough to get a very cheap car. It was a silver Dodge Omni. We ended up packing up to head back to Iowa a month before my due date. He chose to move back in with his mom. I moved back in with Shay and her family that lived two blocks from the group home. Midnight and Blacky stayed with me. The car made the drive just long enough for me to drop Dave off in our hometown and me to Shay's house. It broke down a day or two later and had to be towed to the junk yard.

    As I struggled with whether to keep the baby or not, since I was a single nineteen-year-old living with a friend's parents, I tried to find Charlie. He had always been there when I needed someone or just to give me advice or just to talk to. I went to Charlie's house that he lived in before I had left, but his family had moved out. I went to the high school, but he was not there either. Nor was his teen sister. Taco Bell said he had quit, and they did not know where I could find him. I did not know where else Charlie would be. I had never met his other friends, nor did I know where his mom worked. I confided in Shay about my issues instead. She was great to talk to; she just was not Charlie. She ended up talking to her mom. Shay's mom and stepdad had been trying to conceive with no luck, so they offered to adopt my baby. I did not know what else to do so I agreed. Her mom was going to handle all the legal part of it. I just needed to take care of myself, the baby, and go to my doctor appointments. She even let me use her car for the doctor appointments. She never went to my appointments with me. She would have me take her to work in the morning and either Shay or I would pick her up after she got off work.

Devastated by the consequences of my decision, I found a job to help me with money until the baby was born. Finding a job at eight months pregnant was easier since I was barely showing, and this was a big city. Most people did not know that I was pregnant, and I was not stating so either. My doctor had an intern working with him. I was okay with that, but I still kind of felt like a guinea pig. I had an appointment on my due date which was a Friday afternoon. I had been four centimeters dilated since my first appointment in Iowa. As most would know, the last month of pregnancy you have weekly appointments. This was already my fourth. I think because I was so young and alone, they decided to admit me to induce my labor. At the time I did not know any better, but now I just think they wanted to give the intern some experience with inducing. Anyway, nothing happened. I did not dilate anymore, I did not start contractions, and so I did not go into labor. The next day, Saturday evening, they released me.

A week and a half later, on a Monday, I woke up to get ready for an appointment that I had that morning. As I was getting ready, I felt this consistent tightening of my stomach muscles. It almost felt like it did when I would do sit-ups. Anyway, I pretty much shrugged them off, did not tell anyone and continued my morning. By the time I got to my appointment, the tightening in my stomach started to affect my breathing. I did not realize it, but the lady checking me in noticed and asked me if I was having contractions. When she went to go get a nurse, a pregnant lady standing next to me who was way huge compared to me, asked me how far a long I was. I said that I was almost two weeks overdue. Her eyes grew big as she stated that she was only six months pregnant and that I looked like I was only two or three months. I had gained thirty pounds during this pregnancy though. The nurse came out, looked at me and got a wheelchair. They hooked me up to the belt-like device that measures contractions. They said I was already at one minute between contractions, but I was only six centimeters dilated. They then wheeled me over to the hospital section of the building and admitted me into a room. Once in the room, I did call my work to let them know that I would need to be off for a few days. Six hours later, they had me sign papers to have a cesarean section. Their reasoning was because I was not dilating.

    I focused on the clock, which was high on the wall above my feet during the surgery. I could feel the tugging and shaking, no real pain though, just very uncomfortable. I heard him cry, looked at the time and was out cold before I could see him. When I awoke, I could not move anything below my armpits. The nurse came in. She saw that I was awake and told me that I needed to try to go potty. I informed her that I could not move. She went to go get the doctors. After looking at my charts, they realized that the amount of spinal anesthesia given to me was according to my pregnancy weight not my pre-pregnancy weight. I had a catheter and sponge baths for the next two days. They were confused at why the anesthesia had that effect on me for that long, so the first thing the nurse did as soon as I was able to stand was get my current weight. Three days after I gave birth, I weighed five pounds less than my pre-pregnancy weight. This explained why the anesthesia paralyzed me. They said I must have been all baby during my pregnancy. The baby was in an incubator for about a day longer than my temporary paralysis. When I could finally move, they let me go see him. I had to put on a special gown and gloves before reaching through the little holes to touch him. I do not remember what their reasons were other than he had jaundice. Even though he was two weeks late, he weighed only five pounds seven ounces and was eighteen inches long. One look at him, though, and I could not give him up. I told Shay's mom, with a huge apology.

My son, Daniel, was born on my father's fiftieth birthday. Even though I had not spoken to my parents in over three years, I felt that I should name my son after my parents. His first name was my mom's maiden name and his middle name he shared with my father. He was the most gorgeous baby that I had ever seen. He was born with a full head of dark brown hair and looked exactly like Dave. He also had a purplish triangle on his forehead and a purple bottom. One of the nurses told me that those were normal American Indian marks. There was Indian on both my side and Dave's side.

We were in the hospital for five days, which is not that long considering the trauma that we both endured. I was unable to breastfeed because I had dried up by the time I had feeling in my body. I had lost my job, stating that I did not tell them that I was pregnant, and they could not leave my position open for a six-week maternity leave. I was not going to take a maternity leave, but between the doctor and the boss I did not have a choice. Shay's mom moved my belongings out of her house while I was in the hospital. Shay and her step-grandma picked me up from the hospital when I was released. Daniel, Midnight, Blacky and I all stayed with her. Shay's grandma Sondra was a lovely, sweet lady. She loved having company. She was used to a quiet home, which was too quiet according to her. She also told me not to feel bad about keeping my baby. She said that Shay's mom and her son found out that they were expecting while I was in the hospital, but they were not going to tell me. Sondra did not think they would have been able to financially handle two newborns.

I enjoyed Sondra's company. She said that I could stay with her for as long as I needed. She also made it very clear that she was in no hurry to have a quiet home again. I was having trouble finding work and just felt like everything was going wrong. I had not found Charlie and was feeling alone in a big world with a tiny baby. When Daniel was two months old, I borrowed Patti's (former resident's mom that helped me out when I was eighteen) car. I went to my parent's home and surprised them with a new grandson. My dad was friendly and held the baby, but my mother was distant. She just wanted to know WHAT I wanted. I was not there to ask for help or money or anything else, so my visit was cut short. I then stopped by Dave's mom's house to let him meet his son. We talked a lot about what went wrong and if we thought it was worth working on. I drove the car back to Patti; she took Daniel and me back to Sondra's. I talked to Sondra about my visit and the talk with Dave. She told me that only I knew what was best for me. Sondra helped me move my things back to my hometown while reminding me that she was always there for me if I needed her.

    Dave and I decided to try to make our little family work. I still had some money from when I was working before Daniel was born. Dave and I both got jobs in our hometown. We moved into a one-bedroom apartment about seven blocks from my parents. Everything seemed to be going good at first. I bought a little silver Chevrolet Chevette. After I finally took Dave to get his driver's license, Dave bought a blue Chevrolet Malibu. My mother was too close though. I was quickly thrown back into feelings of worthlessness and inadequacy within a few months. I had regrettably let my parents back into my life. My mother would come over to my apartment, enter without knocking, and start 'fixing' my cupboards to her liking or re-folding my towels. She let me know that I did this or that wrong and Dave became her pet. Dave was still not good with money. I was trying to keep us on a budget. My mother started calling me Dave's prison warden. She would remind me that I was living in sin, since we were not married, and that God was not happy with my decisions. She would undermine me in front of Dave. Each time she would leave my apartment, I would have to re-arrange my cupboards back to how I wanted them and re-fold all my towels and blankets. She never cleaned her own house, so it really irritated me that she would come over to clean mine when my place was almost spotless most of the time. Dave and I did not fight all the time. I would not even say a lot, but when we did it was always about money and his affairs. Yes, he was still cheating on me.

Chapter Seven

When Daniel was about ten months old, Dave moved out and in with one of his consistent girlfriends. This is the one that, back in high school, came to the school wearing his jean jacket when he was supposed to be my boyfriend. I was too busy taking care of Daniel, working and keeping up on the bills by myself to worry about what else I was going to do. It was not too long before Dave came back, literally crying and begging me to take him back. His crying is what made me give in. He also promised that it would never happen again. I think they had a big fight where he thought she was gone for good. We were not that lucky unfortunately. So, I took him back. I became pregnant with child number two within a couple of months. He again started to tell people that this baby was not his either and continued stating that he was sterile. I hoped someone would point out the fact that he obviously was not sterile when Daniel was Dave's identical twin. We moved into my parent's two-bedroom rental house just before baby number two was born. Again, that was a huge mistake. My mother never knocked when coming over and never announced that she was coming at our other apartment. This was her house; she just did not live in it. She seemed to have the perfect timing of popping in whenever Dave and I were having a disagreement even if it was just a small insignificant one. She would always butt in and tell him that if we split up again that she would kick me out so he and the kids could continue to live there.

When I was six months pregnant, my maternal grandma Berta in California was given a few months to live. She had bone cancer. My parents, my brother, Sue, my nephew (Sue's five-year-old son), Daniel (who was nineteen months old) and I all flew out to see her. Tracy was also pregnant, but she was eight months pregnant with her first child and was not allowed to fly. We stayed at my aunt Lorraine's house. My aunt was glad that I was there because she did not know how she was going to deal with my mother. When my aunt gets anxiety, she hastily cleans everything multiple times without even realizing she is doing it. She also drinks wine to calm her nerves when around my mom. During our stay, I found her on her treadmill several times. She said she needed to stay away from my mother and to work through her anxiety. She felt the same feeling of inadequacy and worthlessness from my mother that I did.

When we went to visit Grandma Berta, we were told that she had lost the will to live. She was refusing to eat and would not get up to walk around. I felt like I was close to my Grandma so I thought maybe she would listen to me. She had never met Daniel. She was excited to see him, and we got a picture of the two of them together. We were also trying to tell her to fight to stay alive so she could see the two unborn great grandbabies. They brought in a tray of food. I tried to feed her, but she was refusing. So, I gave Daniel a bite and then tried to feed my grandma again. It was very sad seeing my grandma like this. She was very frail, and in her mind, she was ready to go. She passed away within a couple weeks of our visit, never getting to meet the two new babies.

Dave claimed he could not get time off from work to go to California with us. I do not know if he really could not get time off or if he was just making other plans. When I came home, the neighbors and Dave's sisters told me that Dave had his consistent mistress staying with him while I was gone. The neighbor lady also said there was a second lady who came over after the first one left. Dave's sisters and I could not figure out who the second lady was by the description that the neighbor gave us. When I tried to talk to him about it, he denied it at first, but slipped up in his lie. Then he tried to turn it around at somehow being my fault.

It was mid-spring, Dave's parents from South Dakota were in town and they decided to stay with us that week. Again, with baby number two I was a week and a half past my due date. Daniel was now twenty-three months old. Dave's stepmom said she could tell that I was ready to pop any day. It was a Wednesday morning and I was quietly getting ready for work so that I did not wake his parents. Dave had already left for work. I was feeling those same little tightening sensations in my stomach like I had with Daniel, so I decided to call work to let them know that I was going stop at my doctor's office first. I was trying to be quiet, but when I got off the phone his stepmom was sitting up looking at me. They were sleeping on our pull-out sofa. She said they would take me. We went to the emergency room because the tightenings were happening less than a minute apart. Good thing too. I was ten centimeters dilated. His parents called Dave's work once we arrived at the hospital. He was able to get there just in time. Since my mom was not coming up, his stepmom told the nurses that she was my mom so she would be allowed back in the birthing room with me. I was not given any medications this time, I was not in pain, and the baby was in a hurry. The nurses told me to roll over on my side and pinch my knees together because the doctor was not ready. I saw him over in the corner washing his hands when they told me to roll over onto my back. I was not pushing, but she was coming anyway. The doctor came running over to catch her. He did not even have time to put gloves on or sit on the stool that was at my feet. She was born less than an hour and half after we arrived at the hospital. Baby Joanna was born with a full head of dark hair also, again looking just like Dave.

Daniel was a good helper with his baby sister. He liked to pick out her clothes to wear. When she would cry, he was very worried and would talk to her until I could get to her. He liked to get me her diapers when I was getting ready to change her. I had him potty trained before we flew out to California, so it was nice only having to buy diapers for one. One day when I was breastfeeding Joanna, Daniel asked me which one had juice. He was funny but very serious about his question, so I explained that they both were milk. Once I started to supplement with formula, he enjoyed helping fix the bottles and helping to feed her. Even though he was only two years old, he would still pick up his toys when he was done playing. He kept his room clean; he was his mama's child. I did trade my Chevette for a dark blue Mercury Cougar; it was a bigger car and easier to haul two car seats.

Four months after Joanna was born, we bought a house on the other side of town. I needed something stable for my children that I thought my mother could not control. It was a story and a half home built in 1910. It was on a large corner lot. It had a huge enclosed front porch and a decent sized enclosed back porch. The back porch was completely lined with upper and lower cabinets, so I used this as my pantry. It also included the indoor access to the basement. It had a decent sized kitchen with a built in stove and separate built in oven. It also had three separate doorways. One doorway led out to the porch pantry, another led to the dining room and the third went to the hallway that had access to one bathroom, two bedrooms, and the stairs leading up. The dining room had a six-foot-long window seat which I fell completely in love with. In the dining room, at the opposite end as the kitchen was a good-sized foyer with a huge picture window that I used as a seating area with a bookshelf and two wicker chairs. From the foyer, we had access to the front porch and the living room. The front porch went the full length of the foyer and the living room, very long and narrow, approximately twenty-five feet by five feet. I stored the kids' outdoor toys out there and during rainy days it also worked as their playroom. It was completely lined with windows. The living room also had two large picture windows in it. It also gave access to the backside of one of the bedrooms that we could reach from the kitchen side. We could go in a circle throughout the whole main floor. It also had original hardwood floors throughout. Upstairs were three more bedrooms. The hallway was large enough we could have made another bedroom. I loved this house.

My mother continued to remind me that I was living in sin. His family members kept asking when we were going to get married now that we had two children. We talked about marriage. Neither of us wanted to get married, but between the pressures of extended family and wanting to do what society says is the right thing, we gave in. I also thought things with Dave would get better if it was more official. I had a charge card for a local jewelry store which we used to get the wedding ring set. Of course, I made all the payments myself. When Joanna was a year old, Dave and I were married by a magistrate judge. We had an outdoor wedding at the local park. I wore my mother's wedding dress, Sue was my maid of honor, wearing the same dress that I wore for Tracy's wedding. Daniel was our ring bearer and Joanna was our flower girl. Joanna was walked down the aisle by Dave's mom since she still needed assistance with walking, especially that distance. We had a small reception following the ceremony in the nearby shelter. We made our own food, decorations, and cake. We spent less than two hundred dollars on everything. We did not have a honeymoon. That night, though, Dave looked upset. He said he was not so sure we did the right thing. To change the mood, I started jumping on the bed. That did not help though, instead he brought my mood down as well. We just went on with life as we had been. This wedding and marriage were more for my mother than us.

Within a month, I was pregnant with baby number three. Dave was back to telling people that I was cheating on him again and the baby was not his. This is when it hit me that maybe he said that because he was still cheating on me or cheating on me again. I have heard that the one who accuses is usually the guilty one. It was still hard for me to keep us on a budget with Dave's spending habits, so we each were working two jobs. Before we were married, he was trading cars every couple of months. He would go to work with one car and come home in a different car. Most of the time the new car was in worse condition than the last one, but for some reason he was not trading straight across or getting cash on top of trade. Most of the time he was trading, plus paying cash. After we were married, this habit of car trading grew more often. What I did not know is that he had taken out a couple of personal loans with high interest rates to help with his car gambling problem. Car gambling is what I chose to call it. I do not know what he did with the rest of his money.

Since we were considered low income, I was on a program called WIC (Women, Infants, and Children) that gave out food voucher checks with specific food items on them. They helped with formula, baby cereal, baby food, cereal, peanut butter, juice, milk, etc. They had nurses on staff so they would also do well child checks and test for lead poisoning, etc. One day that I was in there, the nurse said that Joanna had a heart murmur and that I needed to take her to a specialty hospital two hours away. I had always taken my kiddos to our family doctor for their regular checkups, so I was confused at why our doctor never mentioned a heart murmur before. The nurse gave me a form to take to the hospital with her suggestions on it. I could not afford to take Joanna to that hospital, so I took this form and my concerns to my family doctor. He checked Joanna and she sounded normal to him. He scheduled two other appointments with two of his colleagues for them to check at different days and times. All three doctors determined that she did not have a heart murmur. They all signed the form with their findings for me to return to the nurse at WIC. When I did, the nurse threatened to turn me in for neglect because I did not go to the hospital that she chose. I ended up walking out of there with my children in tow and without the WIC checks. I never went back and never again used their program. My doctor continued to monitor her heart and never once did he or anyone else ever hear a heart murmur with her.

 Things were not all bad with us. Sometimes Dave did help me with the household chores, it was a team effort. I would wash the dishes and he would dry them and put them away. I would clear the table and put food away while he swept the floor. We would cuddle on the couch to watch television. I sat on his lap a lot even if there was room next to him on the couch. I enjoyed these moments. These are the moments that I held onto when things were not so good. These are the moments, plus the kids, that gave me reason to take him back after every affair. I could not compete with the one girl who kept coming back all the time. She was married with six kids. At least twice a year, though, she was back in Dave's life and causing waves in mine. She was not his only mistress, but she was the consistent one. She had him wrapped around her finger.

Again, I was feeling like I was all alone in this big world. Dave and I were not fighting, but I did not feel like we were really a couple either. One particular day, he was distant and not mentally present. The kids were napping. I wanted to be alone, I wanted to be in the dark. I do not remember why I did not go outside or for a walk like I would usually do. I do remember that I sat in the bottom of my bedroom closet to think quietly. I just cried and I cried hard. I did not know what to do or how to fix any part of my life. I asked God to please help me, help my family. Then Charlie popped into my head which gave me a sliver of relief. I tried to concentrate on the memory of his voice. I wanted to hear his voice. I concentrated hard enough that in my memory I heard him say "everything will be okay." He probably told me that after my breakup with Sam or my car accident.... But it helped me now even though he was not physically here, he was in my heart. It was what I needed.

When I came out, my mother and Dave were standing in the kitchen laughing. Buying my own house did NOT keep her out. It did not keep her from walking in unannounced without knocking. It did not keep her from rummaging through my house being nosy and changing the way I took care of my own house. She asked what I had been doing. They both knew that I had shut myself in my closet. I am not sure how they knew or how long she had been there, but it was obviously too long. I told her that I needed some quiet time to think about things. She looked at Dave and told him that she believed I was schizophrenic. She told him that he may want to think about having me committed and she would help him. Then she said she would go so he could take care of things around the house. I still do not know exactly what she meant. I do know she thought that he did all the cooking, cleaning, and taking care of the kids by himself. Or at least she made comments to that assumption from time to time. Just because she did not know how to cook, clean or take care of her kids does not mean that I did not learn how.

With baby number three on the way, I kept my Cougar, and got a loan for a dark blue Chevrolet Astro minivan with a white pin stripe down the sides. Every time I decided to upgrade my vehicles, I went to a car lot. I had great credit so I could walk in and they would finance me on the spot. I also paid off my cars as quickly as I could, always early. My plan was to have the minivan paid off before the baby arrived. Dave always traded his vehicles with people he worked with or friends of his co-workers. I do not recall what Dave was driving at this time. He had so many vehicles I could not keep track. I only remember a few of them, probably the ones he hung onto the longest. At different times he had a silver S10 pickup, a black Camaro, a white Trans Am, a black Mustang, a red Camaro......Yes, there is a theme here. None of his cars were car seat friendly.

It was a cold winter evening when I told Dave that my stomach contractions were starting. Third time around I knew that these tightenings of my stomach muscles meant contractions. I did not have the same pain and feelings that I heard other people talk about. I have been told that I have a high pain tolerance and that is why it does not seem the same. When we arrived at the hospital, the nurse hooked me up to everything. The baby's heartbeat was strong, contractions were consistent and close together. I was fully dilated so the nurse said that I would most likely have the baby before midnight. Her twelve-hour shift was almost over, but she did tell me that she would be my nurse the next day as well. She stated that she would be excited to meet the little one in the morning. The next nurse, my night nurse, came in and she was not as friendly. I asked for more ice chips, but she refused to bring me some. At one point she told me that she did not think that I was in labor. I hardly saw her all night.

The next morning the day shift nurse came in. She saw that my water jug was empty, I did not have any ice, the baby's heartbeat was weak, and my contractions had stopped. I told her that I had not had any ice or water since the night before because the night nurse refused. She quickly got me more water and ice chips and told me to drink as much and as fast as I could. Then she brought the doctor in. Their assessment showed that lack of fluids caused me to become dehydrated, dehydration caused the labor to slowly stop, and they could see the baby's head which meant he had been stuck in the birthing canal all night. The doctor ordered the nurse to hook me up to an IV to push fluids so they could quickly get me moving again. About four hours later, baby Brandon was born. His face was purple from sitting in the birthing canal too long. My day shift nurse told me that she was reporting the night nurse and that I would not have her for the remainder of my stay. Brandon did not have the full head of dark hair like the older two. He had a full head of blonde hair. Everyone said, "you finally have one that looks like you."

The day after we were released from the hospital, I was sitting on the couch breastfeeding Brandon when I heard Joanna coughing. It was not a normal cough, it sounded faint and raspy. Daniel and Joanna had been playing in Joanna's bedroom when I originally sat on the couch. The coughing was coming from the dining room though. I got up to check. Her lips were purple, her breathing was shallow, and her cough sounded smothered. Next to her was my glass oil lamp which HAD been on the top shelf of a shelf that was taller than me. Dave was gone at work, so I called 911. An ambulance arrived and took her to the hospital. I could not go because I had the two boys and they were not allowed in the back of the ambulance. Unwillingly, I called my mother to come watch the boys so I could get up to the hospital right away. I knew my mother would be the only one that could get there quickly.

When I got up there, they had contacted Poison Control, which told them that with the oil that she ingested, they could not pump her stomach, so they were admitting her into the Intensive Care Unit. They put her in a huge incubator-looking bed. It looked like a baby bed in a bubble. It had holes in the side to put our arms through. We had to wear gowns, masks, and gloves. Joanna was reaching for me and crying, which made me cry because my baby girl was scared, and I could not comfort her. This hospital was small enough that they knew I had just been discharged from the maternity ward, so once Dave got there, they pretty much forced me to go home and take care of myself and the newborn. I was upset, but I knew they were right. I went home, crying since I did not know if Joanna was going to be okay and I could not be by her side. Instead of comforting me or being there to help me, my mother left to go to the hospital to comfort Dave and be there for him.

When Brandon was about four months old, Dave moved out again. I had been doing first and second shift day care in the home since we bought the house almost two years earlier. I was also still working nights for a cleaning company. I had asked my brother and his girlfriend to move in with me to help me with kids and while I went to the night job. They agreed. One weekend my parents and Sue were camping at a campground near the city that Charlie lived. My brother and I took the kids there for the weekend as well. We all needed a change in scenery and some fun relaxing days. On a walk up to the strip where the store and mini golf was, I saw a payphone. There was a phone book by the payphone. I decided to look through it for Charlie.... I found his name along with a wife's name and an address in the suburbs. I went from excitedly looking him up to being devastated within seconds. I was not going to call and cause tension in someone else's marriage just because I could not succeed at my own.

One day, my brother and his girlfriend had plans so they were not available. I ended up having to work an extra shift for the cleaning company and I did not have any day care kids. After all failed attempts to find someone to watch the kiddos, I broke down and allowed my mother to watch them so I could work. When I came back to pick up the kids, Daniel who was four at the time told me that Grandma gave him some gross candy. My mother claimed that Daniel was allergic to bees, so she gave him liquid Benadryl and Children's Tylenol, so they were in his system for when and if he got stung. On top of that she told me that our family had a history of Porphyria, so she also smashed up Coenzyme Q10 and St John's Wort pills and gave them to him. There were some other pills also, but I cannot remember what they were. The other two stuck in my mind because she continuously brought up that we all should be taking those. It did not matter how much I told her that he had not ever been stung before, therefore no one knew if he was allergic or not. No matter how many times I told her that she was not allowed to give my kids any sort of medication without my permission, she made it very clear that she thought she knew better than I did, and she was going to do whatever she wanted with my children. I took Daniel to the doctor who said that even though there was no reason to give him the Benadryl and Tylenol, if she gave him the correct dose, they would not harm him. The other medications, though, are not meant for children and were a danger to his health. The doctor told me to keep an eye on him for the next couple of days and watch for possible side effects. Needless to say, I never allowed that woman around any of my kids unsupervised again. This is what she did to me as a child and I lost a normal childhood because of it.

A couple months later, Dave begged to come back again. I of course gave in. I still thought somehow our family was worth saving. Why else would God allow us to have three beautiful babies? Dave moved back in and my brother moved out. At first it was great. It had not been this good between us since before any of the babies. We were talking about us, the future, our feelings. We were playful, chasing each other around the house, wrestling on the floor, and cuddling to watch movies every chance we got. One of his co-workers and his wife started hanging out with us regularly. They made several comments over the next couple of months that we were happy, looked like we were madly in love, and acted like newlyweds. We did not act like newlyweds when we were newlyweds, so this was a nice change.

Chapter Eight

One evening I realized we were low on some essentials, but it was late enough that I did not want to drag my three kiddos, plus my second shift daycare kiddos, out to the store. A couple of hours earlier, Dave had come home from his first job, showered and put on the uniform for his second job before leaving the house again. I called Dave's second job to give him the list of items. They told me that he was not working that night. I argued with them telling them that he was probably out on a delivery and just to give him the list when he got back. A few hours after I made that call, Dave came home without the milk, bread, and diapers. He never received my message because he was out with his mistress instead of working. He yelled at me, telling me that I had no business calling his work to check up on him. No matter how many times I told him that I was not checking up on him, he was still angry with me.

I decided to get us set up to see a marriage counselor. We were back to hardly talking and I barely saw Dave. Sometimes he was not coming home between his jobs. I was able to tell him about the counseling and he did agree to go. I let him know when our first appointment was so that he made sure that he did not work his second job that day. He was not home when I needed to leave to go to the appointment so I was hoping that he would meet me there. He was not there, but I did go in and talk to the therapist by myself. This happened with about a handful of appointments. Dave kept telling me that the next one he would show up to. After about the sixth session, the therapist told me that he could not help me if Dave was not willing to show up. I said I understood, but I asked if he would still see me for individual therapy. He explained that he thought I was doing great and did not need individual therapy. He said what he felt I needed was to realize that Dave would never change and that I either needed to accept it or move on. That was a choice I needed to make on my own and no amount of therapy would help me with that answer.

Sometime within these few months, Dave's last car broke down. He could not trade it for anything and did not have the credit that I had. So, he was forced to drive one of my vehicles. I did end up switching the minivan into both of our names during the time we were getting along great. He usually drove the Cougar so that I would have the van for transporting the kiddos. One day I was driving the Cougar and getting ready to pull into our driveway when I was rear ended. The damage was not too severe, but I got out of my car to go into the house to call 911 and my insurance. The young man got out, cursed at me and called his stepdad. He got out of having to pay anything. He also got out of getting a ticket because his stepdad ended up being the magistrate judge that officiated our wedding.

One night our neighbors were having a party. We did not converse with the neighbors too much. They had three generations living there; the grandma, the parents, two older adult sons, a teenage son, a son that was about ten years old and then the little girl was about four. It was my understanding that only the two youngest boys knew English because they were attending school. Dave came home somewhat early from his second job. He took his third shower of the day. First one was before his first job, then between the two jobs and now another one. He told me that he was going to go over to the party. I was shocked and surprised but said okay. I did see him walk over there and talk to the teenage son, but I was busy with the kiddos and was not going to spy all night out the window. After I put the kids to bed, I looked out the window and saw that the party was winding down. I saw the teenage boy in the driveway, so I went out and asked him where Dave was. He told me he was in their house. I asked him to go get Dave for me. I stood there for quite some time and then gave up and went into my house. I was tired of waiting and did not like being outside while my kids were sleeping. He never did come back out, all their guests eventually left, and then all their lights went out. Dave was still not home, and I finally realized that Dave was probably not over there. He probably had not been there for most of the night.

    I could not go to sleep no matter how hard I tried. I cried, went through a few minutes of anger, cleaned the house that really did not need cleaning, and played some solitaire. It was almost morning when Dave came walking in the front door. He was wearing a jacket with the collar up and was not taking it off. I was trying to talk to him about where he was and what was going on. He was not saying a word. He walked over to the recliner and sat down, still with his jacket on, collar up, and head down. I could not even get him to look at me, so I sat on the floor in front of him, between his legs, trying to get him to at least look at me. I was naïve, but not stupid. I smelled a very distinct smell, one that I had never smelled before and have never smelled since. He had sex with someone else and came home with her smell. I tried to ignore it and still tried to get him to look at me or at least talk. I reached up to move his collar and saw that his neck was literally covered in hickeys.

I lost it, I bawled so hard I could barely breathe. All the while he was just sitting in the chair with his head down not saying a word. Not talking to me. All the other times, he would apologize, cry and beg me to forgive him. Not this time, he showed no emotions at all. His infidelity was getting worse. I felt like he slapped me in the face with the fact that he had been with someone else. Before, he would sneak around to do it, and clean himself up before coming home. I knew he was cheating on me, but I was able to ignore it. I could not ignore it anymore. Remembering the words from the therapist, I gave him an ultimatum. I told him that he could not keep doing this, that it was not just affecting me, that it was affecting the kids also. I told him it was either the kids and me OR her. He could no longer have us all. This was two to three weeks before Thanksgiving. He moved out and in with his mistress. I had to take on a third job to pay the bills by myself. I allowed my brother and his girlfriend to move back in with me to help me out with the kids.

I am not sure why, but Dave ended up taking the minivan with him when he left. I have a history of being easily manipulated and being too nice. Dave probably gave me some excuse that made me give in to his wishes. His mistress did not think a minivan was cool, so he traded the minivan for a bright blue 1994 Chevrolet Blazer. Huge learning lesson for me, when having two names on the title to a vehicle, always make sure it says 'and' not 'or' between the names. He did trade the minivan at the car lot that I got it from. Because they knew me, he was able to trade without me and get financed as if I were there. I was confused at the paperwork anyway; it was showing that they gave us so much down payment for the minivan, but the amount of the new loan was still about twice what I paid for the van. It looked like I was going to pay full price for this Blazer and they still took my van. I tried to fight it, but the contract was written, and they said they had already sold my van.

This time this mistress was not hiding their affair. I usually never had contact with her. One day I was standing in my front yard getting ready to walk into the house when a glass beer bottle came flying by me and hit my house. At this same time, I heard "fucking whore." I turned to look at the vehicle driving by and I saw his mistress hanging out the car window. A few days later, she called my house telling me that if she ever caught me outside again that she was going to break my legs and put me in the hospital. I had this recorded on my answering machine, so I called the police to file a report in the hope of getting a restraining order. The police were no help though. They said that I could not file any kind of report for either one of these incidents. They told me that I would not be able to get a protection order until she literally touched me. I cleared this up by literally asking them, "so you cannot do anything to protect me until she has put me in the hospital." Both officers that came, said "that is correct." I must have an actual injury from her attacking me before I can report and request protection. I lost faith in the police that day.

My brother and his girlfriend were out spending the day with her family, so I was alone with my kiddos and my day care kids. There was a knock at the door and a lady dressed in business clothes and a clip board stood in front of me as I opened the door. She introduced herself as a worker from the Department of Human Services and she was there to investigate on a report of neglect and to do a child welfare check. I was shocked, but I let her in since I had nothing to hide and knew that the report was false. I gave her complete access to the entire house; every corner, cupboard, etc. She even got on the floor and looked under my furniture. She looked in every room and inside every garbage can. She even checked all the kids' diapers and clothing. She went through most of the house by herself since I had children to tend to.

When she was done with her tour, she sat on my couch and explained to me what was reported so I understood what she was looking for. It was reported that the kids were not bathed, that their diapers were hardly changed, that there was little food in the house, dirty diapers under the furniture, animal feces all over the house, sink full of dirty dishes, garbage overflowing onto floors, that the kids were wearing dirty clothes, that the house was covered in filth, etc. I was flabbergasted! I never lived like that nor let my house get anywhere near anything that was said. I remember my mouth dropping open and my eyes being big as could be, when she assured me that she found no signs of what was reported. I had three cats and three dogs. She said that she would never have guessed if she did not see my pets. She said my house did not smell like I had animals or as many diapers as she had seen in the garbage cans. She could tell that I kept a clean, organized house and that she was going to file the report as unfounded. Thank goodness, but I was confused at who would report such a fabricated story about me. As I walked her to the door, I asked if she could tell me who reported me. As she explained to me that it was against policy for them to disclose that information, she turned her clipboard towards me with all but the last page folded upwards. I got a quick glance at it just as she dropped the pages back down and turned the clipboard back towards her chest. My mother!

This woman did all kinds of things to me. She treated me awful my entire life. She never apologized for anything, but I always forgave her and continued to let her in my life. I kept trying to do things that I thought would make her happy and finally love me. Then she did this dishonest unforgiveable betrayal that I should not have been surprised about, but I was very surprised and hurt. A couple days after the lady from DHS had been there, my mother pulled up in my driveway. I saw her so I headed straight to my front door before she had a chance to walk in like she usually did. I know I was angry. I do not remember if she said anything before I did, or not. I am not one who usually curses either so what came out of my mouth shocked me. I stood in the open doorway and said, "Get the hell out of my house and stay the fuck out of my life!" Her reaction I believe was a bigger shock than me having the guts to say what I did. She stood there laughing. She said, "I will come back when you are not in the middle of a porphyric spell." She turned, still laughing, walked out to her car and drove away. I stood there still trying to figure out what just happened.

Dave and his mistress moved out to South Dakota... with the Blazer that I was still paying for. I do not know if he quit his job or was fired before they moved. My brother's girlfriend was pregnant, she went into the hospital with complications, so they moved out. I had a friend of mine from high school, Jackie, who moved in to help watch my kids while I worked at my other two jobs. This friend did not have any kids and her husband was incarcerated. I was still doing first and second shift day care as well. The third job I took was an overnight factory job in a small town about forty minutes north of the town we lived in. I would get home just before the first day care child arrived in the morning. I stayed awake until they all had arrived, and everyone ate breakfast. I would nap and then get up to feed lunch and then nap again when all the kids napped. The part-time job with the cleaning company was mostly weekends when I was not working at the factory and had minimal day care kids. I would leave for the factory job right after the last second shift day care child was picked up.

We had Thanksgiving and Christmas without any family from either side of the family. Dave did not try to contact the kids, nor did he get them anything. Jackie cooked Thanksgiving dinner for the kids and me. We had very little for Christmas, but the kids were still little enough that they did not know the difference. I was home with them on both holidays though. I was still working all three jobs and still paying the car payment for the Blazer that Dave had out in South Dakota. I tried to get them to repo the truck from him since I was paying on it, but they would not repo it unless I quit paying. I also found out that a joint credit card that Dave and I had as a safety net was now maxed out. This credit card was hidden away in a dresser drawer and I did not realize it was gone until I received a bill in the mail. Dave took it with him and apparently that is how he and his mistress were living.

After Christmas, I talked a co-worker from the factory into driving me out to South Dakota to get the truck. We went to Dave's parent's house first. The truck was not there, and his stepmom refused to tell me where he was. I had the kids with me, and she never did ask to see them or how they were. We had just driven thirteen hours from my house to theirs minus filling up for gas, food and potty breaks. Then we went to the local police station. They said they could not help me because the vehicle was in both of our names and I did not have a court order stating that I was to get it from him. Now remember, this was a very small town, so it did not take us long to find the Blazer. I did not know which apartment he was in, but his stepmom must have called letting them know that I was in town. His stepbrother was outside telling me that I could not take the truck. Dave refused to come out to talk to me. Since I had a key to the truck, I was able to take it. They threatened to report me as stealing it. What they did not realize is that the officer, even though he would not help me get the truck, he said the same thing went for Dave trying to get it from me. It was in both of our names and there was no court order saying that I could not have it.

I transferred the kids and their car seats from my co-worker's car to the Blazer right there in the apartment parking lot. Dave nor his family came out to see the kids. The Blazer was on empty, so I had to fill it up before leaving town. My co-worker followed me most of the thirteen hours back. He lived in the town where the factory was located. I had to air up the tires almost every time we filled up for gas on the way back as well. The first chance I could, I took the Blazer to the car lot to have them look at the tires. They said they were bald, and I needed to get new tires, but that it was my responsibility. There was no type of warranty on the vehicle. I explained that if I must get new tires then I would not be able to make my next car payment. The guy told me not to worry, just keep him updated. He said he had dealt with me enough that he knew I would pay when I could. I let him know when I got the tires and how much they were. I told him that I could pay him a little for the January payment on my next check but that the rest would have to wait until February. He agreed.

One night I went on break at the factory. I was still a smoker back then, so I went out to the Blazer to smoke.

Standing next to the Blazer was Dave. He said he was done with that mistress because she was cheating on him. I tried to stay somewhat cold towards him, but I could not do it. He ended up just hanging out in the Blazer until I got off work and he rode back home with me. He had someone drop him off, still not sure why he was dropped off at my work instead of our home. We talked most of the next day. The kids were excited to see him back home. I took him back for the kids. Jackie moved out. He got back one of his jobs. I quit the factory job. I quickly became pregnant with child number four.

I made a partial payment of the Blazer the third week of January. I explained that I would try to pay what I could on the first of February and that I had a tax refund coming so that I would catch up on my payments then if not get ahead. I do not know what happened with the verbal agreement that I had with the guy I had been working with, but they repo-ed the Blazer before the first of February. I was only behind on one partial payment. I had made all payments through and including December's. I paid part of January's on the third week of January. I tried to talk to them about the payments and the fact that they took my other car as down payment. Now I had nothing except a lot of money thrown out the window and a mark on my credit that was very upsetting. So, we were down to one vehicle.

Our getting back together was not as smooth as our last try. I had lost about half of my day care families for one reason or the other. Dave was distracted. Once I found out that I was pregnant, he wanted me to get an abortion. I refused even though he continually talked about it. I had let many family members know that I was pregnant again. He started telling them that I miscarried. I tried to talk to him about what his reasons were, but he was just snappy telling me to get rid of 'it'. When I was three and a half months pregnant, Dave was upset with me for not getting an abortion and now it was too late. He kept making comments about wanting to punch me in the stomach or push me down the stairs so that I would lose the baby.

One day in June, he said that he had already told his family that I miscarried so now I really needed to get rid of 'it' somehow. I was in the back yard hanging clean clothes on the line, when a full-sized van pulled in the driveway. I did not recognize the van or the driver. Before I could do anything, I saw Dave carry out one of our toddler beds to this van and then I saw his mistress. The people in the van all picked up speed at putting the bed in the van as I started walking towards it. Then Dave came running towards me. That was how I finally got him to tell me that his mistress was also pregnant with her seventh child. He told me that he could not have two kids the same age from two different women. She was due in August and I was due in October. We discussed the issues at hand. My suggestion was that if he wanted any of the unborn babies 'taken care of' that it should be the mistress's not the wife's. I did not think either of us should have an abortion, but she had a husband and six other children. His only resolution was that if I wanted to save our marriage that I would have to go away somewhere to have the baby and give her up for adoption. He told me that I would have to take the three kids with me because he would not be able to take care of them and work to pay our bills while I was gone. He was told by someone that it would be easier for me to get on low income housing and welfare in Missouri so that we did not have extra expenses. So, to save my marriage I packed up the kids and moved temporarily just past the Missouri/Iowa border. I also did not feel like I had a choice. He was threatening violence in order to end my pregnancy unnaturally. One of our friends drove us down there so that Dave had the car to get to and from work. All the kids and I took were some of their small toys and clothes for us all. We did not take food, furniture, or any other items. I did take Midnight, she was my baby, but I left our other pets there for Dave to care for. We did not have a joint bank account. I transferred most of my money into Dave's account before leaving so he could pay bills.

It WAS easier in Missouri. I was able to walk into the office of low-income housing apartments and walk out with keys within thirty minutes. In Iowa there was a waiting list that I heard some people are on for several years before getting accepted. I filled out paperwork, showing that I was separated from my husband, that I had three kiddos and one on the way, and was homeless and unemployed. These were nice apartments, nicer than any that I had seen before. They were built more like townhomes. There were several different buildings in this complex, each building had five apartments in them. They all had a first and second floor, a front door and a back door plus an attached storage shed. On the main floor was a half bath, living room, dining room, kitchen, and laundry room with appliances. The second floor had three decent sized bedrooms and a full bath that had doors to separate different areas. Walking from the hallway into the bathroom was the sink area, another door, then a toilet with another door, and then the tub and shower with another door that led into a closet to one of the bedrooms which became mine. I had pictures of Dave all over the apartment, so the kids did not forget him. I sent Dave a letter right away giving him our new address. The lady in the office let me know where the local food pantry was and where I could apply for other assistance. I brought very little of our money so that the bills of the house could still get paid. The only downfall was that no pets were allowed. I hid Midnight there long enough to meet a good church family that took her in until I could figure something else out.

 I found a church to get involved in, so I had other resources as well. I was alone in a small town in a new state with three children. Since we went there in the summertime, the kids were able to start vacation Bible school and I volunteered. The congregation started donating many items to us. Before long we had the entire apartment completely furnished along with tricycles and wall decorations. We were given dressers, beds, toys, kitchen and bathroom towels, dishes, pots and pans, bookshelves, coloring books, children's books, a couch, dining table with four chairs, etc. Nothing was new, which was perfectly fine. I loved everything. What people did was go through their homes and parted with things that they did not need. They even gave us food to hold us over until the state assistance that I applied for kicked in.

Chapter Nine

I was told that within a week of the kids and me leaving, Dave had a new mistress living with him in my house. She was not the pregnant one. She was a new one, not one of the other ten that his sisters and I had known about. She was another older woman who had three teenage kids that moved into my house with her. It was harder for me to get ahold of Dave since they were living there and were not giving him the phone when I would call. We did not have cell phones back then, just landlines and payphones.

There was one main lady who helped me and the kids. It was a small town with one small grocery store. We had to drive about an hour away for an OB/GYN doctor and a Walmart. This lady, Nancy, was the one who took in Midnight. The kids and I spent a lot of time at Nancy's, spending time with Midnight and hoping for time to go by. Nancy also took me to my doctor appointments and to Walmart when we needed. She would take us out to eat whenever we would go also. Nancy was married to a man who owned his own business, so he worked a lot. Sometimes I think she may have been needing company as much as I did. She was older, she had a daughter about my age that had passed away years earlier. They were a cute couple. Nancy and her husband would hold hands while watching television, which gave me hope.

Throughout this pregnancy, I had a lot of leg pain. It felt like the baby was pinching the nerve in my upper right thigh that connected my torso to my legs. The doctor said that she would move just right to pinch that nerve. Sometimes it somewhat paralyzed my leg to where I would fall to the floor. Even with knowing that Dave had someone living with him in my home, I was still going along with his plan. Through the hospital social worker, I had signed papers to give her up once she was born. There was a clause where I would have so much time after her birth to change my mind.

Like the three kiddos before her, I surpassed my due date. A week after my due date after Sunday evening service, I felt contractions. Nancy took me to the hospital while her husband kept my kiddos. At the hospital, they hooked me up to the machines. They said I was in full labor, but I had not dilated. I was at about five centimeters, so they sent us across the street to Walmart. They said after a couple of hours of walking around it should be enough to kickstart my labor. Every couple of hours we would go back to the hospital and they would check me. I still had not increased in dilation. By early morning they sent me home, telling me to come back when my water broke or when the contractions were stronger. I had contractions all week. That Saturday, I told Nancy that the contractions had gotten worse and now I felt them in my back. She took me back to the hospital while another church lady watched my kiddos. This time they kept me. She was born that night. I was extremely sick; my vitals were down but they were not finding a reason. Once my daughter was born, I had signed papers to give her up for adoption. I called up north to let Dave know that she was born and to discuss me coming home. He was not home, and I was informed that I was not getting him or my house back.

About four days later, I was finally okay enough to be discharged. That same day her vitals dropped, and she started to have some medical issues. The nurses said she needed human touch in order to flourish. Once I held her and thought about what was happening back home at my house, I changed my mind and decided to keep Ashlee. She had blonde hair also and looked more like Brandon. I knew that meant the end of my marriage, but I would deal with that later. Both the baby and I were finally released the following Saturday. I could not wait to get back to the other kids. Nancy and her husband did bring them to the hospital every day, but I still missed them.

Since I couldn't go home, I stayed in Missouri to raise my four children by myself. I cleaned some homes for members of my church to make some extra cash. Nancy and her husband got me a cheap car that I slowly paid them back for. It was a brown Pontiac. My name got around to some elderly women who needed some caretaking help as well. I was hired to help one lady take her baths, cook her dinner, and do some light shopping for her. Another member of the church owned rental properties and he hired me to clean some of his vacant properties so he could rent them out. The pastor's wife also hired me to help her clean their house as well as help her go through her attic. Dave and I were not divorced nor legally separated. There was no child support ordered and he was not helping me with anything. This was also the first time that I did not go back to smoking after having the baby. I would quit every time I got pregnant but start back up a few months after the baby was born. This time I did not.

It was about two in the morning one night when Dave called me telling me that he needed me to pick him up because she kicked him out of my house. Like an idiot, I loaded up the kids in the car and made the two-and-a-half-hour drive north to pick Dave up from a gas station. All he had were the clothes on his back literally. Over the next few days, I bought him new clothes and other things he needed; socks, underwear, cigarettes, lighter, and then he had me buy a radio to install in my car so that I no longer had the manufactured radio in the car. He applied to a few jobs around town like he was going to stay with us for a while.

About a week later, Dave said he needed to go up to get his last check from the job he had up north. I told him to just have them mail it to us, but he gave me some excuse about having to sign for it. He also said that while we were up north, he would have his uncle help him put in the new car stereo. We loaded up our four babies in the car along with some snacks and drinks for the all-day drive. Two and a half hours later, we arrived at his past employer to pick up his check. The kids and I stayed in the car. When he came out, he said he wanted to stop by the house to pick up some of his things from her. After a long wait in the car, he finally came out of the house. He was behaving differently and just told me to get to his aunt's house because that is where his uncle was. The aunt that he was referring to was the sister to the uncle who was going to help with the stereo. His uncle did not live with this aunt. Keep in mind, this was the late 1990s and neither of us had cell phones so not sure how he knew as much as he did.

I drove out to his aunt's house, shut the car off and started to get out of the car when Dave told me to stay put while he went up to see if his uncle was still there. Again, the children and I waited in the car for a lengthy amount of time. Dave finally came out motioning me to pop open the trunk. I did as I was told and again started to get out of the car when he told me to stay. I assumed he was getting the stereo out of the trunk to show his uncle when I saw him take out a full garbage bag out of my trunk, shut my trunk, and told me to go home. I sat there confused for about ten minutes or so trying to assess the situation. Dave did not even look back as he carried the full garbage bag into his aunt's house. After ten minutes or so, his uncle came out telling me that Dave did not want me here and to go home. I drove away crying and with several different emotions. I was sad, hurt, angry, confused, etc. I felt guilty and felt like a major fool. I admit that I squealed tires and did not stop at the stop sign at the corner. Thank goodness no harm was done to my kids in the car.

During the week that Dave stayed with us, Joanna who was now four, regressed in her toilet training. She had been potty-trained for two years, but while Dave was there, she refused to use the bathroom and kept having accidents. There was a day that I saw her doing her potty dance, so I told her to go potty and her response was "but I don't want daddy to go away again." I remember looking at him. He also heard her response, so he knelt down by her, grabbed her hands and said, "Daddy is never going away again, I promise." In the two and a half hours back home, that incident continued to replay over and over in my head. I felt bad for my babies that ended up sitting in a car for about a total of eight or nine hours. They were five, four, two, and six months old. Considering the circumstances that day, they did very well. Once the kids and I got home, I took them to the park so they could run and play after spending all day trapped in a car. After I put them to bed, I began to think about that garbage bag. What did he have in it? I went through every inch of my apartment. I realized that all the clothes, cigarettes and car stereo I had bought were gone. He knew before we left that day that he was not coming back. The only thing I found that he did not take was the partial package of socks that I had bought for him. It enraged me that he basically took the food right off the table from my children. I did not have the money to spend on clothes and cigarettes for him. I put some of that stuff on my charge cards. That was another point at which I realized that my marriage WAS really over. I could not let him do that to my kids ever again.

 I started getting mail sometime after Dave went back to Iowa, from a variety of places, stating I owed them money. One of the letters was from my bank stating that they believed there was fraudulent activity on my account. They needed me to contact them as soon as possible to verify this. This is when it hit me that, since I had planned on returning to my home, I left all my unused checkbooks at the house and Dave had this other woman living there. After I called and explanations from both sides were told, they sent me copies of the bounced checks that had come in on my account. Most of them were in Dave's handwriting, making checks out to his girlfriend, out to gas stations for cash, and one was even made out to his cousin. These were not made out for small amounts; they were a couple hundred here and a couple hundred there. I also received mail from Figi's, Fingerhut, Columbia House, and several other mail-order companies. Everything was in my name, with my address but shipped elsewhere. Again, they were not small orders, they were hundreds of dollars to each company. I contacted every one of them to get copies of the order forms. Again, all of them were in Dave's handwriting. I kept everything that I received so that I could file identity theft charges. I wrote back to each of these places explaining what really happened and who they should be charging for these items. I kept copies of all the letters I wrote also. I also let my bank know about these other fraudulent encounters. When I tried to file a report, they stated that I could not do anything since everything was in Dave's handwriting and we were still legally married. If anything had been in his girlfriend's handwriting and I could prove it then I could have charged her, but they were all in Dave's handwriting. As long as we were legally married our credit was linked.

  Two or three days after Dave left, I received a call from a local factory wanting to schedule an interview with Dave. I scheduled it, but I went in for the interview. I explained to the gentleman behind the desk what had happened. He had me fill out another application while in his office and hired me to start right away. I was able to get on childcare assistance, so the state helped me find a lady to watch my kiddos while I worked in the factory. Most factories you think would have mostly men who work at them. This factory had two separate buildings, the one I was assigned to work in was mostly women. That was probably a good thing that Dave did not stay and start work there. He would have been too excited to be the only guy and the affairs would continue in a new state.

Well these ladies were not like any women that I had ever known before. They spoke like sailors. They cursed hard core, smoked, and talked about sexual encounters constantly. I was not one to curse and I had quit smoking. I did not like sex and quickly found out that I knew nothing about sex. I was called 'miss goody two shoes' many a time in my lifetime. I never thought of myself as being a goody two shoes, I was just an average person. I was uncomfortable, but I was glad to be getting a paycheck to pay off the debt accumulated by Dave's expenses. These ladies talked about drinking, bar hopping, male strippers, blow jobs, and a list of sexual terms that I still am not sure what they all mean. This is where I learned what it meant to go commando. One of the other ladies talked about how underwear bothered her so the only time she wore them was on her time of the month. I was shocked and way out of my comfort zone.

After about the second week working there, the women decided they would get a little nosey in my personal life issues.

They told me how I need to forget about my husband, file for a divorce and get a new penis. They were a little more vulgar though. There was a man who came into our building daily. I believe he was picking up our finished products to take to the main building. The ladies would tease him, telling him that I was looking for a new penis to get my mind off a no-good husband. He told me one time to just ignore the ladies because they were just playing. I think they got a kick out of me being a prude which is exactly what I was in comparison. The lady that seemed to be the ringleader made comments that she had given that guy a blow job before and that he would be happy to help me learn how to do my first one. I tried hard to ignore the comments but remained friendly since I did have to work every day with these ladies.

    With this job, I now made too much money to stay in the low-income housing. The church member who had rental properties had a two-bedroom, two-bathroom house available so the kids and I moved. I put the two boys in one room and the two girls in the other. I slept on the couch in the living room. I felt like they needed the bedrooms more than I did. I also could have Midnight here which made me very happy. This house was a one-story bungalow. It had an enclosed front porch which led into the living room. The door to the left was the front bedroom with an attached bathroom that I put the girls in. Straight ahead was an arched doorway that led to a dining room. A door to the left off the dining room was a small hallway that led to the second bathroom and second bedroom which I put the boys in. Straight ahead was another arched doorway that led to the kitchen. There was a tiny enclosed back porch off the left of the kitchen that had been made into a laundry room which had a back door that led into a big back yard. No play equipment for the kids in the yard, but this house was across the street from the local park.

One of my co-workers, Dayna, had a boyfriend who worked with a guy who was single. Dayna and the other ladies bugged me every day about going on a blind date with this guy. I told the entire factory that I was not interested in dating. I was not interested in a divorce. My concentration was raising my children and being able to provide for them. I was not getting help or support from any family members. I lost touch with many of the friends that I did have. The relationship roller coaster that I was on with Dave isolated me. I made some friends from church, but they were all older ladies that would not understand these women that I was working with.

After a month of telling Dayna and the others that I was not interested and politely asking them to leave me alone about the date, I decided to change my tactic. I asked Dayna that IF I went on the date, would she leave me alone. I gave in and agreed to go on the date with the understanding that I did not want to be alone with the guy and after the date, the nagging was to stop. She set up the blind date for that Saturday. One of my other co-workers agreed to watch my children, and we went on a double date. Dayna and her boyfriend went with us. I made the mistake of letting Dayna pick me up from my house, though, instead of driving myself. She picked me and the kids up in her car. We took the kids over to the other co-worker's house and then we went back to Dayna's house so she could finish getting ready for our double date. I was sitting on her couch waiting while she was down the hall getting ready, when three guys come walking in the door. Only one of them said hi to me. He then proceeded down the hall towards where Dayna was getting ready, so I assumed he was her boyfriend. The other two started playing video games and proceeded to act as if I was not there which was very awkward. At this point I did not know who my date was supposed to be, if either of them. Neither of them was very attractive, which may have been more so their rudeness than their actual looks. I did not think either of them was dressed for a date either. When Dayna was ready, she marched into the living room. She said "let's go" like a mother corralling her children and continued for the front door. One of the guys playing video games got up, went to the refrigerator, grabbed a rose, handed me the rose, all the while still not even looking at me, and said "here." He then turned and headed for the door. I found myself standing there alone except the one guy still playing video games. The three going on the date with me were already out and in Dayna's car. At this moment I was thinking how I was supposed to get home. I already wanted the date to end when it had not even started. I did not feel comfortable around any of these people that I was supposed to spend the evening with.

  We had about an hour and twenty-minute drive to the town they chose to have this date. Dayna drove, her boyfriend sat in the front passenger seat while I was stuck in the back with my date, Richard. They played music that was not my type of music. It was the loud screaming kind that I could not make out the words to. This did not help with me already being uncomfortable and feeling out of place. During the drive, Richard did nothing but talk about himself. He talked about his dad, mother and two siblings. How they are a close family and he does all sorts of things for his siblings all the time. I found out later, this was his stepmom and his father's other two children. He had three more siblings with his real mother that he did not mention at all that day. He talked about drugs and some friends of his that he gets his drugs from. He talked about having a bunch of friends in a biker gang. He told me about his job and how many cars he had but never once asked me about me. I could not get a word in edgewise even if I wanted to. I even wore my wedding ring on this date.

Our first stop was a Target. They all did a little shopping while I just browsed. Next stop was a mall where they were looking at CDs and sunglasses. I still used cassette tapes, but I also had children that came before my wants. I felt like I was an old lady in the store with a group of teenagers. I am the kind of person to use things until they break. I had a working cassette player and all my cassettes still played music. Richard ended up getting a Lenny Kravitz CD and a two-hundred-dollar pair of Ray Ban sunglasses. I just cannot grasp spending that much money on a pair of sunglasses. I always bought the ones that were five dollars or less. I could already tell this guy was materialistic and that was not me. We had nothing in common, so even if I did not already plan on not being interested, there was no chemistry there. Then we went to a Mexican restaurant where Richard tried to touch my knee. That is when I was finally able to speak up. I said that I had four children, I was married, and no intentions of getting a divorce, while holding up my left hand with my wedding ring still on it. I also mentioned that I was not interested in dating him or seeing him again after this date. The rest of the dinner was conversations between Richard, Dayna, and her boyfriend. The long ride back home was also filled with conversations between the other three. I felt out of place. I could not wait to get my kiddos and go home.

 I was hoping she would take me home to get my car so I could go get my kids. That did not happen. Instead she went straight back to her place. When we got back to Dayna's house, I asked if she was going to take me to get my kids and then home. I do not remember if she answered me or not, but I did sit on the couch to wait for her as she headed straight back down the hallway to her room/bathroom. Her boyfriend also followed her. The guy that was there earlier was still there playing video games and Richard joined him once we got back. I know it was a couple of hours before Dayna's boyfriend reappeared. I asked him if she was ready to take me home and he said he would check. He went back down the hall and again seemed like forever before he came back out. He said that she fell asleep and that I would have to wait until she got back up. It was already getting late! I needed to get my kids picked up and in their own beds. We had church in the morning. I was getting very anxious. I must have dosed out a bit though while waiting for Dayna to come out of her room because I remember waking up to everyone being asleep. It was about two in the morning. I had no choice but to wake up Richard to see if he could take me home. I initially did not want him to know where I lived, but at this point I was just worried about getting my kids and getting home. He creeped me out because he was asleep on the other couch, but his eyes were slightly open. He did wake up, drove me to pick up my kids, and drove me home. I said thank you, we said goodbye and I got my kids in their beds. Phew.... the nightmare was over...or so I thought.

Chapter Ten

The kids and I got up Sunday morning for church as usual. This Sunday in particular, was a potluck day, so the kids and I stayed to eat and socialize. I think we got home about two or three in the afternoon. I laid everyone down for their naps since we also always attended Sunday evening services. Before evening services, I fed the kids dinner and then we were back at church until about eight or eight-thirty. Once back home, I bathed the kids and got them ready for bed since I had to work Monday morning and they had day care.

That Monday at work, Dayna was upset with me and gave me the third degree about not being home on Sunday. I told her that my kids and I were very active in church. I did not realize I was to check in with her before attending my normal Sunday routine. She said that Richard tried to come over several times on Sunday and that I was not home any of those times. I reminded her that the agreement was one date only and then everyone leaves me alone. The co-worker who watched my kids was also upset that I did not pick the kids up until late on Saturday night, basically early Sunday morning. I tried to explain that I did not have my car and was waiting on Dayna but that did not go over so well. They had all worked together for a long time, so I was considered the outsider. I felt like they were ganging up on me. Dayna started telling everyone that I was psycho and they all stopped talking to me. I kept to myself and started taking my breaks in my car since I did not feel comfortable around any of them anymore.

During this time, I was in the process of evicting Dave and his girlfriend from my house. I was ready to go home to Iowa and stop living in Missouri. My job had gotten tense and unenjoyable with working with all those gossiping women. Two weeks had gone by since the blind date, so I thought it was behind me. I was using the front enclosed porch on my rental house as a toy room. One day I was cleaning the house when I heard a man's voice coming from the porch. I walked out to the porch to find Richard sitting on the floor playing with toys with Daniel and Brandon. The boys were six and two now. Daniel admitted to unlocking the door and letting the man in because the man said he knew his mom. Richard looked up at me and asked if he could hang out for the day. His job consisted of traveling, so he was usually out of state and that is why it had been two weeks since he had come over. He said he got to come home about every other weekend. I like peace and was not comfortable with confrontation. I was timid and compliant because of my low self-esteem. When he started talking about the Sunday that I was not home, I again had to explain where I was the Sunday after our date. I wish I had not explained this because it really was not any of his business. I again reminded him that I had no intentions of starting a relationship with him. I also told him that within a couple of months I was moving back to the house I owned, which was over two hours away. I let him stay for a little bit longer, but I made him leave before I fed the kids dinner.

Another couple of weeks went by without a word and then he showed up with a package of diapers. I did not want to seem ungrateful by refusing the diapers so instead I offered to pay him for them, which he refused. I then offered for him to stay for dinner to pay for the diapers. I did not have a television, so other than talking and watching the kids play, we did not do much else. Some moments were awkwardly silent because we did not have a lot to talk about. Other times it was awkward due to something he said that made me extremely uncomfortable. He took advantage of me being a nice person who could not figure out how to tell him more aggressively that there was no interest in him. I told him every time he came over that I was not interested, I still wore my wedding ring, and I also said that even if I were not married, I had no interest in him. There were many reasons, but I had also been obsessed with the man needing to be older than the woman. He was two years younger than me even though I felt about twenty years older because the things he was interested in were more like a young teenager, not a man in his mid-twenties. He lived in the basement of his parent's house when he was not on the road and drove a company truck. He was a short man, a couple inches taller than me. He was stocky with long hair, a beard and a mustache. He had brownish hair and hazel eyes. Both of his ears were pierced, and he had tattoos. Dave also had piercings and tattoos, so it was not that I judged anyone for those things, but they just were not my thing. If I ever decided to date again, I would pick someone opposite of Dave, not someone similar.

For the next couple of months, he would stop over unannounced. At first, I would make him leave before I fed the kids dinner. Then he started staying for dinner, but I would make him leave before I started their baths. Then he started helping me with baths, but I would make him leave before putting the kids to bed. I was getting frustrated with myself because this guy did not accept my rejection or my reasons for him needing to leave. He had a way of pushing me to get what he wanted. I had no knowledge or experience dealing with someone so demanding and pushy. Repeating myself in my normal friendly personality was going in one ear and right out the other with this guy. He would not take no for an answer. I just kept hoping I would be able to move soon and never see him again.

One day he brought over a small television. It was a prize he got from his senior prom and was going to let me borrow it. I told him thank you, but that I did not want to borrow it. I also told him that I did not want it to stay at my house when he was not there, but he refused to take it. It had a VCR player attached so we started watching movies with the kids. I would still make him leave before putting the kids to bed. He tried many times to stay later, but I was not comfortable with that for a variety of reasons. The main one being the fact that I did not want to be alone with him. Another time after he left, I noticed that there was a small bag of his clothes somewhat hidden between my washing machine and the wall. This concerned me a great deal.

The kids and I took a trip up to the house after the eviction notice was served. I was checking the condition and signing some final paperwork, one of which was a quick claim deed to remove Dave's name from the house. They were still living there but were preparing to leave. I realized that Dave got rid of most of my pets. One dog remained so I decided to take him with me. Dave's girlfriend for some reason told me that she was pregnant with his baby. It did not bother me like I think she thought it would. When I asked Dave's mom about it though, Dave's mom laughed saying that his girlfriend could not be pregnant because she had a hysterectomy several years earlier.

Another weekend that I took a trip up north, Dave's mom was wanting to see the kids. So, I went over to her house. We hung out for a little while, so she had some time with the kiddos. As we were getting ready to leave for our two-and-a-half-hour drive back home, Dave pulled up in front of my car blocking me. I had not gotten all the kids in their car seats yet. Dave was getting in my face about something. Brandon did not like it; he was a protector of his mama. Brandon either tapped or poked at Dave's leg. Without skipping a beat, Dave reaches down and picks Brandon up while still talking to me. Brandon was about two years old now and his feet hung about to Dave's private area. Brandon kicked him in his testicles at the same time as he was telling Dave to leave his mommy alone. Dave almost dropped Brandon, but he did get on with his way and let me finish loading my kiddos in the car.

On our way back to Missouri, we ended up in a car accident. I wrapped my car around a pole. Luckily, we all made it out with just scratches. I had my dog with me, but when the ambulance came, they would not let my dog in the ambulance. They did not give me the option to refuse the ambulance either. One of the bystanders said he would take my dog until I could come get him. He pointed to a house not too far away and said that it was his house. Richard was the only person that I knew in Southern Iowa, but he was out of town. I was still in Iowa and closest to Richard's parents. I called him; he called his parents to come get the kids and me from the hospital. They took me back to that town to get my dog, but I could not find that kid or my dog anywhere. The town that I had my accident in was almost nonexistent; it literally was a couple blocks worth of houses and that was it.

I was a light sleeper when my kiddos were little. Since I had hearing loss, I did not want to miss waking up to my kids needing me or a noise outside. I slept on the couch and the bedroom doors were always left open. There was a specific night that I remember feeding the kids dinner, locking the doors behind Richard as he left, and then tucking the kids into bed. I would never go to sleep right away. I would usually do another sweep through the house double checking locks and windows. Then I would lay down on the couch for at least thirty minutes before falling asleep.

This night though, the next thing I remembered was waking up on the living room floor with my pants at my ankles and Richard inside of me. I was still fully dressed otherwise. I did not wear pajamas and never took off my bra. I do remember pushing him away and asking what he was doing, besides the obvious. My stomach was turning like I was going to be sick, so he left the house. Just thinking back to that night makes my stomach turn and gives me the same sick feeling. This ended up happening a few more times. I told him that I did not want to have sex with him and that I felt sick about it. I did not know what to do though. I asked him how he was getting into my house after I locked up. His response was "I have my ways." I had no one to talk to about it. All my education told me that it was not rape. I think we even discussed it because I remember him telling me that it was not rape because I allowed him into my home, that he was not a stranger, and he dared me to try it. I also remember him telling me that since he was from that area, he knew more people than I did so everyone would believe him over me. I did know that the ladies at work were not supportive of me. He was friends with Dayna, so I did not feel like I stood a chance.

Soon thereafter, I found out that I was pregnant. I had so many mixed feelings but did not know what to do. I already knew in my mind that my marriage was over, but I do not think my heart felt it until this moment. Now it would be my fault that my marriage failed. Richard and his stepmom told me that I needed to get a divorce. I did not want to have a baby with Richard. I loved babies and would have a dozen if I could, just not with him. I did not believe in abortions for myself. I hated myself for letting myself get into this horrible situation. I was getting ready to move back home to the house I owned until I got this news. I had already put in my notice at the factory. My mother's shrilling voice kept repeating "you are living in sin, it is God's will that you are pregnant, once you have sex with someone then you become one in God's eyes." All these things kept playing in my head. I don't know if I was more afraid of my mother or to get struck by the hands of God. I had not even spoken to my mother since I moved to Missouri, but she still haunted me. I felt like I should at least stay until the baby was born and make visitation arrangements with Richard. I found a young religious couple with a small child to rent out my house as soon as Dave and his girlfriend moved out of the house. I also learned that my mortgage was a couple months behind in payments as well as learning that my mother had made the payments in the past year instead of Dave and his girlfriend. The renters gave me first and last month's rent, plus deposit, which I used to catch up on the late payments. Their monthly rent paid me just enough to cover my mortgage payment and then they were responsible for all utilities.

When I first told Richard that I was pregnant, he did not believe me. He said he thought he was sterile because he had been with many women unprotected and never got anyone else pregnant. Looking back, I think that was part of his game plan. He quickly accepted the news without proof and was quickly planning for us to live together, all the while still trying to push me into filing for divorce from Dave. I reminded Richard that I still did not want to be with him and that this was just temporary. Richard and I moved into another two-bedroom house on the Iowa side of the border, two blocks from his parent's house. He continued to travel for his job, I quit my job at the factory to move and take care of the kids. I went back into childcare and watched a few kids from town for extra money. It was not too bad of an arrangement because I only had to see Richard every other weekend. Sometimes it would be three weeks before he would come home. He did not want me telling his family about our temporary arrangement because he claimed that they would not help me while he was away if they knew that I was not going to stay with him. I needed their help since I had no vehicle and was in a small town that did not even have a store. I complied.

I quickly became scared of this man. I felt like I had to comply to keep the peace and keep my kiddos safe. I could keep the house clean all week long with all the kids running around, but when Richard was home, I could not keep it clean for anything. He was the biggest slob I ever met. He complained about everything, including the kids. Ashlee had a rash from her diapers even though I changed her regularly. I took her to the doctor about it and the doctor's conclusion was that she was allergic to the cheap generic diapers that I felt like I was forced to buy. He even said that a rash from an allergic reaction is different than an actual diaper rash. This is one of the things that Richard used against me. He said that his stepmom, who was a volunteer EMT, would testify that I was an unfit mother due to Ashlee's rash. He said his stepmom would help him take my kids away from me. I experienced several red flags with him, but I did not know what to do since I did not really have any type of support system. He was constantly making comments that if he wanted someone to disappear, all he had to do was let his biker friends know who, and it would be done, no questions asked.

A few years earlier, a newswoman from a northern Iowa town had disappeared. Her body was never found, and she was presumed dead. One of Richard's stories is that one of his uncle's and a cousin kidnapped, raped, killed and buried this newswoman somewhere in Alabama. The way he told it scared me as much as the story itself. I was not sure what to make of these things he said back then, but now I believe these were intimidation tactics to scare me into never crossing him. They worked because he had me scared into complying with everything.

One night his stepmom invited me out to watch the male strippers at a bar in a neighboring town with her and her friend, while Richard's teenaged sister watched my kids. I did not drink nor did I touch any of the strippers because I had no desire to do so besides I was in the first trimester of pregnancy. I did not even spend any money as his stepmother paid for everything. Richard apparently called the house while we were out and got his sister who he yelled at about me not being home. When I got home and called him back, he again yelled at me for being out in a bar. This bothered me since he went to bars almost nightly while he was on the road and I did not technically consider us a couple. A few days later, his stepmother told me that he called her too and yelled at her for taking me to the bar to see male strippers. Laughing, she told me that she put him in his place so that I did not need to worry about what he would do when he got home.

During these months of living near Richard's parents, I learned a lot but not directly. I had to piece together a lot of everyone else's stories. Richard's stepmom would tell some stories about him during his childhood, I would hear some from his grandpa, some from his dad, and some from his teen sister. His sister hated him, said that they never got along because he was mean to her for as long as she could remember. Richard's stepmom is only ten years older than he is and ten years younger than his Dad. She was sixteen when she met his dad. His dad was a truck driver, so she traveled with him for the first two years. When Richard was eight, he went to live with his dad so his stepmom, who was eighteen, came off the road to stay home with Richard. Richard complained about his stepmom always locking him out of the house, grounding him then telling his dad so that he always got punished twice, and the list went on. His stepmom's stories did collaborate some. She said she locked him out of the house so he would go play, otherwise she could not get him away from the television. She also said that he did not like to get up in the mornings so she would sit on him until he got so mad that he could not go back to sleep. Richard always said that it felt more like he had a mean older sister or babysitter, not a stepmom. He believes she was punishing him because she could not travel in the semi anymore.

Richard always said that his mom did not want him, and his stepmom hated him because she had to become a parent to someone else's kid. Richard said his sister bit him when she was about a year old which made him hate her as well. They have never gotten along even through today. His stepmom actually admitted to not letting Richard talk to his mom when she would call or giving him birthday or Christmas cards from his mom. She said if there was money in it then she would take the money to the store and buy Richard something with it. Her reason for doing this was because she said he would act up and she was the one who had to deal with his behaviors after he would speak to his mom or see a card from her. His grandpa told me that one of the times he was locked out of the house, Richard badly skinned his knee, so his grandpa poured rubbing alcohol on it and tried wiping the gravel out of the wound. Richard complained about this incident because he said his grandpa was not gentle about the whole thing.

    I still had that partial package of men's socks that I had gotten for Dave a few months earlier, so I decided that I was going to start wearing them. Richard saw them on my feet and accused me of stealing his socks. I had to show him the package and show him that they were not the same brand as his. Then he accused me of lying about where they came from and reminded me that he had people watching me while he was gone so he would know if I had another man in the house. Another red flag I experienced was one day that he was home. He was looking for a key for a jobsite and could not find it. He yelled at me and the kids about touching things that were not theirs. He scolded them to high heavens about not telling him the truth of who took it and where they placed it. I interrupted and told him that the last place I saw it was on my dresser where he would usually empty his pockets out onto. He informed me that he looked there, but the key was not there. He said he knew that one of my brats took it. I proceeded to walk to the dresser as I was starting to learn that there was no arguing with him. I picked up his stocking cap, and there appeared the key right where he last laid it. I told him that it was under his hat. That it was still in the place that he put it along with his change and pocket fuzz. He continued to argue with me, still convinced that my children were messing with his belongings and they moved the key. He never apologized to them or me.

He was always telling me that my kids were pussies because they loved their mom. I do not remember what Brandon was doing, but he was not quite three yet and Richard was pissed off at something. Richard put a dress and a diaper (Brandon was toilet trained and wore underwear) on him and told him if he wanted to be a sissy baby then he could look like one. Brandon was crying and Richard took a picture of him. When I confronted Richard, he said that I was not a proper parent and that he knew better than I did. I was angry and told him that I was going back to my hometown because I did not like the way he treated my children. He threatened to kill me or take my kids away. He reminded me that he knew plenty of people that would vouch for him that I was not a fit parent and the state would take my kids. I believed him. I did not have the money or means to move back home without help so I felt trapped... stuck.

These were just a few of the situations that I found us in.

Chapter Eleven

About a month before my due date, my renters decided they were going to move and instead of finding new renters, I planned to move back into my home. Richard did his same threatening manipulation tactics. I did not want to keep him away from his child, so I gave him the option to move with us. I did not think that he would agree to move, but I also thought that once she was born, he would split. The shop he worked out of was in the same city as the group home that I had lived in. Living in my hometown was still over an hour closer to Richard's employer than the town his parents lived in.

The kids, Richard and I all moved back into the house that I owned. It was not a very easy transition as Dave's failure to pay bills came haunting me again. I called to put utilities back in my name and found out that Dave and his girlfriend left an electric bill that was over nine hundred dollars and a water bill that was almost six hundred dollars. I had to pay these bills in full before I could have service turned on. Since I was the homeowner, I was responsible for delinquent bills of my tenants. I filed these bills along with the other fraudulent documents. It did not stop there either. I went to take one of the kids to the doctor and also found out that Dave had an outstanding bill of almost two hundred dollars that had to be paid in full before any of my kiddos or I could be seen by the doctor. I even tried to remove him from our family file so that he had to be responsible for his own doctor bill. They would not allow me to remove him until after our account was no longer delinquent.

Dave lived at the other end of town with his girlfriend. He would drive by the house occasionally, but he would never stop to visit with the kids even though sometimes they were outside playing. He would just slow down and kind of creepily watch us. I tried to motion to him that he could come and see the kids, but he drove off quickly as if he would get into trouble for talking to me. One of my neighbors came over to talk to me once she realized that I was back. She told me that she was glad that I had moved back. She said the people I had living there had sold drugs to her grandson and a few other teens in the neighborhood. Many of the neighbors were apparently glad that I had come back as well. At first, I thought she meant the religious couple that I rented out the house to, but after a lengthier conversation with her, she informed me that it was Dave and his girlfriend. Apparently, there were all kinds of problems coming from my house while Dave and his girlfriend were there. Police were called frequently, lots of yelling and loud music at all hours of the night. Sketchy people coming in and out at all hours of the day and night. This kind of explained the fact that after they moved out, I noticed one of my windows was broken and I had to get that fixed before the renters could rent from me. The neighbor also claimed to have known about a local police officer buying drugs from them as well. That one I left alone because I really could not do anything about it anyway. Not that I could do anything about Dave's girlfriend's issues, but it was good information to have as far as the safety of my children.

Dave did file for divorce once he knew I was pregnant, I think. The reason that I believe this, is because he did not file until after we had moved back, and he saw us outside. I clearly looked pregnant since I was eight months along. Even though I now lived in the same town, he made no effort to see the kids. I would let them spend the night at Dave's mom's house and she said he still refused to go see the kids. One of Dave's sisters even loaded up my kids one day to take them straight to his apartment. She said she pulled up and told Dave that the kids were in the car if he wanted to see them. Before he could get to the vehicle, his girlfriend came out onto the deck yelling something about getting the kids away from Dave. I shared pictures of the kids with his family, even giving extras for him to have, but all the family members said that it was a waste of money because his girlfriend did not want him to have anything to do with his kids.

In the summer of 1999, I gave birth to my fifth child, third daughter, and Richard's first child. He was initially upset that she was a girl because he thought that his first child was supposed to be a boy. Something about all the other men in his family had boys first so he was too. Besides he had only picked out a boy's name, not a girl's name. He was going to name this baby after himself. Since we had a girl, he now decided that an affair with a married woman from a couple years earlier resulted in a child of his. Now all of a sudden, he believed her son was really his instead of the lady's husband's. This is the first that I had heard about him supposedly having a possible son by a woman. Apparently, he had a fling with her at his last job. She was married and she got pregnant around the time they had the affair. She had a son so now he thought the child was his, but he did not want to disrupt her family. I still thought it was odd that less than a year ago he told me he was sterile and now he thought he fathered a child two years before just because I gave birth to a girl. I did not think this was normal behavior.

While in the hospital Richard informed me that she was HIS daughter, not mine, and that he would name her since I had named four other children. I should have stood up to him then, but I was trying to keep the peace, so things did not escalate. He named her Cole. She was not named after anyone that I am aware of. Once we got her home, he did NOT get up in the middle of the night with her. If she started to cry, he would wake me up to take care of her. I was breastfeeding, but he had no interest in helping with the real care of a baby. He did not change her diapers because he thought he would vomit. He would not even give her a bath. I breastfed, but even when I would bottle feed her for supplement, he still would not feed her.

After Cole was born, Richard finally told me about his real mom and siblings in Nebraska. Yes, I heard a little, but not as much as he let out now. He decided he wanted his mom to know that she had a granddaughter. So, a couple weeks later, his mom, stepdad, his thirteen-year-old sister, Elizabeth, and five-year-old brother from his mom came to visit.

He also had another brother from his mom side, but I met him years later because at this time he was already an adult out on his own. This was the first time they met me, and they gave me hugs as if we had known each other for years. Elizabeth and I became really close, very fast and she is still one of my best friends and favorite sister. We have claimed each other as sisters since day one, leaving out the in-law all together, and most of the time she says she is my sister not Richard's.

I talked to his mom and Elizabeth on a regular basis. Richard was also not very nice to his two brothers and Elizabeth when they were growing up. He had a lot of behavioral issues that his mom had trouble handling. He often cursed at her, broke things, and told her he hated her. She had sent him to stay with his dad for the summer when he was eight years old. She did that in the hopes that he just needed a break from her. From my understanding, he ended up staying with his dad for about a year, then was returned to his mother. Around age twelve, still having behavioral issues both at home and at school, she sent him back to his dad's, again, originally only for the summer. His mom told me that she decided he liked it better at his dad's and was better off there because every time she would call to talk to Richard, his stepmom would say he was gone or busy. His mom said that the stepmom would say how good he was doing. Elizabeth told me that her mom had a really hard time with Richard not being with her, that sometimes she would cry because she missed him.

I had not been able to start my childcare business back up yet, so I went back to work outside the home. Richard chose the childcare provider since he was 'picky' about who was allowed to watch his daughter. My older kids did not really like it there. They said the provider was mean. I noticed that every time I picked up the kids, the provider had Cole sleeping on the cold porch. Cole had ear infections almost the entire time we used this provider. I finally was able to get Richard to listen to me and remove the children from her care. The kids were there for about three months. Again, he worked out of town for two to three weeks at a time, which was still nice for us, but I had to wait until he came home before firing this provider. I picked the next childcare provider for the kids. The kids loved it at the new place. Since Richard was on the road, it was at least six months before the new provider ever met him. After she met him, she told me not to take it the wrong way, but he was not what she expected. She said she expected me to be married to a tall good-looking man in a suit and tie. She said we made an odd couple. The kids and I loved her though, so she watched my kids for the next two years.

A couple months after Cole was born, I received a court order stating I was divorced. We did not go to court nor did Dave or I sign this document. His lawyer was none other than the magistrate judge that officiated our wedding, plus the stepdad to the kid who rear ended me. I did not have a lawyer, so his lawyer and the judge signed the papers and finalized the divorce. Several things concerned me about the order, so I did decide that I was going to need a lawyer. This order was giving Dave every other weekend visitation plus Wednesday evenings. It stated that I was responsible for all joint bills. There was no child support ordered. One day I saw Dave parked on the side of the house in the street so I quickly ran over to him before he could drive away. He said that he did not sign the divorce papers because he did not really want a divorce. I told him that I did not either. Dave said he did not agree with everything that his lawyer put in the papers and that he also told his lawyer that he no longer wanted a divorce. It is not that I wanted Dave back because after everything that he had put me and the kids through, there was no way that I could do it, but I did not want the divorce either. I think it may have been a protection barrier for the other mess I was in.

I hired a lawyer to modify the court order. I also took in copies of all the fraud and the receipt for the new window I replaced after I evicted Dave. Along with those documents I also had the copy of the Quick Claim Deed and eviction notice showing what dates everything took place. The new court order gave him supervised visitations for a few hours a day on a few certain days of the month, ordered him to pay child support and also listed a property settlement amount to cover all the bills and fines I had to pay. The courts ordered a third-party person to do the supervised visitations. I would drop the kids off at a certain time, Dave was supposed to show up about a half hour later, visit with the kids and then I was to pick up the kids about a half hour after he left. The only reason we were not supposed to be there at the same time was because Dave had told the judge the only reason that he had not seen the kids was because I would not let him and that he could not handle being around me. I knew that was a lie, and probably something that his girlfriend was demanding. Dave's family had already told me that she was physically abusive and controlling.

A few months later my lawyer went to court for me again. I was not ordered to appear, just my lawyer had to be there. The lady who had been ordered to do the visitations had complained that she was an unpaid babysitter because I was dropping the kids off, but Dave was not showing up. My lawyer filed contempt, I believe, because of the lady's complaint and the fact that I was still not receiving child support OR the property settlement. The only change to the order was the removal of any kind of visitations. Apparently, Dave was also ordered to spend a night in the county jail for not complying with the child support order. I did not find that out until several years later though when he told Aimee.

I was still not receiving any child support. In a conversation with Dave's mom, she said that she had seen one of his pay stubs that showed a deduction for child support. With this information I went up to the local child support recovery office. They informed me that they did have an order for me, but that a previous order surpassed mine. When I asked what it was for, the lady behind the counter said that she could not give me that information because it did not involve me or my children. She then said that if Dave wanted to know who was receiving his garnished support payments that he would need to come up himself. I relayed all this information to Dave's mom. We decided that it had to be the mistress that was pregnant when I was pregnant with Ashlee. I have never been told for sure. I do not even know if Dave ever went up to find out.

When Cole was six months old, Richard had not made any attempt to find his own place and his behaviors towards my kids were not getting better, so I kicked him out of my house. About two weeks later, he called me crying about missing the kids and me. He said he was sorry about how he treated us and that he really was hoping we could have a relationship. I knew that his crying was fake because he had told my boys several times that real men do not cry. That only pussies cry. He had made fun of me on a few occasions for crying over a sad movie. I tried to explain to him that we had nothing in common, other than a child, and that we were not in love. His response was that opposites attract, which was a statement he used continuously throughout the next several years. It was not until I went to college in my 40's that I learned this is a myth, opposite attraction is short lived due to a thrill of change, never meant to be a long-term relationship. When I did not give in to his crying, his tone quickly changed into anger and he made threats. He again threatened that his stepmom would help him report me and get my kids taken away from me. Again, I found myself without a support system and unsure of what to do to protect the kids and myself other than to comply with his requests.

About this same time, I received a letter from Dave's live-in girlfriend. To summarize it, I think she was trying to make me feel inadequate. She mentioned how I could not satisfy

Dave with my sexual missionary positions, then goes on to say how Dave's whole family knew that I was allowing Richard to abuse my kids, that they may try to get custody and how she guaranteed that Dave would never leave her because she would turn him in for the fraud. I never responded to her letter. I disagreed with her missionary positions comment, but that was something I thought should stay between Dave and me. I also realized that she did not know that Dave could not be charged for the fraud since we were legally married. She must not have known that I had already tried to press charges on him for all of it. I did show the letter to Richard when I was making my case about how his threats would not hold up if others knew how he treated us.

Like usual, Richard knew exactly how to keep me in his little 'mental' cage. He got upset at the letter, saying that Dave's family did not know shit. He ripped the letter to shreds. Little did he know, I dug the letter out of the trash and have kept the pieces in a Ziplock bag. Then he reminded me that the only way I could keep my kids was to do what he wanted, that he had people to back him up so Dave would not have a case. He also mentioned that since Dave lost his visitations, most likely no lawyer or judge would allow him to take me to court to take custody. Now that my divorce was final though, I had nothing to keep Richard from manipulating me into marriage. Which he did, he said the only way that I could keep my kids was if I married him. He said that it would be a business contract just until Cole turned eighteen.

Two months before Cole turned a year old, we got our marriage license. Again, we used my charge card from the same jewelry store, and I made all the payments myself. I was very stressed out about it because I had been trying to figure out how to get out of this union with Richard. Dave's sister told me that Dave and his girlfriend got their marriage license a week after we did. She said Dave found out about us getting a marriage license and was hoping to make me jealous. My thoughts were that it was a little late for that, but I was confused at the same time. This was not a game; this involved the lives of several people including my children. They also were married two weeks after we were. Again, Dave's family told me he did it once he found out what I was doing.

A month before Cole turned a year old, my mother's pastor officiated a very small generic ceremony. It was on a Tuesday afternoon, with sixteen people counting my children. Richard and I both wore jeans and t-shirts. I wore tennis shoes; he wore work boots. A guy that I met from work was a witness and Richard's mom was a witness. My dad took pictures. The only picture with Richard and me both in it looked like it was from the 1800s with color. Neither of us were smiling and we both looked like we were mad at the world. My mother was the happiest person that day. Again, there was no honeymoon, we both returned to work after the ceremony. The only people in attendance were the pastor and his wife, my parents, Richard's mom, stepdad, Elizabeth, and his youngest brother, Scott the witness, Richard, my five kiddos, and myself.

A few months later I was served with a sheriff's sale notice on my house. I was totally confused because I lived there now and was not behind on my mortgage. I took the papers to my lawyer. He found out that the day before Dave signed the Quick Claim Deed, Dave signed a contract with American General Finance that he had several personal loans through allowing them to use the house as collateral. These were some of the loans he had from trading cars; he had apparently not paid them. We went to court. I had my lawyer present and a representative with my mortgage company and a representative from AGF were both on the phone. My lawyer showed the judge the Quick Claim Deed, explained that the children and I resided in the home and that I had been paying all other bills accordingly. He explained that I had no knowledge or legal responsibility to the personal loans through AGF. He told the judge that he thought there should be another way for AGF to get their money from Dave instead of the home that the minor children lived in. My mortgage company agreed with my lawyer. They also stated that I had been paying my mortgage as agreed and that the only time there was ever a delinquency was while Dave was living there, but once I became aware of it, I caught the payments back up. The judge ruled in favor of AGF stating that at the time of those debts we were still legally married. I lost my house. We were given ten days to move out.

Chapter Twelve

We moved all of our belongings into storage as quickly as we could. My lawyer helped us get emergency housing vouchers to live in a hotel temporarily. Those only lasted two to three weeks though. It was hard living in a hotel room with five kiddos plus Midnight, which I still had with me. About the time the vouchers ran out though, my parent's rental house became vacant, so we moved in down there. Again, it was temporary, so we did not move any of my furniture out of storage. Since the experience of renting from my parents last time was not so pleasant, I was in a bigger hurry now to find a permanent place to live.

When I met Richard, he had extremely bad credit. He owed money to all kinds of places, including some medical bills. While we lived near his parents, I was helping him pay on his debts to help fix his credit so that he could get a place of his own eventually. My credit was excellent before the repo of the Blazer and the joint credit card with Dave which I never paid on since it was all expenses from him and his mistress. My credit was not horrible, but it was not the greatest even though I had been trying to repair mine as well. Richard and I were trying to find a house to buy instead of rent since I had built up his credit.

Not surprisingly, we were not agreeing on where to live or what type of house to buy. The company he worked for was an hour away in the bigger city. I was wanting to start my in-home day care business back up so I thought we should move closer to the big city. He did not want to be IN the city. He said he had always lived in small towns and that was where he was most comfortable. I did not like small towns. They were too gossipy, and everyone knew too much, or at least they thought they did. I also preferred being close to shopping and doctors, especially with five kiddos. We had argued enough that I said that he could live wherever, and I would find my own place. He reminded me that we had a business contract. Unless I wanted to lose my kids, I should do what he wanted. I tried to talk to him about the problems that I was still having with his behaviors towards my kids. He did not like to talk about serious issues. He would always overpower me for sex and then make the comment that sex fixed everything.

We looked at several houses in small towns within a thirty-five-mile radius of the big city. My parents found one just fifteen minutes from their house in a small town with a population of less than five hundred. That was the house that Richard decided we would buy. Built in the mid-1970s, it was described as a twenty-five-year-old split foyer home with six bedrooms, two bathrooms, a family room with a fireplace, living room, dining room, double detached garage on a third of an acre lot. It had been a foreclosure and sat empty for over a year. We could not move in right away because of several issues. When they tried to turn on the water, pipes started spraying water everywhere, so we had to get those fixed before trying the water again. There were no appliances so that was another expense. It had never been updated. It had brown carpets with pink walls, yellow linoleum with brown paneling, white countertops with the gold glittery spots in it on dark brown cabinets, the kitchen and dining rooms both had carpet. My lawyer suggested that we put the house in Richard's name only because he had a hunch that Dave still had some outstanding debt that could cause us more financial troubles. He suggested that in a few years we could probably add my name to the title. My name however WAS on the mortgage loan.

 We were finally able to move in about a month after signing the purchase agreements. We continued to have other issues with the house. When we checked the breaker box, it contained a paper stating that the house was from Wausau Manufactured Housing. Basically, the house was a double-wide mobile home that they stuck on top of a basement. While we were trying to remodel, this became increasingly clear, from the basement we could see where the two halves were connected. On the main level, because they were two halves combined together, we were limited on what we could change. The vaulted ceilings throughout the upper level gave us no attic and no way to put up ceiling fans in any of the rooms. I made the comment that this was a temporary house anyway so if we could just fix it up the best that we could then we would still be able to sell it for more than we bought it. Richard informed me that he would only buy a house one time so he would die in this house. In my head I knew that I would be moving in sixteen and a half years at most so there was no need to continue that discussion. Cole was eighteen months old when we bought this house. After buying this house, with him on the road all the time, we did get a joint bank account so that I could pay the bills using both of our incomes when he was traveling.

I soon found out that I was pregnant again. We hardly ever had sex due to the fact that I did not like him touching me, or even looking at me. We probably had sex at most four times a year and that was only because he either forced himself on me or he threatened my kids in order for me to comply. Because of this, I knew I became pregnant before we bought the house, when I was threatening to end our business contract. This pregnancy caused a huge disagreement between us because he was trying to say that this pregnancy extended our business contract. I said that it did not, our original agreement was to expire when Cole turned eighteen and I was not going to agree to an extension. I dropped it only because I still had sixteen years before the original agreement ended so there was no reason to continue arguing with him now. Besides, less stress for me was better.

About four months later, my lawyer called me stating that Dave walked in his office asking how he could terminate his rights. His reason was that he did not want to pay child support. I was not getting child support, or the ordered property settlement money anyway so was not sure what he thought he was getting out of. My lawyer also stated that Dave was claiming that only two of the four kids were his biological children. The lawyer explained to me the same as what he explained to Dave, that he could order paternity tests for all four kids. Dave would only be responsible to pay for the paternity tests that came back positive and then they would order child support accordingly as well. I was all for it, ready to take the kids in for the tests when my lawyer said that Dave refused, stating he would rather sign his rights away to all four than take any paternity tests. My lawyer said that statement told him that Dave knew all the kids were biologically his and he just did not want to have to pay anything. He gave me my options and told me to get back with him soon with my decision.

First option was to deny Dave his request. He would eventually be forced to pay child support and all the delinquent child support as well. Second option was to let him sign away his rights, but by law someone would have to adopt the kids in order for the courts to finalize the termination of Dave's parental rights. I cried for two days. I did not know what to do. I did not want Richard to adopt them, but I did not want to force Dave to be a father either when obviously he did not want to be one. I thought about how Dave used to be with the kids. He used to play with them. I have pictures where the kids would be napping on his chest. I could not for the life of me figure out why anyone would want to abandon their kiddos. I knew he had not been around anyway, but I just thought eventually he would be in their lives again. This tore me up inside. These were good kids, beautiful kids, that did not deserve any of this. In these two days, I got to thinking about Charlie again. How I wished I could call him and talk to him about my dilemma. What would his advice be?

I did not talk to Richard about this at first because they were not his kids and I really did NOT want him adopting my kids. I believe the only reason I mentioned it was because he knew that I had been upset and going through old pictures. With no hesitation at all, he said he would adopt them. He said he knew this conversation was coming and he had already thought about it. He did the "I told you that Dave would not fight for custody" rant. Hesitantly I called my lawyer with the decision to give Dave what he wanted. This is one of the biggest regrets that I have, a decision that I wish I would have made differently.

We were in court within days. Dave and his wife were there. They did not look at or even acknowledge the kids which I brought to court with me. I was hoping that Dave would see the kids and change his mind. No luck, the judge asked him if this was his choice, he said yes, that he wanted to sign away his parental rights. The judge then asked Richard if he was willing to step up and be the legal father of the kids. He agreed and all I could do was cry. One of the phrases my mother used to say was, "you lay with the dogs long enough, you are bound to get their fleas." Right now, I felt like this was all my fault because I had children with the worst men ever. Richard was already abusive; I just did not realize it would get much worse now that he felt there were no restrictions.

All the delinquent child support was expunged. I knew that would happen; it was part of the court order. I received one check after court for seventy-five dollars. That apparently was for the property settlement that for some reason was also expunged. When I asked my lawyer why, he said that was part of the agreement that Dave had made with the courts. I was not aware of this agreement and wanted to know why I did not have a say. The property settlement money had nothing to do with the kids or custody of the kids. Those were expenses of Dave and his now wife that they had accumulated and not paid. I was forced to pay their expenses and never reimbursed. I just felt like Dave got away with everything. He had not been responsible for his kids for the past four years, he committed fraud and got out of that, he racked up loans and other expenses that the kids and I ended up paying for with either cash on hand or our home. I found out a few years later from Dave's sisters, that Richard threatened Dave into signing away his rights and making the deal that I would not come after him for anything else.

A few months later, I went into labor with baby number six. This was the first pregnancy in which I went into labor early. The other five were all one to two weeks late. The doctor said he assumed that I went two weeks early because of stress. I did not tell him but yes, I had been extremely stressed lately, fighting with Richard and some issues with our neighbors. Richard named her Renee, again because I had named four kids, so he thought he needed to be the sole name giver of his babies, I guess. He did not give me the same demands with Renee as he did with Cole. He would still refer to the girls as his kids not ours, but he was not as strict with what I could or could not do with Renee.

Every time I had a baby, I repeated the discussion with the doctor about birth control. The test results showed that I was still allergic to the main chemical in all the methods. There were a few new methods, but the doctors still thought that it would be too dangerous for my health. I even discussed the possibility of a tubal ligation since I did NOT want more kids with Richard, but they thought that I would be one of the slim percent to end up having a tubal pregnancy after the tubal ligation. They explained that I was so fertile that I usually had multiple eggs that dropped during my ovulation period. He also explained that my insurance would not pay for the termination procedure or the reversal of the tubal ligation if this scenario were to happen. He again told me that my options were abstinence or condoms. I talked to him about the condoms apparently not working. He suggested that it was a user issue and not the fault of the product.

I knew what he meant even though we did not discuss that in detail. I was told by Dave's sister that he admitted to poking holes in the condoms because he said I was happiest when I was pregnant. Cole was conceived without consent so there was not a discussion with Richard about birth control prior to having her. While I was pregnant with Cole, Richard and I never had sex. After she was born, we only had sex when he was threatening, and I needed to keep the peace, but I told him that he had to wear condoms also. There were actually a few times that I fought him off of me because he refused to put one on. I assumed he took the same approach that Dave did so he could continue to trap me. I did try to talk to Richard about him getting a vasectomy. His response was that a real man would not let anyone near his 'junk' with a knife. He also said that just because I had six kids did not mean he was not wanting to have more, with me or someone else.

A week after Renee was born, I was driving Ashlee to preschool when over the radio was the announcement of the planes crashing into the twin towers. I pulled over to cry and listen. I was shocked. I tried to think about whether I knew anyone out there or not, then I hoped and prayed that no one that I had lost contact with was out there. Sadly, my thoughts were more selfish than what I would like to admit. I thought about what if more attacks happened around the country. What if something happened here, I would want to be with people I loved and loved me if I was going to be a victim soon. I would want to be around someone that I trusted to keep me and my kids safe if possible. I thought about Charlie and hoped his life was happier than mine.

Richard was still working out of town, usually out of state, two to three weeks at a time. I loved the time I had with just the kids and me. We would listen to music, sing and dance. We would all make cookies together, watch movies, cuddle on the couch, and play games. I always tucked each of my kids into bed at night, pulled their blankets up under their chins, gave them a kiss on the cheek or forehead, and told them "I love you! Good night, sweet dreams!" and then blew them a kiss to catch as I walked out of their rooms. These were things that none of us felt comfortable doing when Richard was home. He made fun of us for singing and dancing, he made fun of the music we chose because he did not like my type of music. He also made fun of our movies, calling them gay or stupid. If any of us would cry during a movie, he would laugh and call us pussies or titty babies. He would make fun of us, telling us that it was stupid to cry over movies. He did not like me tucking the kids into bed because he said that I was babying them and turning them into pussies. At this time the kids were nine, seven, five, three, two and one month old. None of which were too old for affection from their mother, but to keep the peace with him, I did not tuck the kids in if he was home and able to see what I was doing. Sometimes he would go to bed before the kids did or be playing his video games so I would be able to tuck in the kids without him knowing.

I did not go back to work outside the home after Renee was born. I took on a few local kiddos to slowly start my childcare business back up. Richard had gone on a couple longer projects where he was gone six weeks at a time. He would call to check on me every night. Most of the time, he would call me from a bar. I could hear the background noise and knew exactly where he was. We could not afford for him to spend money on alcohol at a bar, but I think he was there for more than that. He said several times that his co-worker would pick up women and that sometimes "the women needed a paper bag over their face." I guess that was his way of saying they were too ugly for him. His co-worker was married. I said something about that fact when Richard informed me that "it is not cheating if you are in a different area code." He ended up making this same comment many times over the years. I heard this from him often enough that I am pretty sure that it was not just his co-worker picking up women. I did not really care if he was picking up women though. I thought maybe if he was with other women then maybe he would leave me alone.

Richard got a cellular phone a couple of years earlier through Sprint, I believe. He was always complaining that it did not always work around home. When Renee was about nine months old, we went to the local US Cellular store. The main reason that I agreed with this was because I was driving the younger children fifteen miles away to attend preschool while the older children were in a public elementary school in the opposite direction. After the 911 attacks, I wanted to know that if something happened to me or any of my kids that I could be contacted, or I could contact someone if needed. The account for some reason went into my name, he picked the newest top of the line data phone, and I picked one of those simple Nokia brick phones. I did not need anything fancy, all I wanted it for was to make emergency calls when I was away from home. This was my very first cellular phone.

When Renee was about a year old, Richard's employer closed the doors on the business. Some of the other guys, including his supervisor, went to another similar company. His supervisor was in a management position at the new company as well, so he hired Richard and some of the other guys to work at the new place. They did the same type of work, but more locally, which meant less travel. For the first few months, it was not too bad having him around more. Once in a while he would work out of town for a night or two during the week but was home every weekend. He still was a slob, so it was harder to keep the house clean with him there all the time. He did start to play a little with the kids, promised the boys that he would teach them to throw and catch a baseball. Renee refused to speak, she would point to what she wanted, and her five older siblings would get it for her. She acted half afraid of Richard. My assumption was that it was due to him being gone so much, and she did not really know him. She finally started talking at about eighteen months old. Then we could not get her to stop.

About a year after he started at this new company, Richard was laid off. Work was slow, they said it was an impact from the 911 attacks that were just now starting to affect the Midwest. I had my day care in the main living room so it would be near the kitchen. Richard could not stand being around all the kids, so he usually hid out in the bedroom or the family room in the basement. There was a television in our bedroom as well as his gaming system. There was also a television and a different gaming system in the family room that my kids would usually use. Richard was usually watching something that my kids did not want to watch or that was inappropriate for them to watch OR he would be playing the game system and refuse to play any two player games so that the kids could join him. After a few weeks of this, the kids just started going straight to their rooms to stay away from him. He would curse at them or when it was a show that was inappropriate for them, he would call them pussies.

Also, with him home more, he kept getting dogs but did not keep any of them for more than a couple of weeks. He got a Dalmatian, an Irish setter, a bulldog, and a few others. He got a shock collar for the Dalmatian I think, but Richard and his dad thought it would be funny to put it on Daniel. When I found out, I was very angry, I yelled at Richard, but he laughed at me saying it did not hurt Daniel and if it did then he was a pussy. I said then he should put it on himself, but he again laughed at me and said hell no. Daniel said that it did hurt, but he knew that Richard would call him a pussy, so he toughed it out. He did say that it just made his hatred for Richard grow that much more.

    Since he was on the road for the majority of the first five years that I knew him, I was able to manage the house and the kids the way I wanted, including Cole, who he said was not my daughter. I had a whiteboard with all the kids' names listed on it. Each week I would switch the chore of the week next to their names to a new chore. I was also on this list even though I did more than one chore a day. The kids all did their chore on a daily basis, but they had the same chore for a week. They always knew what was expected of them. I usually added the kids to the list when they were between two and three years old. They would start out with the easier chores even though I would help them until they could do it on their own. Richard was never on this list even when he was not working. He always made the comment that the only reason to have kids was to make them your slaves. I did not agree with that and would usually just ignore him. The older kids did not like it though and could not ignore him. Their hatred for him grew as well. Richard would not even go get the mail. It was a stand-alone box at the end of the driveway. He always said that if you cannot get there in thirty seconds or thirty steps you should drive. The driveway was only about two and a half car links long but took longer than thirty seconds to walk out there.

Cole had been on this list for a couple of years, helping out with chores like everyone else. I had not yet added Renee, but it was getting close to her time to be added. Richard did not like Cole having chores so when he realized what the chore list was all about, he started telling one of the boys to do Cole's chores. She immediately caught onto the role he had for her in this so-called family. She had the attitude of a teenager before she even started kindergarten. She learned quickly that she did not have to do chores or even listen to anything that I told her to do. She figured out that she could tell Richard that either one of the kids or I had hurt her, and he would come unglued on us. One day, I spent the day trying to get her to do her chore. As soon as Richard walked in the door from work, she told him that I had grabbed her arm. He got in my face telling me that I had no business touching his daughter and that she was not to be doing chores. Even after I told him that I had not touched her, he did not believe me. He took her side.

Another day, he was watching television in the family room on one end of the sectional. I was folding clothes on the other end. Cole was standing maybe two feet in front of Richard, Brandon was about four feet to the right of him, I was maybe four feet to the left of him. Cole calls Brandon a fucking asshole and Brandon fires back calling her a dumb brat.

Before I could say anything, Richard yelled at Brandon to apologize and sent him to his room. I said, "Excuse me, Cole was cursing at him with words she should not be using." Richard claimed he did not hear her, only Brandon and continued to yell at Brandon and me.

There was an incident that took Daniel a few days to finally tell me about. There was a day that most of my kiddos were upstairs with me because Richard was downstairs watching his shows. Daniel came upstairs very mad but tight lipped. I asked him what was wrong, and he said never mind. A few days later, when Richard was not home, Daniel said, "Mom, something is wrong, and I do not know what exactly, but it hurts my tummy." He continued to tell me that he was coming out of his bedroom at the same time that Richard was coming out of Cole's bedroom. Their doors were right next to each other. He said that Richard threatened him that if he told me that Richard was in Cole's room, that Richard would accuse Daniel of touching his sister's private part. Richard obviously used different words than Daniel did, but I believed Daniel was telling me the truth. The only reason that I could think of why Richard would threaten to this extreme was if that was what Richard had actually been doing. Since he did not tell me right away, there was no way for me to go check. I understood why he waited though. I could not figure out how to bring it up without throwing Daniel under the bus, so I just tried to be more observant of what Richard was doing and where he was at all times.

For about a year after this incident, many of the kids would tell me that Cole was being gross when playing in the sandbox. This included many of my day care kiddos. It got to the point that no one would even play in the sandbox except for her. The kids would call her "stinky butt fingers." No matter how much I told them that was not appropriate, I would still catch the kids doing it. Like I said, this was not just my other kiddos but day care kids as well. They told me that her fingers smelled like dirty butt, which they did. I smelled it too, but I did not know why. I gave her baths and the smell seemed to always be there. Then the kids told me that Cole would sit in the sandbox with her hands down her pants or up the leg of her shorts. They said she was sticking her fingers in her private or her butt. This is sometimes a sign of sexual abuse, but I did not know that until years later.

Richard was always making comments about how stupid my kids were and that Cole was smarter than all of them. He said many a time that "stupid people shouldn't breed," referring to Dave and me for the most part. I mentioned about wanting to go to college, but Richard laughed at me, said that I was too old to go and not smart enough to pass. At this time, I was about thirty-one years old. I believed him. He also told me that I would never be more than minimum wage and the only thing I was good for was taking care of his house and kids, and for "putting out." He had Cole on a pedestal. He treated her better than me and all the other kids, including Renee. When I would help any of the kids with their homework, Richard would say that Cole should help them because she was the smart one.

He started telling the kids these things also... saying they were stupid, would not amount to anything, would not make it into college. He kept calling my boys gay and saying the girls would both be pregnant before they finished high school. He started calling Ashlee crazy, telling Joanna that she had a big booty, and Cole would repeat him, etc. He was getting more aggressive and he liked having a sidekick who repeated him. I was standing in the kitchen washing dishes when a pan hit the upper cupboards above my head and then fell to the floor next to my feet. I think it would have hit me if I did not duck when I heard it hit. When I turned around, Richard stood several feet behind me glaring at me. No words were said; he just turned and walked out of the room. That pan gained a dent in its side that would not come out. Other times he would come walking towards me with a look of evilness in his eyes, I would walk backwards into a corner, like they do in a typical scary movie. He would puff up his chest, shoulders back, arms straight to his sides, and when he had me in the corner, would hover over me making it difficult for me to get out. Sometimes he would take a swing at me but punch the wall right next to my head, then laugh and make fun of me because I would flinch.

Almost daily he would walk past me and grab my crotch saying he could carry me like a six-pack. I did not like that at all, it hurt and was uncomfortable, besides he would do it in front of the kids...mine and childcare kiddos. If he was not grabbing my crotch, he would grab my breasts, again it hurt and was uncomfortable. I told him multiple times that I did not like when he did either of those. I also told him that I preferred that he not do it, especially in front of the kiddos. He said they were his and he had every right to grab them when and how he wanted. It was degrading and made me feel like an object, not a valued person. Richard's favorite joke was "How do you turn a dishwasher into a snowblower? You give the bitch a shovel." He would tell this to anyone who would listen and every chance he got. He admitted to it being his favorite. I do not know if it was because he knew I hated it so much or because he was a real male chauvinistic pig.

Chapter Thirteen

Since Richard was laid off anywhere from three to six months out of the year now, he decided to attend college. Of course, I asked why it was okay for him to go and not me. He said because it is different for men than it is for women. Plus, he said he was smarter than me and could use a college degree more than I needed one. He enrolled part-time at the community college in my hometown. I believe he took a total of three classes. His classes were in the evenings so it would not interfere if he got called into work. One night he forgot his paper that was due, so he called asking me to bring it in before the class ended. When I did, everyone in his class just stared at me. I assumed he said something negative about me, so it made me quite uncomfortable. He later told me that his whole class was in awe, they all imagined his wife to be "some rough old biker looking chic." He also said that they wanted to know how he got me because they thought I was "out of his league." I never asked what he told them. I was surprised that he told me as much as he did. He only went for two semesters though. He was getting C's in all his classes. He has yet to finish to get a degree in anything. When Elizabeth got married a few years later and her husband first met us, he too asked Elizabeth how Richard 'got' me because he also thought I was out of Richard's league.

I bought a desktop computer and printer for business reasons. I was now state registered, on the Quality Rating System or QRS certified, and on the food program as well as teaching an age appropriate curriculum to all ages that were in my care. I had to continue childcare classes for a certain number of credit hours each year to maintain my certifications and registration. I had childcare policies in place, contracts, and mandatory forms for my families. I needed the computer to help keep these files easy to access and to print off as needed. Along with this process, I made my first email account. Richard also decided to use my computer once in a while for personal reasons. I think part of it was to monitor my usage. He joined chat rooms, he said mainly to connect with other players for his gaming. I noticed a couple times that he was actually instant messaging women from other parts of the country. Again, I let it be, hoping he would leave me alone. It also got me thinking about if there was a way to find my old friends that I had lost contact with.

The three oldest kids took on paper routes so they could make their own money. Richard was not wanting us to be responsible for their clothing needs or other expenses. At first it was just Daniel who had a paper route, then about a year later Joanna and Brandon also got routes. I took the kids up to open bank accounts at the bank that held our joint account. Even though I took the kids up, for some reason the bank put Richard's name on them as the parent and linked their accounts to our joint account. This bank was in the small town where we lived, and Richard was on the volunteer fire department, so I assumed that was why. The only people in town that knew anything about me were the day care families that attended my childcare. I kept to myself partly because I was shy, but I also had a family to take care of, my kids were my everything. The kids would put fifty percent of their checks in the bank and I would let them spend the rest however they wanted. I still bought their necessities regardless of what Richard said.

Midnight was still with us. She was still my baby, sleeping with me, sitting with me, following me throughout the house, etc. We also took in an older female Sheltie named Lady. Lady was already eight or nine when we got her and had health issues, but she still needed love. She was great with Midnight and the kids. Then one of Daniel's friends was moving and could not take her cat with her so she asked us, while we were on the paper route, if we could take care of her cat temporarily. I agreed. What I did not know is that her cat was pregnant. It also became evident that they were just dumping the pregnant cat on us. They did not come visit the cat, they did not give us a forwarding address or a phone number to contact them if something were to happen. This kitty was not friendly to us or my other pets. She seemed to prefer to be outside, but I kept her inside, so that she would not run away.

About six weeks later, she had a litter of four. I kept my distance at first so she could give birth in peace, but I soon realized she was not doing very well with it. I noticed one was not moving at all. I assumed it was stillborn. The other three were moving and trying to drink from her. She kept moving away from them as if they were bothering her. She even hissed and swatted at them. Before I could grab it, she sat on one and broke its neck. I used gloves to grab the two deceased ones and bagged them up. Using different gloves, I moved the other two into a box for safety (she started to sit on the male, but I saved him) and used damp towels to clean them since she was not. Then I had to hold her down for them to eat. I did this several times a day for several weeks until I thought they could live without her. I also started feeding them with a dropper when she was being to mean to me and them. I eventually let her out and never saw her again. I let her outside because she was attacking Lady, Midnight, her own two kittens and all of us humans. We named the kittens Princess and Fluffy. Princess had calico markings with a white chest and Fluffy was a dark gray furball. Fluffy eventually grew out of the gray color and was pure black, looked a lot like my Blacky, Midnight's brother.

    About a year later, I was driving the kids around on their paper routes because it was chilly and rainy, when I saw something white in the middle of the street. Initially it looked like a white plastic grocery bag, but once I got closer, we realized it was a white cat just sitting in the middle of the road, facing away from us. I honked a couple different times, but he did not even flinch. I got out of the car to chase him off, but he still did not move. I slowly walked towards him. He finally jumped a little from being startled once he noticed me, but he still did not move out of the street. Being hearing impaired myself, my first thought was that he was possibly deaf. I let him sniff my hand, I pet him from the top of his head down to his tail, and then slowly reached over to pick him up. He had chunks of fur missing, he had sores all over him, and he was so skinny I could feel his ribs. I went straight to the local veterinarian. They said most completely white cats are deaf. After a quick evaluation, their diagnosis was that he was a stray, they had never seen him before, he was malnourished and had probably been living outdoors for a couple of months. Their suggestion was to put him back where we found him. I morally could not do that so I told them I would just take him home. I was a regular there so they knew me and said if anyone came looking for him that they would send them my way. Within a couple weeks, his missing fur had grown in, his sores were healing, he had gained some weight and was a sweet beautiful kitty. The kids named him Oliver. No one ever claimed him, and he fit right in with our family.

 Richard had a couple hunting rifles when I met him because that was supposedly a pastime of his and his father's. I am only aware of one time that he went hunting in all the years that I have now known him. That one hunting trip was within the first three months after I first met him. Now he was buying handguns and a lot of ammunition. We had to buy one of those large gun safes to keep his guns locked up so that I could guarantee my kids were as safe as could be. It was so big that if I took the shelves out, I could fit in it with a lot of room to spare. I originally told him that I did not want guns in the house due to the fact that you hear all the time where kiddos are getting ahold of loaded guns and accidentally killing each other. He did not care or agree with my concerns, so he kept the guns in the top of our closet. It was my idea to get a gun safe because I knew the more that I complained about them the more he would continue to possess.

At night, anytime there was a noise outside or in the house, Richard would always wake me up to go check on it. I would look in on all the kiddos, look around outside, double check all the windows, and head back to bed. I never knew what type of noise he had heard or from where. He would just wake me up and I would do my rounds checking to make sure everything was alright. He was usually sound asleep when I returned. He also slept on the side of the bed furthest away from the door, no matter how the bed was positioned in the room. I never gave it much thought though until one day I heard a conversation. I was with a group of women and one of them started telling a story about her husband waking up to a noise, he told her to stay low, and he went to check on the noise. This group of women all agreed that their husbands all do the same. They continued saying that all the husbands had the wives sleep furthest from the door, that staying low meant staying on their side of the bed using the bed to shield them until their husbands let them know that it was safe. It was clear that they had men who cared for their well-being, where I did not.

Around this same time, I watched something on television that mentioned someone accidentally getting shot through a wall. I do not remember if this was a news broadcast or a crime show. This got me thinking about the gun cabinet full of ammunition in my house. I decided to ask Richard if any of the ammo that he had in the house were the types to go through walls. He said yes that most of the ammo he bought was that way. One night I had a dream that someone broke into our house. Richard woke me up to go check like usual. In my dream, I came around the corner into the upper living room to see a man coming up the stairs. The man stops when he sees me. Richard comes up behind me, using me as a shield and tells the guy if he moves, he will shoot. In my dream he shoots through me, hitting the intruder. As the bullet exits my body, the bullet goes through the intruder, comes out of his back and it goes through a wall that has one of my kiddos on the other side. This dream scared me tremendously so I asked Richard how true that could be. He laughed at me and said very true. He said if it were the only way to ensure that he shot the intruder and if it meant saving himself then yes, he would shoot through me. I asked him if he had bullets that would go through two people and a wall to possibly shoot my children. He again said yes, depending on which gun he chose to use.

With that conversation I heard with the women, the dream I had, and the uncomfortable answers he gave, I decided to converse a little more about this with Richard. I wanted to get a feel for what I was really dealing with. I asked him why I slept closest to the door, why he always woke me up to go check on the noises, why he thought he needed guns in the house, and why he felt those types of bullets were the best to keep on hand. His responses were that I slept closest to the door so that I did not wake him up getting up or coming back to bed after checking on the kids, a noise, or getting up for the day. He said that he woke me up because it was my job to take care of the kids, and if an intruder did come in, by sending me out first gave him time to get to his guns. His reason for having guns was for home safety, but he could not give me a good explanation as to why he needed so many guns for home safety. He liked those types of bullets and wanted to make sure that whatever he was needing to aim at was going to get hit. Whether these answers were to intimidate me or not, they did. It did not help that he threatened to kill me on a weekly basis.

Other than constantly buying or trading guns, he was also constantly getting new tattoos, video games, and earrings to stretch his ear lobes. None of those things were my type of thing. I do not have anything against piercings, tattoos or guns. I just am not into those things for myself. I do not have any tattoos, I have one piercing in each ear lobe, and I have never touched a gun. Besides, we did not have the money for him to be spending like that when he was laid off so much of the year every year. He was not sharing the video games with the kids either, most of which were inappropriate for them anyway. Also, with the constant threats from him, I feared more and more what his real intentions on keeping that many guns and that much ammo in the house may have truly been.

Our joint bank account started to become an issue as well. I was making more money than Richard since he was not working a full year. When I would put money in the bank, I would pay whatever bills I knew would be covered with that deposit amount. Some of the checks were bouncing. After looking closer at the bank statements, I realized that Richard was spending more than he was putting into the account. I saw the charges for the tattoos, guns and video games, but there were also many ATM withdrawals for large amounts that he would not explain. He would say they were for a drink, snacks or beer from the gas stations, but he also had smaller point-of-sale charges from the same gas stations as he was withdrawing cash from and on the same day. He sometimes would also tell me that it was none of my business what he spent his money on. I decided it was time to open my own separate account. I took my name off the joint one so that it would be only his. I did not want him on mine, nor did I want him to have a reason to argue with me about it. I opened one for myself in another town and at a different branch than where his was located. I did not want him to have any chance at being able to access mine. I found out that he was also taking money from the children's accounts. I tried to close out their accounts also so that I could move them to my new bank, but his bank said Richard would have to sign off on them. At this time the kids were thirteen, eleven, nine, seven, six, and four. I quickly realized that I was paying all the bills out of MY account. He was not putting money in my account. He was not paying any of the bills with his account. He was always saying he was broke and could not help me when I would ask him to cover a bill here or there.

For the entire few years that we shared a bedroom and bed, I would sleep as far over on the edge as I could without falling off. Sometimes I even had at least one of my legs hanging off the side. I slept fully clothed as well. I wore t-shirts, sweatshirts, sweatpants, socks, underwear obviously and my bra. I wanted it to be as difficult as possible for him to access any part of me including my skin. We did not cuddle. We had a queen size bed and there was enough room between us that two other adults could probably fit comfortably. I would usually wait until he was asleep before I would go to bed and was usually up before he awoke, even when he did work. My first day care child usually came at least an hour before he would even get up to get ready for work.

For the last three of Renee's four years of life, she slept in our bed with us. I had never allowed any of my children to sleep in my bed before. I initially told Richard that it was not a good idea. There was a night that she would not go back to sleep, and she was keeping Richard awake. He was getting mad and finally told me to just put her in bed. He did not care what my opinion was on it, he needed to get some sleep. After that, she would only sleep in our bed. I could not get her to sleep in her bed for nothing. I no longer fought him or her about her sleeping in her own bed. After a while I welcomed the idea of her being in our bed because it guaranteed him to not try anything with me while I was sleeping. That ended abruptly one night. I woke up to him yelling and standing next to the bed. She had been potty trained for over two years, but for some reason had an accident. I could not help but laugh. He was livid because she wet the bed, and she was scared. He scared her so much that she never slept in our bed again.

There were several times that Richard would try to overpower me or the kids. He would sit on the kids and hold them down to see if they were strong enough to get him off. When he would do that it made me think of the stories from his stepmom where she told me that she would sit on him, holding down all his limbs, trying to make him angry enough to get out of bed. I would tell him to get off the kids, explaining to him how inappropriate his behaviors were. One day he had Daniel on the floor, he was holding him down and Daniel looked at me saying "Mom help me, he is hurting me." When I told Richard to let him loose, he laughed and said he was fine that he was just being a pussy, so I grabbed the landline to dial 911. It did get Richard off of Daniel because he jumped up to knock the phone out of my hand. When I picked the phone back up, I heard talking but it did not sound like dispatchers, it sounded like it was a husband talking to his wife. All I heard was a guy say "Honey, I am hearing something that I shouldn't be....". Before I could ask whoever for help, Richard took the phone from me and told me that if I called the police that I would go to jail with him for enabling him. He also reminded me that he had a gun cabinet full of ways to do away with me and my kids if he wanted to.

He still would grab my kids by the throats and hold them up against the wall, feet off the ground, to get me to do what he wanted though. Even if I had day care kids, I would agree to go down the hall to our bedroom just so he would let loose of my kids. I would always tell him that I did not want to have sex, that I was not interested in it. I would also remind him that the kids were in the house, awake, and how I thought it was very inappropriate for his behavior to keep me from my job. Sometimes once in the room, I would still fight him off, then he would get so angry he would give up for the night anyway. I learned that my legs were longer and stronger than his. I figured out that I could wrap my legs around his and lock them as straight as possible so that he could not get his penis anywhere near my vagina. I could hold that position so long that he would tire himself out trying to get loose. When I would finally let him go, he would be so angry that he would punch the wall and slam the door on his way out. There were a few holes in the walls because of this exact reason.

There was an upcoming concert for the hard rock band that one of my high school friends was the lead singer of. It was not my normal type of music. It was Richard's type of music though, so I got us tickets to go. I just wanted to see my old friend even if it was from a distance. I knew I would not be allowed close enough to talk to him. Before going, though, I dug out the old pictures of him and me at the group home standing next to the pool table in the rec room. I had about five 4x6 pictures, plus his school picture that he signed the back of for me when we were still in high school. It felt good to reminisce in the good old times, even if I had to do it alone and quietly. After the concert, I laid those pictures on my dresser. The next day I put them in my top dresser drawer with my undergarments. I did not have time to put them back in the box where I was keeping all my old pictures from the past two decades. This box is the box I was keeping these pictures in for most of those years, just adding more pictures to that box as I accumulated more. This box always kept my pictures safe. Well a couple days later, I noticed they were no longer in my drawer. Richard claimed he put them somewhere safe for me because he "was afraid they would get lost or ruined." When I asked him where they were because I wanted them back in my picture box with all my other pictures, he conveniently forgot where he put them. I asked if he put them in his gun safe because my logic was that would be the safest place if he truly was worried about them. They were not in the safe.

I started writing poems and short stories when I was in the group home. I continued to write during all my adult years as well. I had four notebooks full of my writings. After moving into this house with Richard, I got a couple of my poems published. I had copies of those two hardcover books that contained my poems. I kept my notebooks and these hardcover books on the shelf that was in our bedroom. I eventually realized that they were missing. I do not know how long they had been missing. It was not regularly anymore that I was writing. Richard claims he knew nothing about them. I also had a cabinet in the basement that was filled with Dave's baby pictures and other pictures of Dave. I was saving these for my kids when they got older to have and keep. Those also came up missing and I again had no clue how long they had been missing. Once more, Richard claimed he knew nothing about them.

It dawned on me that a few months earlier, after the concert, Richard was running the fireplace. When I had asked him what he was burning, he said it was his old school notebooks and old work papers that he no longer needed. I started to wonder if this was actually where my missing notebooks and pictures disappeared too. When I asked him about that, he became very angry, reminding me that he already said that he did not know anything about them. I made a few points of fact. They were missing, no longer where I had put them, that the kids did not have access to the places these items were kept, and he had no interest in helping me find them. He supposedly still did not remember where he put my pictures from my dresser drawer either. His behavior with my questions I felt were dramatic and defensive even before I accused him of taking them. I never did find any of them. I feel like he may have been jealous of my past, possibly trying to erase my past to where he was all I ever had.

Richard had a subscription to Playboy magazine. For whatever reason, he put them in my name. He got a new magazine every month, for several years. He made a footlocker-like box just to keep them in because he had acquired so many of them. He also subscribed to receive regular shipments of videos called *Girls Gone Wild*. I am not sure if it was with these shipments or if he had subscribed to something else, but he also started acquiring other videos that were pornographic. There were at least some that were about threesomes and some were girl-on-girl action. He told me that since I was not interested in sex then maybe these videos would help get me turned on for him. I humored him by agreeing to watch some of them. He showed me the girl-on-girl video first. I got grossed out and told him if anything it turned me off even more than I already was. A few months later, he showed me a threesome video which included a man. Again, it grossed me out. He said that his fantasy was to have a threesome sometime in his lifetime. I told him that maybe someday he would get his wish, but that I would not be one of the three. Richard called me a prude and told me that I was no fun.

In all the remodeling we were doing, we did make a seventh bedroom. We started almost every room in the house, but never finished a room. He would get bored or something and decide to start the next project. I tried to talk to him many times into letting me have my own room. We did have six kiddos, but they were young enough that it would not hurt some of them to share a room. He knew what my reasons were, but he told me that we were married, therefore we did not need separate bedrooms. Even when his dad and stepmom moved into separate bedrooms in their own home, I could not get Richard to agree with us having our own rooms. Richard would just say that he did not want a marriage like his dad and stepmom had. I told him that we did not have a marriage anyway, and definitely did not have what his parents had. At least they wanted to marry each other.

Richard was not a religious person. He did not attend church or really say whether he believed in God or not. He made fun of me for going to church, he made fun of me for reading my Bible, and he really did not like when I said prayer at the dinner table. He would usually somewhat participate in it but never said the prayer and continued to ridicule me for it.

He participated in the holding of hands around the table, probably because the kids did, and they would take his hand to complete the circle. Even with all this, he would use passages from the Bible against me. He would constantly tell me that the Bible said that I was supposed to obey him and that I was not supposed to deprive him of intimacy. I tried to counter argue with the fact that he was not leading our family in church, therefore those verses did not pertain to him. I also told him that he was not supposed to be treating the kids and me like he did. If he wanted to use the Bible as a reference for our marriage, then his behaviors needed to change.

Chapter Fourteen

When Richard would go to work, he would always call me. He would call ten to twenty times a day, not exaggerating. I am pretty sure he was just checking up on me, but he did not like me talking to anyone else while he was on the phone. Sometimes it made it a bit difficult to do my job. He would call just to ask what I was doing, what was for dinner, and tell me which of his co-workers were annoying him that day. Then on his forty-five-minute drive home from work, he would talk to me the entire drive. He would get mad if any of the kids interrupted. I tried to explain to him that he was actually the one interrupting. When he was on his way home it was usually after school so besides my kiddos, I also had after-school day care kiddos. My rule was they all were to come straight home and do their homework, even the day care kids. So sometimes he would call while I was helping someone with their homework, but Richard wanted my full attention on the phone while he was on his drive. When he was home, he would continue to interrupt the kids by wanting my full attention. Even if I was on the phone with someone else, Richard would still try to get my attention and interrupt me. The kids started to do the same, copying his behaviors, but Richard would get angry and tell the kids how rude they were being.

Richard was increasingly getting more controlling. He did not like me or the kids leaving the house. The kids went to school and came home. He did not want them hanging out with friends at our house or away. I would go to town once a week to the grocery store and Walmart to get our necessities. Sometimes he would go with me, stating he could not trust me. It was a fifteen-minute drive to town; the grocery store was on the north end of town and Walmart on the south end. I was usually only gone about a total of three hours. I would come back with a carload, receipts showing the time of checkout at each store, and how much I spent. There was never time for me to stray as he wanted to claim. If he did not go with me, he would call me every five minutes, or sometimes stay on the phone with me for the entire time that I was in the store. This is when I would regret ever getting a cellular phone.

Richard did not approve of the kids being in sports either. He did not want them gone from home for more than the normal school day. I had always planned on letting my kids go out for whatever sport or school activity that they wanted to go out for. I wanted them to be as active as they wanted to be since my parents did not allow me to be. I felt that it would be good for them and they could have a social life. With the tension in our home, I felt that getting the kids out of the house was in their best interest. No matter how much he yelled and complained, I did not give in to him wanting to deprive my children of this normalcy. I paid for whatever they needed for whichever sport or activity they chose; I drove them to and from the school. I did not get to go to very many events because I either had childcare kids or Richard would not allow me to attend them anyway.

I had always been family oriented even when I was not speaking to my own parents. I thought it was important for the kids to know their extended family no matter which side it was. I felt like just because Dave signed away his rights, did not mean that his family did. Richard disagreed with this and made it very hard for me to visit Dave's family. He made it hard for me to visit or stay in touch with my family and his own family as well. He completely hated my brother and did not like me talking to him at all. Anytime I was on the phone with any family member, he would listen to the entire conversation. Even if I went into another room so I could hear over the background noise, he would follow. For holidays, I would still go wherever we were invited to go, or sometimes family would come to our house. When I would go to Dave's family, Richard would get really mad telling me that it was not my family and that I had no business attending their family get togethers. Dave never attended these get togethers because his wife was just as controlling as Richard was so it was not because he thought I would see Dave.

By playing around, trying to learn how to use my computer, I found a site called classmates.com which did list the high school that I graduated from. I searched for Shay, Charlie, and a few of the other friends I used to have, but no one popped up. I found a couple other sites that I could search for people on also. With those sites, though, I either did not find a match or if someone did pop up, it would not give me any information or a way to contact them without spending money. We did not have the money anyway, but I have always been very frugal. I would just have to keep searching for another way to find my old friends.

After several months of not finding anything, I finally got an idea to look up Charlie's sister, Aimee. It was winter of 2005. I searched her name in classmates.com, one was found but there was no picture. I sent a message asking if she was the same Aimee that had a brother named Charlie. I was so excited, I kept checking back to see if I had gotten a response. It was a few days later that I got a response saying that yes indeed it was the right Aimee. We exchanged phone numbers and started talking on a daily basis. The reason it had taken her a few days to respond was because she was letting Charlie know that I had made contact. He did not want to talk to me though. As soon as she mentioned my name to him, all of his heartbroken feelings came flooding back like it happened yesterday. She decided she still wanted to reconnect with me even if he did not.

Aimee told me that she did not realize that Charlie and I were just friends back in high school. She said by the way Charlie handled me leaving, she was positive that I had broken up with him. She told me that the day I drove away, he stood out in heavy oncoming traffic hoping to get killed. She continued to tell me that all of his girlfriends have all been the opposite of me by both physical appearance and personality. By her viewpoint, he never let anyone get as close to him as I had been. She did not believe he ever loved anyone as much as he did me. Never married? Love? I was astonished. She explained that Charlie was a junior sharing the same name as their dad, but their dad had not been in their lives until they were adults which explained why I did not know about that. I did not know he loved me, and I think I still played it off as a teenage crush. Aimee also told me that their mom gave birth to twin girls about six months after I left which makes them six months older than Daniel. Then when Charlie was nineteen years old, their mom passed away from breast cancer. She passed away a month after my grandma Berta passed. I was sad and confused, but I was happy to have a new old friend. I had been craving adult interaction other than the constant ridicule from Richard.

Aimee and her family drove the forty minutes to our house to have a mini reunion. The kids hit it off great. I think it was a little awkward for us adults, partly because Richard was not being very hospitable. Aimee had two sons who lived with her, plus two stepchildren who she had part of the time. Each of her four kids were close in age to at least one of my kids. From this moment on, the kids were treated like cousins and Aimee and I like sisters. This visit with her made me feel alive again, like there was hope for at least a little happiness even if it was temporary. Brandon's birthday was coming up, so we planned a party for her kids and mine to spend time together. We took the kids all to a skating rink in the town we went to high school in. Aimee also brought her three younger sisters.

I felt horrible for Charlie though. I apparently was not a good friend. I could not blame him for not wanting to forgive me. He had always been there for me. I bailed on him when he needed me the most. He obviously did okay without me being there, but I was not there when his mom was sick. Aimee and Charlie were teenagers watching their mother deteriorate in front of them while they helped care for three siblings under the age of five. Something like this is difficult for a seasoned adult to deal with, I cannot imagine two teenagers going through this alone. Once she passed away, the younger girls went to live with a friend of an aunt.

It took a couple months before I did finally hear from Charlie. I think Aimee might have helped convince him that we could still be friends. We started out just instant messaging through email. He had a girlfriend, but they did not live together. They lived in the same apartment building though. We talked about things that happened in our lives. Mainly surface stuff to regain trust I suppose. I did not hide any of these conversations from Richard. I had no reason to. Richard was not happy that I was talking to old friends but that was nothing new. I was starting to feel alive again, like there was sunshine in my days. Not just from finding Charlie but having adult conversations and talking to people I connected with.

Aimee was invited over to their aunt's house for a jewelry party. It was like a Tupperware home party but with jewelry instead. I had never heard of the company before, it was called Premier Designs. Aimee did not want to go by herself, so she asked me to go. I was always thrilled to get out of the house so of course I was ready to join Aimee at this party. Joanna went with us also. I always broke out to jewelry unless it was fourteen carat gold, therefore, I was not too interested in the party itself. I was there as support for Aimee. After the presentation, guests were looking through catalogs and the displayed jewelry while Joanna and I sat talking and waiting for Aimee. The presenter, Cathy, came over asking if she could help me with anything or if I had questions. I told her that I was allergic to cheap jewelry, so I was not interested in anything. Cathy then explained to us that this jewelry was made differently. She had heard from other customers that they could wear this jewelry when they could not wear other fashion jewelry. She made me a deal; I purchase a piece of jewelry and wear it every day for a week, if I break out to it, she will buy it back from me. If I do not break out from it, then I have a new piece of jewelry and I will know that I can wear this brand. Joanna and I looked through the catalog for the cheapest piece they sold.

    I purchased a long rectangular pendent. It took about five days before it came in my own personal mail. I thought that alone was pretty cool because most parties like that the order gets delivered to the hostess and then you have to wait until the hostess gets around to delivering it to you. I put the pendent on a chain that I already owned. I wore it inside my shirts so that the pendent laid directly on my skin all day every day. After a week, I called Cathy (her name and information was on everything she had given me). She was excited to hear that I did not break out and asked me about hosting my own party so I could get free jewelry. I said no, I was actually interested in selling it. Cathy was excited. We started our new friendship and a new adventure. Richard was not thrilled with my new adventure, but he did like seeing the extra money I was making from selling this jewelry.

Aimee wanted to get a dog. Lady had passed away and it was hard on the kiddos, so I was doing my own research to find out what the best family dogs were. Aimee and I both decided we wanted black Labradors. There was a breeder not too far from where we lived. I usually did not get my fur babies from breeders. I preferred to get the ones who were orphaned. The kids and I went to visit the breeder and his pups. It seemed like a pretty decent farm, it was clean, and the dogs all seemed happy and well cared for. Aimee could not make it to go with me so while there I called her. They had two males left which is what we both wanted. I took pictures and texted them to her. She wanted one of the males and could pay me back for hers at the end of the week. I paid the breeder for both and he gave me the AKC papers for them. The kids and I took the two male puppies' home. We named ours, Brutus. They named theirs Bruno. I put Brutus through obedience classes. He was such a good dog, fast learner, and well behaved.

Charlie was finally comfortable talking to me on the phone instead of just instant messaging. I told him a lot about my life, but not everything like I would have fifteen years earlier. We agreed to meet up in person at a midway point somewhere we could eat, talk and let the kids play. He did not live in the big city either but was in the opposite direction that I lived. Richard knew where and when this meeting took place.

I was excited and got there a little early. I had sent Charlie a few texts; one when I left home, one verifying the place we had agreed upon, and then letting him know that I was there. He did not respond to any of them, so I called him after sitting in the parking lot for a few minutes. He groggily answered. He had fallen asleep and was about forty-five minutes away. I told him that I would meet him inside when he got there because I was going to take the kids in to eat and play. He must not have been as excited to see me as I was him. When he did show up, I knew it was him. He looked the same, except he was bald and muscular. Like a puppy grows into his large paws, Charlie grew into his hands. We had a good talk and I think it helped us move from being old acquaintances back to being friends.

About a month before school was letting out, I realized that I was going to be at my maximum for childcare for the summer which meant I needed a full-time assistant. Elizabeth, now twenty years old, was on summer break from college and needed a summer job. This was perfect for both of us, so she came to Iowa for the summer. We paired up some of my kiddos so that Elizabeth would have her own bedroom. I paid her every Friday when I got paid. I introduced Elizabeth to Aimee and Charlie. Elizabeth also went with me when I would present my jewelry shows. She helped out a lot with the day care, my own kiddos and being a great support for me.

Having someone else in the house did not deter Richard's aggression like I had hoped. His behaviors did not change at all. The more I would tell him to stop the worse he became.

Poor Elizabeth witnessed more than she bargained for, she already knew some of his behaviors, but being in the house with him caused her unneeded stress. Richard would pick Brandon up off the floor by his nipples and make fun of him for crying. He would make fun of Joanna, telling her that she had a shelf butt. I knew his behaviors were wrong, but he would say things that made me feel crazy and question whether I was wrong or not. Elizabeth being there helped me realize that I was not crazy because she felt the same way. She said he was bad news and we were living in a very bad situation. She did not know how to help me either. We talked about everything, more than we had before she came to stay with me. I loved having her around.

 Elizabeth and I took a few of my kids to Aimee's one weekend. We needed some away time, some girl time. Richard knew we were going to spend the night. I took kids for a few different reasons. The main one was because Richard would always make me take some of the kids so he could ask them all kinds of questions when we returned home. I also did not like to leave them with Richard, but I did not want anyone left alone with Richard either. Another reason was they needed time away as much as I did plus if I took some kids, I felt like Richard would be more apt to let me go. While the kids stayed at her house and hung out with Aimee's kids, us three women went out. Aimee decided to invite her cousin as well and somehow Charlie was also invited as our bodyguard. We would dance as a group together and he was just keeping the other men at bay. I also thought it was the sweetest gesture ever when he would stand outside the women's restroom until we came out just to make sure we made it safely. Even Elizabeth thought he was a sweet guy and wanted to know how I let him get away from me so many years ago. A couple more times that summer, we did a weekend girls night at Aimee's. We always took some of my kids. That first time was the only time we went to the bar though. These other times, we would just hang out at Aimee's, talking and drinking Boone's Farm.

One day, some of the day care kids were outside playing with my kids, while Elizabeth and I were inside with the younger kiddos. The doors and windows were open so we could hear and keep an eye on the kids outside. I was sitting on one end of the couch, she on the other end, just talking. Richard came home from work, came in the house livid about something. He called me a fucking whore. He stomped over to me and swung his fist at me like he was going to punch me in the face. I closed my eyes, but I opened them once I felt the air from his swing pass me. He said, "you're not worth it" and stomped back outside. He punched the hood of his car, leaving a dent, and yelled all types of curse words in front of the kids. Elizabeth and I watched this all happen. She told me she jumped, thinking that he was really going to hit me. Now we were just trying to figure out what I did wrong, if anything. He came storming back into the house telling me that I needed to take him to the emergency room because he was positive that he broke his hand. I had to wait a few more minutes for a couple of the day care kids to get picked up so that Elizabeth was in legal numbers. On the drive, he explained that he knew that

I was having a lesbian affair and apparently that was what he was mad about. No matter how much I told him that I do not lean that way, that Elizabeth and I were just close as sisters, he did not believe me. He mentioned that he also thought that Aimee and I were having an affair, again I explained we were like sisters. I admitted to starting to really hate men after dealing with him and Dave, but that I was not attracted to or curious about women in that way. He did break his hand and he had to get a cast.

Once Elizabeth went back home, she told her mom some of what was going on here. Richard's mom called me telling me more things about his childhood. She apologized to me for not getting him the help he needed as a child, but that she did not really think that it would follow him into adulthood. She thought his behaviors were for attention because of the divorce of his parents and both parents moving on with new families. She also thought it was a phase that he would eventually grow out of. She told me that when she was eight months pregnant with him, they had gotten into a really bad car accident which made her go into labor with him early. They thought they were going to lose him. She had felt lucky and felt like he was a miracle. She continued to apologize; I think because she did not know what else to say. I think she felt somewhat responsible for what my kids and I had to deal with. She had also told both Elizabeth and me that his behaviors made her wonder if he was born evil. I, too, had that feeling.

Richard liked movies that had vampires or some sort of evil entity. Since living with him, I had watched many movies that I normally would not have watched if he did not turn it on or rent it for us to watch. He always wanted the kids and me to watch the movies that he liked whether we wanted to or not, but he would never watch anything that we were interested in. These movies had me thinking that maybe Richard was evil because he was not supposed to live through that car accident his parents had when he was in the womb. I cannot recall which scary movie it was, but there was one that I watched with Richard that was similar to that thought. I actually think it was that specific movie that put that thought in my head. I just could not fathom any human being born to behave like Richard had since I met him, without some underlying cause.

The parents to one of my day care families were having a party at their house. For whatever reason, Richard was invited instead of me. The Smyths lived about five blocks to the north of us. Richard left to go up to the party about eight-eight thirty. He came home about two-ish and was as drunk as could be. He went to bed fully clothed and on top of the blankets. The next day he showered right away, saying I would not believe what happened at this party. He said Mrs. Smyth ran around the yard and house completely naked in front of all their guests. He said there were a lot of people up there, including some of my other day care parents. He then told me that she invited him upstairs to look at something, but once upstairs she asked him about a threesome. He said that her husband was sitting in a chair in the corner ready to watch because, apparently, he liked watching his wife have sex with others. He said that was when he bailed because it became too weird. Even before this party, Mrs. Smyth did a lot of flirting with Richard. I cared for her children for a couple of years. During these years, she was constantly coming over to hang out when he was home, but she would wrestle with Richard on the floor. She was a bigger gal with humungous breasts. She seemed to like to rub them all over him while they wrestled. So, his story did not surprise me at all, but I did get the feeling that he did not tell me the whole story.

The Smyths divorced soon after this incident. She and the kids moved to the town my parents lived in. A couple of years later, Joanna and I were sitting on a corner in my van waiting for my day care kids to get off the school bus. Mr. Smyth came walking towards me. He asked me if I was interested in a threesome with him and his new girlfriend. I said that I was not into that type of stuff and that I was still married to Richard. He then told me that he knew that I liked kinky sex because he knew that my husband did. He continued with stating that you do not stay married as long as we had without having that in common. I asked how he thought he knew anything about what Richard liked. He just smiled, told me to let him know if I changed my mind and walked away. It took everything I had not to vomit. I looked at Joanna and shook my head. It was at that moment that I decided that most of Richard's story about the party was probably true, but I now thought he left out some huge parts. Like possibly staying for a threesome or to have sex with Mrs. Smyth while her husband watched. I do not know for sure and I really did not want to know all the factual details.

It did however add to my already growing list of reasons why I should not stay married to Richard.

I continued to try to have a girl's night out with Aimee at least once a month. Even though it caused more tension between Richard and me, it was something that I needed for my sanity. It did not matter what I did or did not do, Richard was always angry no matter what. I tried to keep the peace and I tried to make him happy without sacrificing my morals, but I realized that he was never going to be happy. He told me multiple times that he hated women and did not trust any of them. He said his mom hated him and did not want him, that is why she 'threw' him away. He said his stepmom hated him and did not want him around. He said that she was always trying to turn his dad against him and get him into trouble with his dad. He said that all his ex-girlfriends always lied to him or cheated on him. I tried many times to tell him the stories that I had been told to let him know that he was loved and wanted but he did not believe me. I asked him what I had done for him not to trust me. He said nothing yet, but that since all the women who had ever been in his life had screwed him over, he knew that I would too eventually. He did not trust me though and said that many a time even though I had not yet given him a reason. Part of me felt sorry for him, but another part of me hated him for not even giving me a chance. I had never hated anyone before him, not even my mother. I felt hatred and it was not a good feeling. He was the first and only person that I ever hated.

Aimee and I also started attending church together where her dad and stepmom attended church. I wanted to get back into being involved in church and this gave us another day to hang out. I got to know Charlie and Aimee's real dad and stepmom during this time. All the kids were also enjoying attending church regularly again as well. I invited Richard to go, but he always refused. He would also want me to come home immediately after services were over. I met a few new friends there. One of which, Mandi, was very concerned with my home life without me saying too much. She made it very clear that she was always there if I needed her. Sometimes I wondered if either the kids told her something or if Aimee had, but I never asked.

Chapter Fifteen

Usually if I was not going to have day care kids on the weekend, I would try to plan something either for just my kids and me or with Aimee's family. One weekend I had not planned anything, but Richard was already angry at me and the kids more than usual. He was so angry that he took the emergency cell phones and my cell phone. He turned them off and hid them. He also took the landline out of the wall. I had added two phone lines to my cellular bill so that the kids could share them. I called them emergency phones so whoever was away from home either for sports, school activities, or paper routes; they could still get ahold of me. This specific weekend, he was not going to allow us to go anywhere, not even to church on Sunday.

I spoke with Aimee every day, so she became worried when she did not hear from me and I was not answering my phone. I had talked to her Friday morning; this was Sunday afternoon. I believe she may have also tried to call the emergency phones. She decided to call Elizabeth who obviously was in another state. Elizabeth had also not heard from me and could not get me to answer my phone. So together they conference called my mother. My mother also could not get ahold of me. They were all three very worried. They decided to call the police to do a welfare check on us.

When the deputies showed up at the door, Richard was livid, he wanted to know how we called the police. He told me that if he went to jail, he would take me with him. One officer took me outside to the end of the sidewalk, while the other one talked to Richard at the front door. Some of the kids walked out with me while some stayed in the house. I told the officer we were fine. He told me that he had seen situations like this and that he could help if I needed it. He explained that I had people worried about my safety because they had heard Richard threaten my life. Richard was staring at me from across the yard and I was too scared to tell the truth, so they eventually left. The officer also told me that they would have to make a report since they came out, and that I could always reference the report if needed in the future.

A few weeks later, at church, it was announced that another church was offering classes called "How to be a good Christian wife." I decided that maybe I was causing Richard to act like he was, maybe I needed to be a better person. At the beginning of this so-called relationship, I told myself that I was going to treat this like an arranged marriage. Other cultures marry without love and still make it work. I even told myself to try to learn to love him, I did try very hard. I tried to find good things about him and concentrate on those good things. His behaviors made it very hard though. I was willing to do anything to make life easier for all of us. I still had many years to go before Cole turned eighteen. I decided to sign up for these classes along with Mandi, Charlie's stepmom, and a few other ladies. I took notes and was trying to learn anything new that I could. I wanted to be the best wife possible even if he was not a good husband. A problem arose, I realized that most of these things, I was already doing. The ones I was not doing, I did not think that I could. The one that stuck in my mind was telling him how strong he was and letting him do something for me. The example they gave was to let the husband change the light bulb and comment about how strong and helpful he was because men like praise. I kind of laughed yet, shook my head, because I felt like the only way that I could pull that off, was to lie to Richard and I did not like that idea. I thought about this for weeks, trying to figure out how I could praise him for a real job well done. He was not helpful around the house; he did not help when I asked something of him. I did everything myself, including moving heavy furniture, interior painting, hanging pictures, any maintenance needed around the house, etc.

 Charlie only knew some of my marital issues. He was having issues of his own with his girlfriend as well. I gave him advice on what to do with his relationship, and he gave me some according to the information that I did give him. Aimee knew more about my home life than Charlie because she would be on the phone with me and overhear Richard's behaviors. She was shocked by some of it, but I do not think that she told Charlie. One day Charlie asked if Richard and I had tried marriage counseling. We had not. Since my previous marriage counseling attempt was not successful, I had not thought about it this time. At first, Richard said no way that counseling was only a way for them to con money out of people. I found out that his insurance would cover it. Then he agreed only if we could get a female therapist. I thought that was odd since he did not like women, but I had no preference, so I requested a female marriage counselor.

Richard pulled out new tricks that I did not expect. In our first session, she allowed him to speak first. He literally cried telling her that I did not love him or show him love. In her perspective I did probably look heartless, but I turned to him saying that he knew that since he forced his way into my life. She scolded me for interrupting when it was his turn to speak his feelings. When I mentioned that he made fun of my kids for crying because he said only pussies cry, he denied it and again she acted as if I was making things up. I was frustrated but after we left, I thought, she is a professional, she has to see through his deceit at some point. At our next appointment, the same thing happened except he told her that I kept comparing him to Dave and made fun of him for being short and fat. I again tried to correct his lies, and she again scolded me for interrupting him. She handed him a magnet and said whoever was holding the magnet had the floor and the other one had to remain quiet until it was their turn. I did not get a turn.

On the way home, I asked him what he was doing. He said I was the one who wanted to go so whatever happened was my fault. I explained to him that if he did not tell the truth then nothing could be repaired. He said that nothing was broken in our marriage so there was nothing to fix. He then told me that I was just jealous because our marriage counselor had the hots for him. I could not help but laugh and that made him even more mad. He turned the music up extremely loud. It was his hard head-banging, screaming-like music. While he was driving, he started punching the dashboard, and driving somewhat recklessly. I made sure my seat belt was tight and hung onto the door handle. Looking at me he yelled, "What? Don't trust my driving, afraid I'm gonna wreck?" I just looked at him and prayed that I would get home safely to my kids. We never went for a third session.

Since the Christian wife classes and the marriage counseling did not work, I tried to talk to him about the problems in our house. I tried to explain to him that he was making it very difficult for me to stay per our agreement. He refused to listen or talk about it. He acted as if the problems would go away if he ignored them. I think he may have even made that comment. I was trying to have a normal adult conversation with him about our issues that clearly needed our attention and some sort of solution. I felt like he was ignoring me, he was not participating in any part of the conversation, he would not make eye contact or converse back with anything to make me think that he heard anything that I had said. A few times, he would sit eerily cleaning his guns, and that intimidated me more, possibly being his intention. So, I decided to write him a letter so that he could read it, ponder it and maybe have something to say. One thing that I did learn from my mother was to make copies of anything of importance. So, I made a copy of the letter with my printer so that I knew exactly what I had said. He had a habit of twisting my words or telling me that I said something that I did not say or that I did not say something that I actually had said.

The letter read as follows:

3-14-2007

Richard,

Things aren't getting any better and you being pissed off about how I'm feeling isn't helping. I'm depressed and very sad and all you care about is that you aren't getting sex. Your anger is making me hate you even more, the kids are wanting to get away from you, and you have been accusing me of sleeping around. You aren't getting any because of your anger and how it's making me feel. When I make the comment that I can go the rest of my life without sex you say, "I know you could", but then you turn around and accuse me of sleeping around. You are contradicting yourself. Which one do you really believe?

I'm dying inside- I'm losing myself and it's going to get so bad I won't be able to find myself again. That young man who died last week made me realize that we could go at any time! I don't want my last days to be in misery and sadness. I don't want my kids to remember me this way. Do you want your last days to be in anger? Do you want the kids to remember you as an angry beer drinking ass that is hard to live with?

Neither one of us is happy. Why do you want to live like this? When you use to talk about your dad and stepmom not being happy, you said they would be better off splitting up. I think we would be better people and better parents if we were not together. I have said several times that I'm not talking permanently right now. If we can work things out separately like Tracy and Todd, then fine- if not then we go our separate ways permanently.

I don't want to fight over who gets what. I don't want to tell the kids where they have to live, I want them to feel comfortable in deciding. I don't think you should tell me that I can't take either vehicle. Why can't we share? Whoever has majority of the kids has the van? I have some ideas on how we can do this civil wise. I'm scared to death to talk to you right now.

When I'm around you I feel like a worthless piece of crap that can't do anything right. If the kid's feel like I do then that would explain why they act like they do.

I hope you understand this note and don't get even more mad. Let me know your thoughts!

Jorgie

I set the note on his dresser next to his wallet and keys so he would definitely see it. I do not remember if he was working at the time or not, but I do remember seeing the letter ripped to shreds in the garbage. I asked him if he read it, and if he was ready to talk about its contents. He glared at me and did not say a word. It was never discussed, and nothing changed. He continued to bully the kids and myself. I talked to Elizabeth about this. Her advice was to leave him, which was easier said than done. I talked to Aimee about it. She also said that I needed to leave him, and that the kids and I could stay with her.

I was so scared. I did not know what to do. Richard threatened to take the kids away if I left him, he threatened to take my life if I left him.... I did not know which would be worse. I could not stay; I could not continue to put my kids through this hell. I struggled with taking the younger two away from their dad. I had already put the older kids through one divorce, I felt like it was a no-win situation. I felt like no matter what I did that there would be devastating consequences. Brandon and Cole had been having problems at school for the past several months. Our family doctor suggested counseling for them. I started taking them about a month before that letter to Richard.

I decided to talk to the counselor. Because of patient confidentiality, she could not tell me what the kids had said in their sessions, but she did tell me that she had a few concerns. First one being that their school was not in their best interest. She suggested open enrolling into another district. She also had other clients with similar issues at this same school and since they had already switched schools, those kids were doing much better. Her other concern was Richard. She said she did not support separation of families without cause, but she said either Richard needed to get some mental health help, or I needed to get the kids away from him until he did. I did know that Brandon was getting bullied by both students and teachers. I had gone to the school a few times to discuss issues and they were not nice to me either. Then there was a day that I stood in the hallway and witnessed the teacher being inappropriate with Brandon, so I took him out of that class. I tried to file a report, but the principal backed up the teacher. With Cole, she was refusing to do her worksheets. She was in second grade and was writing along the four bordering sides of her worksheets that her teacher was stupid, that her teacher was mean, that she wanted to go home to her parents, she hated her teacher, etc. In a meeting with her teacher and principal, they thought the problems at home were causing the issues at school. The counselor and I both agreed that even though there were problems at home, that Cole's problems with her teacher were even worse.

Richard was still not wanting to talk or discuss anything. I wanted to give it one more attempt before I took Aimee up on her offer. So, I wrote another letter to Richard. The letter read as follows:

5-31-2007

Richard,

You don't seem to understand my side of things. I also don't think you really know me because of different things you say. I don't like being controlled, getting yelled at, made to feel like everything I am is wrong, everything I do or want to do is wrong. That's not a relationship., that's not what one is supposed to be.

You seem to only want sex. Well I have to feel something in order to do it and I only feel anger and resentment towards you. I don't know what to do either. I'm tired of being miserable, tired of not being myself. I feel dead and I might as well be if this is how it is gonna be. I still think a separation would be best, but you won't listen!

You say I'm hiding things from you – I have told you things but you either get mad or act like I didn't say it. Me leaving is a guarantee! I've been debating the when for over three years. First, I thought I would just stay until Renee was eighteen. Then it was when I get the money. But now it all is affecting the kids and I don't like the way you treat them, and they see the way you treat me. Then the problems with the school are pushing me to get out sooner. When would you rather me leave? Now, next year, five years from now, or in 2019? The longer I wait the more hate I'll feel and the harder it will be to fix anything.

I don't believe you love me either. You love who you want me to be and I can't be that person. If you loved <u>me,</u> you wouldn't treat me the way you do. I want what is best for the kids and it isn't the way we are living now. We NEED to talk!

Jorgie

Again, I set the note on his dresser next to his wallet and keys. Again, he did not acknowledge the letter and refused to talk about it. Aimee and I discussed the plans. We were going to double up the kids. She was buying her house on contract through the owner. Her house was a five-bedroom, three-bath on a cul-de-sac with a large partially fenced yard. Daniel and Brandon would share a room with her stepson since he was only there every other weekend. Joanna and Ashlee would share a room with her stepdaughter for the same reason. Her two boys were going to share a room when currently they had separate rooms. Then Cole and Renee would share the remaining bedroom. The lower level family room was big enough that we would use half of it for my room. We were going to bring the cats who would stay in my quarters and Brutus who would be happy to play with his brother. Aimee had a knack for finding good deals on housing. So even though we had this planned out, I told her to keep an eye out for a good housing deal for me, so we did not have to disrupt their house any longer than needed. I gave my childcare families a forty-day notice, which took us to about the middle of July.

I think Richard got wind that my plans were not just talk but were going to happen. I told him we were leaving before I even gave my notice to my day care parents. He told me that he was ready to discuss issues. I started to tell my side of things when he started taking off my pants. I tried to hold my pants up. I explained that we were talking, and I was not consenting to sex. He laughed and stated that sex would fix everything. I continued to say no and talked about the issues that needed fixed. He overpowered me, got my pants off, and five minutes later he was zipping up his pants and walking out of the room. He got what he wanted so he was no longer letting me discuss the issues I thought we needed to work on.

I was busy packing and preparing to move in with Aimee, so we had not spoken much. I assumed she was also rearranging her house preparing for us to move in. About three weeks later, I was feeling sick, so I went to the doctor. I was pregnant again. I sat in the parking lot crying so hard that I could not breathe or see to drive. It was probably a good thirty minutes before I was able to call Aimee to tell her. The first thing I asked when she finally answered was what was she doing because she sounded busy and out of breath. She was moving.... moving...to where? She had found another house deal on the other side of town that she was moving into. A smaller house, three bedroom, two baths, with a small yard. I was not going to be able to move in with her. I asked her if I would be able to move in and take over her contract at the other house, but she said no because they upset the owner. I ended the call to let her get back to moving without telling her my news.

I was devastated beyond belief. What was I going to do now? I sat there and cried another thirty minutes or more. Then I called Charlie. He said that sounded like something Aimee would do, that he would not expect anything less. He told me that she was motivated to help herself not others. I did not want to believe that was who she was, but I also could not believe she did this to me. It took me a few days to call her again because I was so hurt. Charlie acted somewhat distant like he did not want to talk to me either. He said he was confused how I let myself get pregnant if I was trying to leave Richard. That is when I realized he was upset about that part of our conversation. Elizabeth did not answer when I called her, but this summer she was working with her uncle, so I assumed she was working. With no one else to call, I calmed myself down enough to drive home. At this time my kiddos were fifteen, thirteen, eleven, nine, almost eight, and five years old. I told the kids and Richard the news. The only one that was happy about it was Richard. He did make the comment several times that he thought that I was going to try to abort the baby. I told him that he did not know me very well if he thought that was something I would do just because I hated him. I decided to let all my day care families know that I was withdrawing my notice. Luckily most of them had not been able to find other childcare so they were also happy that I was staying.

 I had bought a used pop-up camper with my childcare money. I loved camping and thought we should do it more. The kids and I loved fishing, hiking, camping, etc. We had gone a few times over the years without Richard and stayed in tents. I also was able to get the kids open enrolled in the school district nine miles to the south of us. I would just be required to provide transportation since we lived outside the boundaries. Before school was to start, we all went camping. The boys and Brutus stayed in the tent while the girls, Richard and I stayed in the camper.

 One evening, we had the campfire going. We roasted marshmallows to make smores. Then I put the kids to bed, tucking in each of them. Richard was sitting in a lawn chair a few feet from the fire all evening with his arms crossed, beer in hand and not saying a word. He was sitting on the far side of the campfire, so his chair was facing the camper and the tent. He did not participate in the smores or anything else the kids and I did that evening. Once all the kids were tucked in, I decided to stand near the campfire to warm up and just enjoy the warmth on my face before I turned in for the night. Out of the blue, Richard said, "You're lucky you're pregnant or I would push you into that fire." Not sure that I heard him correctly, I asked him what he said. He repeated it, and I did hear correctly the first time. I did not know how to respond. I was stunned but not really shocked. I decided that was my cue to go to bed. I do not know when he came into the camper to sleep, but that was our last night camping before heading home. It was a very quiet and tense drive home.

Chapter Sixteen

Right around Renee's sixth birthday I had an ultrasound. I was now about three months pregnant. Richard went with me mainly because he was still positive that I was going to abort the pregnancy. When the ultrasound technician told us it was a boy, Richard excitedly said, "Yes, I am finally getting my son, my boy!" On the way home, I asked him why he was so excited when he had two sons, my boys that he adopted. He said it was different and continued to say he finally got a son. He also slipped up by saying getting me pregnant this time worked in his favor. The way he said it was odd so I asked what he meant and with a mischievous grin said he purposely got me pregnant so he could try to get what he wanted before I bailed. He also said that he always tells his buddies to "tap it one last time, before the bitch splits." So, that is what he did, he claimed. I had heard him make that comment multiple times in the years I lived with him.

About this same time, the counselor that Brandon and Cole were seeing told me that she did not feel like she could continue services. She explained that she had helped the kids as much as she could, and until Richard got some much-needed help then she did not feel like she could do anymore for them. She said that she would be happy to schedule them back in once I either got them away from Richard or he got some help. I could not understand why, but I agreed to discontinue their services until something changed. Richard did not want the kids in counseling anyway so that was one less fight that I had to have with him. I did however tell him her reasons for discontinuing services. To my surprise he chose to start seeing a male therapist in the same office as the kids had been going.

His therapy was short lived. I think he only went weekly for about a month. That is longer than I expected him to go though. He started ranting and raving about how stupid the guy was and he must not know how to raise children properly. Apparently, his therapist put him on anti-depressants, told him that he should slow down or quit his drinking, told him that his ways of punishment were borderline abusive, and that he wanted to sign Richard up for anger management classes. Richard did not think there was anything wrong with his disciplinarian skills, he also did not agree with the anger management, and there was no way anyone was going to tell him how much to drink. He did however fill his antidepressant prescription. He had already been on a doctor-prescribed sleeping pill for the last several years as well as acid reflux medications. I found out later that his real reason for therapy was so he could get his permit to carry. Apparently, that was one of the questions and requirements for qualifying for this permit.

The next six months were very stressful and tense. I was frustrated and depressed because I felt like I was in prison and could not find a way to get out. I was feeling worthless and little, while his ego seemed to enlarge. He figured out a way to continuously trap me. I wanted to die instead of living in this hellhole, but I trusted no one to care for my children. My kids were what kept me going each day. His therapy did nothing except add to his already distrust of any type of psychology professionals. He referred to them as quacks.

I was in a lot of pain with this pregnancy. I felt like the baby picked up on Richard's aggression. Sometimes when he would kick, it hurt so bad I thought he was going to break out of my stomach. I never experienced anything like that during any of the other six pregnancies. I dropped about a month before my due date. The doctor kept saying that I would not make it to my next appointment. Then when I would, she would be surprised and wonder how I had not gone into labor. I did keep getting this sharp pain in my belly button that felt like he was ripping the umbilical cord out. They just brushed it off like he had hit or kicked instead. My due date came and went. Everyone kept saying that I had dropped really low. I was having trouble walking because it did feel like he was hanging between my legs. Obviously, he really was not hanging that low. Since I passed up my due date, Richard started hoping for a Leap Day baby. It was Leap Year, but I was hoping I would not hold out that long. On February 26, I had Richard take me to the hospital because I felt like something was horribly wrong. My doctor was not the one on call. I told them that the baby was not moving as much as he had been and that I was still getting the same pain from my belly button. They checked me out and released me a couple of hours later. The nurses told me that there was no way possible that I could feel him pulling on the umbilical cord even if he was.

The evening of the 28th, we headed back to the hospital, again I felt that something was not right, and I was in extreme pain. They got me hooked up to the machines. I was having contractions and they could see his head. After a few hours of trying to push, they even had me stand next to the bed leaning over the bed to push because he was not coming out. Every time I would push, his vitals would drop dangerously low and I would get weak and dizzy. When I first got there, a different doctor was on call and checking on me. One of the times they had me leaning over the bed to push, my doctor actually walked in to help out. I did not know if she was on call now that it was the next day or if someone called her stating there were complications. My doctor was this itty bitty very petite woman with very small hands. She made me look like a giant. She agreed something was very wrong. She had the nurses help me lay down on the bed. She checked and I was fully dilated. She touched his head, stating that it should be lower than it was, so she put her hand up in there and was able to feel the umbilical cord around his neck. My doctor told the nurse to give me terbutaline, which is a medicine to stop or slow down contractions. I already had an IV in my right arm so that was how they administered the terbutaline.

Before the terbutaline kicked in, though, my vitals and the baby's vitals both became dangerously low. I may have been going in and out of consciousness, because I do not remember very much after this. I do remember the doctor saying they needed to move fast because they may lose one or both of us. I also remember someone telling Richard to get out of the way and that he may want to pray. They wheeled me out to prepare for an emergency cesarean section. Because of my doctor's fast reactions, she was able to save both of us. Sabastian was born on Leap Day like Richard was hoping. He was put in the Intensive Care Unit because he ended up with holes in his lungs and they needed to monitor him. The doctor told me not to worry that babies heal quickly and that the holes were caused from him fighting to breathe.

My doctor did let me know that she believed he had been wrapped up in the umbilical cord for at least the last two months. That was why I was dropping but nothing was happening. She also told me that she believed the pain I felt WAS in fact him pulling on the umbilical cord, possibly trying to move since I did say his movements slowed way more than normal. I was not able to see him right away because since I also came close to death, they needed to keep me hooked up to machines and monitor me. I cried because I wanted to see my baby and start my bonding with him. I always breast fed my kids, except Daniel, and wanted to get that started. Richard came into my room and told me that he was able to see him but not hold him yet. Richard said that Sabastian looked like me with red hair.

An older nurse came to wheel me to see Sabastian. They wanted him to try to eat since I wanted to breastfeed. They apparently already gave him some formula, which I was not happy about. Anyway, I went to feed him. This was not my first rodeo, so I did know what I was doing. He was not latching on though, so I told the nurse something was wrong. She told me that I was holding him wrong and took him from me to reposition him. I told her that I had breastfed five other children that same way, so I knew what I was doing. She could not get him to latch on either. She told me that she had gotten him to take a bottle for her earlier, so she knew nothing was wrong with him, but thought that maybe I was doing something wrong or he just did not want my breast. I was mad.... I do not typically get mad, but this lady was acting like I was some dummy. She finally gave him back to me while she called the on-call pediatrician. I looked over Sabastian while she was on the phone. I noticed that he could not stick out his tongue. The skin under his tongue, frenulum, was all the way to the tip of his tongue. Normally it is attached closer to the back of the tongue. When the pediatrician came in, I showed him right away. He said that was a quick and easy fix. He said he could clip it and he would heal quickly. After that little procedure, I no longer had any issues breastfeeding. I did however make it clear that I did not want that nurse back in my room. She did not apologize.

 I also had that same recurring conversation with my OB doctor. This was my seventh child. I was interested in any birth control that she could recommend. She said she would look over my previous doctors' notes and talk to me about it at my follow up appointment. At the follow up appointment, she said that the chemical that was listed in my files as an allergen was still a main component. She retested me to see if I still had the allergy, it came back positive, so it was back to abstinence or condoms. Which obviously did not work in my favor over the past sixteen years.

Something changed in Richard though, he was being nice and helpful. At first, I thought it was a show for the hospital staff, but even when no one was in the room he was smiling and asking if I needed anything. This smile was different than his usual smile. His usual smile was creepy and mischievous. This smile was normal, friendly, pleasant. This continued when we returned home, even the kids asked me what was wrong with him. I decided to jokingly ask where the real Richard was. With a serious look on his face, he said "I almost lost my only son and you." He explained that when our vitals were dropping and they said they may lose one or both of us, he couldn't take it. He said he kneeled by the chair in my hospital room after they wheeled me out and literally cried and prayed for the first time. He prayed that he would try to be a better person if God let us live. For the first time since I had met the guy, I saw feelings, sadness, and honesty in his eyes. I felt relief that maybe this guy did have potential and we would be able to make it work.

He was sweet, lovable and seemed to care about me and ALL the kids. He was helping out more around the house without me asking him. He would ask me what I needed help with. He was nicer to the kids, watched movies with them and even played some two-player games on the game systems with the boys. I could not believe the new man that was in our house. He offered to do the grocery shopping and pay a bill or two. He did a complete one eighty. I did not feel love for him yet, but for the first time since I met him, I actually liked him. There was potential to possibly learn to love him. I finally felt like we were a real family with a bright hopeful future. Nope, he found a new way to con me. This new person disappeared about four months later. Literally like switching off a light switch, one day he was still sweet, the next day he woke up pissed off at the world and taking it out on the kids and me. I did not understand.

Sabastian was not a fussy baby, but he did not like to be in his crib. I could not get him to sleep in it for anything, no matter what time of day it was. If he fell asleep in my arms, he would awake as soon as he touched the crib mattress. I even tried to let him lay in there and cry for fifteen to twenty minutes. Richard did not like that though, he thought I was being mean to his son. He also said that he could not sleep if the baby was crying. So, for close to a year, Sabastian and I slept in my day care room. I in the recliner, sometimes with him, but sometimes he would sleep in his car seat. I knew those were big no-no's, but I could not break him of this.

Richard would come home telling stories about his coworkers. I do not know how true or untrue they were. He would say that so and so was complaining about his wife. That the wife kept spending more money than they had, or that the wife did not like the husband playing video games, etc. He would even talk about how all of his co-worker's wives would spend hundreds on their hair and nails every month or hundreds of dollars on purses and shoes. He said he bragged about having a wife who let him do whatever he wanted and never spent money on herself. He bragged about having more freedom than the other guys and how they were all jealous. Even though I am sure it was true that the women spent money on themselves like that, I assume the men allowed them to. They wanted their wives to look pretty when they took them out. Richard and I never went out, my kids were what my concentration was on so spending money on myself was never a thought. I rarely wore makeup. My clothes were older than my children, unless they were hand-me-downs from a friend. I did not get my nails done or my hair done. I did have a day care parent that would cut and color my hair occasionally, but if I paid her, it was usually at most sixty dollars. Sometimes I would just subtract it from her childcare bill. She did it in my kitchen when she would come pick up her children.

Richard was also telling me that he said this or that to his co-workers or boss. He made it sound like he spoke to them like he did me and the kids. I heard him on the phone a few times with his boss and it was complete opposite. He was polite and did not curse. He would say yes sir or no sir. He would laugh, and just be someone I did not know. I went to a company party with him once. He stayed by my side the entire time. He again was polite to his co-workers and did not curse. At home this man could not say a sentence without having multiple curse words in it. Usually at least every other word was a curse word. He was never polite; he was always belligerent.

I continued to fight for some sort of normalcy for my kiddos. I did not really care anymore if he hit me, forced me to have sex, or yelled at me. I felt like as long as it was to me and not them, then it was okay. I would plan birthday parties for the kids; usually at a bowling alley, hotel swimming pool, or pizza place. I let the kids choose and they invited whatever friends they wanted. Richard attended a few times, my guess is just to make sure that we were actually doing what we had said, but usually it was just the kids, their friends and myself. Most of their friends liked me and thought I was a cool mom. Most of them were also afraid of Richard. My four oldest kids did not even call him dad except to his face. They told their friends that he was not their real dad.

Besides having continued issues with Richard, Cole was learning his ways. One day she got a hold of a kitchen knife and was chasing Brandon around the house with it. She was laughing saying she was going to stab him. He was yelling for help. I safely got the knife from her and she made it clear that she was going to tell on me. After that incident, I took all the kitchen knives and put them in the very top of the pantry closet, hoping that she would not be able to reach them or even know where they were anytime soon. I sent her to her room, but like any time that I tried to properly discipline that child, she never listened. She was told that she did not have to listen to me.

Another incident, the older kids came running upstairs yelling for me to come help. Cole was sitting on Renee holding a pillow over her face. Renee was trying to get free and the older kids said they tried to get Cole off of her without success. I took the pillow from her first and then took her off Renee while she was kicking and screaming. Renee was having trouble catching her breath, but after a few minutes she was okay. Cole threatened to tell her dad that I touched her. I told her to go right ahead because what she was doing was very inappropriate. After she told Richard that I grabbed her and hurt her arms, I explained what happened. His excuse was that she was just trying to play with Renee because no one ever plays with her.

Richard's stepmom and sister taught Cole to say "take your Midol" whenever she did not like something. So anytime that I would tell her to do her chore, or leave her siblings alone, she would tell me to go take my Midol. Even though it was very frustrating, I never blamed Cole. I knew that she only behaved this way because her dad taught her and allowed her to. Now I also had his family enabling the dynamics in our home.

Daniel confided in my brother with some of the incidents in our home. I do not know which ones or what all was said but my brother did call me one day. He said that he had seen signs of abuse and knew things were not right in our home, but since he thought he and I were close during childhood, he was waiting for me to ask him for help. He knew that until I acknowledged there was a problem, he did not believe he could convince me. He was hurt that I had not confided in him prior to Daniel doing so. My brother and his second wife had bought a house, so he offered for the kids and me to move in with them. It was very tempting, but my brother lived in Minnesota and that would be a big adjustment for the kids. I was also told that I could get into legal trouble by moving the kids out of our home state even though the courts were not involved yet.

I was usually upset with Richard, but I kept my emotions to myself, which eventually made me feel like a robot. One particular day though, I apparently was showing my emotions. Richard, sitting at the dining room table, asked me if I was mad at him. I said yes, always. Then he asked me why, what did he do that was different than normal. After a few minutes, I realized that I was actually mad about the dream I had that night. He laughed and said that was a stupid reason to be mad, but he continued to ask what the dream was about. I told him that I had a dream that he slept with my sister. He stopped laughing, and with a serious tone asked me which one. He looked guilty and tense. After being with him as many years as I had, I noticed his eyes changed colors depending on his moods. When he was nervous or uncomfortable, they turned a yellowish brown. Well at this moment they were a yellowish brown. I tell him the sister in my dream was Sue. He relaxed, his eye color went back to his dark hazel, and he laughed. He said, "not with that sister." I asked him what that meant, had he slept with Tracy? Without looking at me, he stood up from the table and said it was just a stupid dream and walked downstairs.

No, he did not admit it with words, but something was definitely going on between him and Tracy. Obviously, this would not be the first time this happened with Tracy. For birthdays, she would usually take my kids for the weekend near their birthday and spend about twenty to twenty-five dollars on them. She would usually get Richard a gift card to somewhere. Her reason for not doing anything with me or getting anything for me was that I was always busy with kids. At Christmastimes, she would spend twenty to twenty-five dollars on each person, including me, our parents, and our siblings. She would usually buy something for Richard that was around the same price range BUT there was always a hidden gift card in there for about twice what she spent on everyone else. She was a big drinker also so whenever there were any get togethers, Richard and Tracy would become drinking buddies and be off in their own little conversations. One of their conversations that I had overheard was talking about how crazy my mother was and that it only took two signatures to have her committed. Putting these facts together with his odd behavior about my dream made me feel pretty positive that they either had, or were still having, an affair.

All my kids told me that they tried to tell Aunt Tracy what was going on in our home. Joanna said Tracy acted like she was lying and always treated her like she was worthless. Joanna was uncomfortable sometimes with Tracy, that most of their birthday weekend activities were what Tracy wanted to do and they spent a lot of time in the bars. Daniel and Brandon said she would just ignore what they said or play it off like Richard was just disciplining them. They also said their birthday activities were spent mostly in the bars and whatever Tracy wanted to do. Tracy's son, Bryan, was two months older than Joanna. It was hard for me to be around them because I was a mandatory reporter and there were a lot of situations that made me very uncomfortable. She was constantly calling him stupid or dumb, or a fucking idiot. She would smack him in the head on a regular basis. I always felt bad and wondered if it was worse behind closed doors like it was with Richard. According to Daniel, Brandon, and Cole; Tracy treated Bryan like crap and them better than him. Joanna, Ashlee, and Renee had opposite experiences. Joanna said one day Bryan hit her with a bat and he begged Joanna not to tell, but she did anyway. Bryan told Tracy that it did not happen, that Joanna was lying, and Tracy believed him. Tracy scolded Joanna enough that she did not want to go to Tracy's ever again.

After many stories from the kids and knowing how she treated Bryan, I was also getting to the point that I did not trust her around my kids. I also learned that before Bryan was old enough to drive, he was having to drive her home from the bars on a regular basis because she was too drunk to drive herself. She left her first husband, Bryan's dad, when he was about a year old. She said her first husband was too controlling. She lived with this other guy for many years, but again left him because she said he was abusive to her and Bryan. Both of these men owned their own homes before meeting Tracy, so when she wanted to end it, she had to move. Bryan would see his dad on his court ordered visitations and did not seem to think that his dad was as bad as Tracy thought he was. Bryan also continued a relationship with the ex-live-in boyfriend and again did not seem to have the problems that Tracy had. I always believed Tracy and was on her side of things, supporting her decisions, mainly because I thought that was what sisters were supposed to do, whether we agreed or not.

Chapter Seventeen

Richard's behaviors continued. It was getting harder for him to pick the boys up by their throats since they were getting to be taller than him, but it did not stop him from trying. He would still grab them by the throats and push their backs against the wall, but it was easier for them to fight him off. He did more sitting on them now. Joanna felt very uncomfortable when he would sit on her or try to overpower her. She started to work out so that she could get stronger than him and once she did, he would become livid with her. The boys called him a bully, he acted more like a teenage bully rather than a man who was supposed to be their stepfather. He called the boys gay, called the girls whores, and continued to intimidate all of us with his fists and degrading words. He made fun of the boys for wanting to wear sandals and shorts. He said that only girls and pussies wore sandals and shorts. Outside of Joanna's bedroom window was the dog kennel, so in order to get to her window from the outside you had to go into the dog kennel and avoid poop. Even with that Richard was accusing Joanna of sneaking boys into her room at night so he put a nail in it to where she could only open it three inches.

One evening I had heard some yelling from downstairs and I went down to check. Richard was taking the lock off Joanna's bedroom door. When I asked what was going on, he said she was being sneaky and he did not trust her, so she did not need a lock on her door. Her bedroom was the one that we added, by splitting the family room in half and we put up a wall with a door. Her door opened into the family room which is where Richard spent a majority of his time. I found out years later, that the argument was over him constantly walking in on her while she would be changing her clothes. She started locking her door when she was going to get dressed so that he could not get in. She would unlock it as soon as she was dressed. Well that pissed him off, so he took the lock off the door so he could walk in any time he chose.

Some rules that Richard had made with the emergency phones were that they had to be on the kitchen counter by 8:00 pm every night, they were not allowed in the kids' bedrooms at all at any time for any reason, and they were not to text or call anyone without his permission. At the beginning I was okay with that because they were little, and I was still new to the technology. Once they were teenagers, though, I thought socializing with friends was important. I still agreed with the 8:00 pm rules though. When Richard was not home, I did allow the kids to talk to friends. Richard did find out because he went through both phones every night. He also went through mine daily, but no one, not even me, was allowed to touch his cell phone. They were all in my name, including his, and he still did not give me access to his phone.

Once he realized that Daniel had phone numbers to some girls in his classes, Richard told Daniel that he should ask for nude pictures. Daniel was not dating, not because he did not like girls, but because he had respect for them and was always friend zoned. Richard thought that was the best time to ask girls for those types of pictures. Since Daniel would not do it, apparently Richard did after 8:00 when he had full access to the phones. I do not know if any of the girls actually sent a picture, but they did tell Daniel at school that they received those messages from the phone he used. One night, a 'dick pic' popped up on the other emergency phone. Joanna usually used that one. Anyway, it came in after 8:00 so no one saw it other than Richard. He did show it to me briefly and then made the comment that he did not want me liking another penis so I should not look. He grounded Joanna, not that she ever went anywhere anyway, but he chewed her out, then yelled at me saying that I was probably the one who wanted to see the boy's penis. At school the kids found out that the reason the boy sent Joanna a 'dick pic' was because he thought that Daniel had asked his girlfriend for a boob pic. He wanted to teach Daniel a lesson on staying away from his girlfriend. I believe Joanna had to explain to the kid that it was not her brother that did it but her nasty stepdad.

 I had always been petite, built like my grandma Vera. I was always the smallest in my classes at school. I was the shortest out of my parents and siblings. When I graduated high school, I weighed ninety-five pounds and was five foot one. The biggest that I got during any of my pregnancies was one hundred forty pounds. I was usually all baby so after they were born, I quickly got back down to under a hundred pounds. I did not watch what I ate and was told that it would eventually catch up to me someday. After Sabastian was born, I was thirty-five years old, but Tracy had made the comment to Richard that I still looked and dressed like a twelve-year-old boy. I did wear size twelve in young boys' shorts, but that was because I did not like the style of the girl clothes. When Sabastian was between seven and twelve months old, I gained weight for no reason at all, but I was happy that I was finally over a hundred pounds without being pregnant. I gained ten pounds. I stopped breast feeding him at seven months old. By my thirty sixth birthday, I was one hundred and eight pounds.

Richard always told me that if I ever gained thirty pounds or more, he would leave me. He started saying that sometime after Renee was born. My rationale was I gained weight due to age. I continued to gain until I turned forty. I had gained a total of thirty-five pounds since he first met me. I pointed that out to him hoping he would make good on his threat of leaving me. Instead he said that I did not look like I gained that much weight, instead I actually looked healthier now.

When it was time for the kids to get their permits and driver's licenses, Richard made it very difficult. He was constantly telling the older kids that they were not smart enough to pass. He also insisted that he accompany them to take their tests. When they would be studying, Richard was always telling them that Cole could pass the tests without studying, but she was not yet old enough. When Daniel was fourteen, Cole was only seven. After a few attempts, Daniel finally passed. I signed him up for driver's education classes through the county sheriff department. I paid for it, even though Richard was not happy about it. When it was Joanna's turn, Richard would put her down and make fun of her all the way to the Department of Motor Vehicle which was about a fifteen-minute drive one way. It took her several tries because he would make her so nervous. I was never able to sign her up for driver's education. The same thing happened with Brandon and Ashlee.

I encouraged the kids to go out for anything they had an interest in. Daniel went out for football, cross country and track, but not at the same time. He only went out for football for one season. He did track and cross country for all four high school years. His coach for track and cross country was also the school superintendent. Daniel did not tell me until years later that his coach had confronted him about suspicions about Daniel's home life and that he was concerned. Daniel admitted to telling the coach a little about Richard's behavior and the coach let him know that he was there for him if things got too bad at home. Joanna went out for basketball for one season and track for a couple years. Brandon went out for track also. Ashlee and Cole were in Girl Scouts for a year or two. I was able to attend a couple of each child's different activities each year. I wished I could have made it to more, but between day care kiddos and fighting with Richard about me attending, I did the best that I could.

Once Daniel was able to get a car, he quit the paper route to get a job at the McDonald's in the town fifteen minutes away. Ashlee helped take over the paper route. Richard was not thrilled with Daniel getting a job. He was glad he was making more money, but he was always accusing Daniel of not going straight to work or coming straight home. Within about six months, Joanna also started working at McDonald's with Daniel. They were gaining experience, getting out of the house, making new friends, and making more money. They were still putting most of their checks into their bank accounts.

In January 2011, we lost Midnight to kidney failure. She was nineteen and a half years old. It was the hardest thing I have ever had to do. She was getting weak, she was barely moving, and not eating nor urinating. I even tried to feed her with an eye dropper. She wanted to be held or to at least be near me all the time. So, for her last few days, I slept on the floor with her. I took her to the vet and held her as she took her last breath. She continued to purr through it all. I was so devastated that I could not stop crying and could not drive back home. The only people I wanted to call were Dave and Charlie. She had initially been mine and Dave's kitty so I felt like he should know, but I had no way to contact him, nor would his wife allow me to talk to him. I could not talk anyway since I was crying so hard so it would not do me any good to call Charlie.

About two months later, I added a new business to my life. I started selling women's accessories through a business I started myself. It meshed well with the jewelry that I was already selling. After getting an employer identification number through the IRS, I was able to become a member to a few different wholesale factories. I would order my inventory through them and then sell to friends and family. I had also opened a business Facebook page that Elizabeth would help me with. I was selling so much that I was having to order new shipments almost weekly. Most of my business came from out-of-state customers that I had no connection to other than them finding me on Facebook. I sold purses, wallets, scarves, fashion shirts, Bible covers, beach bags, etc.

When Daniel turned eighteen, Richard tried to kick him out of the house. I objected since he was still in high school. He was not going to graduate until a few weeks before his nineteenth birthday. Once he graduated, we had the discussion again, but since Daniel planned to go to college, again I objected. Joanna and Daniel continued to work through that summer, but since the college was forty minutes in the opposite direction of where he worked, Daniel needed to quit working to attend classes. Joanna did not have her license or a car so she also had to quit since Richard would not allow me to drive her to and from work.

While in college, Daniel started dating this sweet girl who liked to make wallets out of duct tape. Kallie was in some of Daniel's classes and their schedules were similar. When not in class, sometimes he would hang out at Kallie's house, which was about ten minutes from the college. Sometimes she would hang out with us at our house. She said she enjoyed spending time with us. She loved the girls and me. She showed some of the girls how to make things with duct tape. She also brought over some clothes that she no longer wore for the girls if they wanted them. Kallie usually came around when Richard was not home. She slowly stopped coming around and Daniel was spending more and more time with her in the bigger city. Daniel came home from Kallie's one day, anxious to talk to me.

He had sex for the first time, told me that it was not as exciting as he thought it was going to be. I explained how normal that actually was and that I was glad he could come to me about something as important as this. He did make me promise not to tell Richard. I did not tell Richard, but somehow, he found out anyway. Richard made fun of him, making a pleasant experience turn nasty.

Kallie came over one day when the kids were at school and Richard was at work. She apologized to me for not coming around because she really loved my family, except Richard. She said she did not feel comfortable around Richard anyway, but he had been inappropriate with her so she definitely would not be coming around if Richard was there. She told me that there were a few different incidences. The only one she went into details about though was that he had seen a picture that she thought she sent to Daniel and Richard had made inappropriate comments about. It was a picture of her in a lacy white nightgown; it was somewhat revealing, cleavage was showing, and she obviously did not have on a bra, but she was covered. He continued to text her from Daniel's phone for a little bit after the picture was sent. She got a weird feeling, so she ended the conversation with the excuse of going to bed. She waited until the next day to ask Daniel about it in person. Daniel had no knowledge of any of the conversation and it had been deleted from his phone. She on the other hand still had the messages. Daniel was angry, but they did not know what to do. She chose to come to me with the information. I reassured her that I was not upset with her, that I knew it took a lot of courage to come to me. I apologized to her for Richard's behavior and explained that I completely understood her reluctance to visit. We hugged.

Richard was laid off almost the entire nine months that Daniel was in his first year of college. His unemployment was about to run out. He was also frustrated because, he found out somehow, that he was the only one not working from his company. When he would ask or check in with his supervisor, he always just told Richard that work was slow, and they did not have any work for him to do. One of his former co-workers who had left months earlier for another similar company, told him that his new company was hiring. His former co-worker was up for a promotion into project manager if he could get someone hired to take over his technician position. Richard was torn on whether to take it or not. He would have to take a pay cut and would not have a company vehicle to drive home. It was also not a union company, the other two were union companies. Feeling like he had no other choice, he took the job in early April 2012.

Daniel only took two semesters. He was more girl struck than wanting to finish college. For some reason he thought that he would have more time to spend with Kallie if he was working instead of attending school. I was not happy about it, but he was not about to listen to reasoning. I had also done the same thing when I was young. Since he did not go on to a second year, Richard kicked him out. I had nothing to bargain with this time. I tried the 'he is not ready, prepared, etc.

speech' but I did not win the argument this time. Besides, Joanna was now eighteen and we were having the same argument as two years earlier, just about a different child. Joanna was still in high school; she would not graduate until after her nineteenth birthday. We got Daniel into a two-bedroom apartment that was a few blocks from our house. I also ended up spending two to three hundred dollars getting Daniel kitchen and bathroom supplies; dishes, silverware, towels, cleaning supplies, food, etc. Daniel got a job at the same place Richard now worked.

A couple months after Daniel got his apartment, I again put in my thirty-day notice to day care families, which took us to the end of August of 2012. I had not completely planned what would come next, but when I was ready to move out, I did not want anything causing delay. I did keep the two part-time families just so I still had money coming in along with my profits from Premier Designs Jewelry and my personal business until I could find an outside job. I also sold most of my day care toys and turned the day care room into my office/shop area. I had a purse rack to keep most of the merchandise on and then shelves for the jewelry. Richard's aggression was continually getting worse. None of the kids nor myself could stand to be around him. The tension was so thick when he was home, that outsiders were noticing. My cousin Matt came over a couple of times and told me that the tension was so thick it made him literally sick to his stomach. He also said that he could feel the daggers from Richard's eyes. Richard was not friendly to Matt.

Daniel and Kallie broke up and Richard was making Daniel's life at work a living hell, so he came to me to vent. Richard was constantly making fun of Daniel and telling other co-workers embarrassing things, some of which were not even true. As long as Richard was around, the other co-workers joined in making fun of him and making him feel like a worthless piece of crap. If Richard was on another job site, Daniel said it was not as bad, that the other guys were nicer to him. The problem was the boss put them on the same job site more often than not. He told me that he could not handle it anymore. The more I seemed to try to talk to Richard the worse things got. He apparently started calling Daniel a "titty baby" among other things at work. Daniel ended up quitting his job and moving over an hour north of us with some other friends that he had met.

For the past few months, I had been going through my belongings, getting rid of anything that I no longer needed. I also boxed up things that I never used or touched but that I did not want to get rid of. I wanted to make whatever transition we did make as easy as possible. Richard asked me if I was getting ready to move out. My response to him was that the outcome was up to him. He did not like that response, but he did nothing to change my mind either. During these few months, I was also applying for jobs within about a thirty-five-mile radius, with no call backs.

Aimee decided to have a jewelry party for me at her place of work in April of 2013. She was now a property manager at a large apartment complex and single. She did not have very many people show up so for most of the two-hour slotted time, it was just her and me. We did a lot of talking like we used to. I asked a lot of questions about the apartments and the area. Realizing the reasoning behind my questions, she said with her position she would be able to help the kids and me get into one of the apartments when I was ready. She also said her boss would be hiring another office person soon and she would let me know when and how to apply. If I worked in the office, I would get a discount on an apartment like she did. I kept that information in the back of my head so when the time came, I knew what all my options were. About a month later, I had my first interview in a suburb of the big city. I thought it went well. I did not get a call back though. I continued to apply for many jobs in the same initial radius.

In July 2013, Heather, my second roommate from the group home, was getting married and invited my family. She had met my kids but, not Richard. She wanted him to come so she could meet him. I had not given her any details on my so-called marriage. I think that I was embarrassed because I never talked about the actual details with anyone unless they had witnessed an incident. Aimee had witnessed some. Elizabeth had witnessed a lot. Even Richard's stepmom had witnessed a little, but her comments to me were that I "needed to nip that in the bud" and that it "would take me leaving him for him to change."

Richard did not want to go to the wedding. He did not want me or the kids to go either. There was going to be a reception immediately following the ceremony and the invite stated to bring swimsuits as well. The kids were excited about the swimming part of the invite, so everyone had their swimsuits and towels ready. Richard finally decided he would go; his reason was so that I did not stay too long. So, we all loaded up to attend the wedding. It was an outdoor wedding. There was lemonade and water available prior to the ceremony since it was hot. Once Heather saw that I was there, she came over right away to give me a hug and introduce herself to Richard. Like usual he did not smile or look thrilled that anyone was even talking to him. Before the ceremony even started, he was already complaining about the heat and that he was ready to go.

As soon as the ceremony was over, Richard was already trying to corral the kiddos to start walking to the Traverse. Most of them wanted to stay and eat, and I wanted to at least talk to Heather before we took off. Everyone was wanting to congratulate and talk to Heather, so it was hard for me to get over to her. I did finally get Richard to agree to stay and eat, at least so the kids could get something to eat. We did have almost an hour drive back home. Once the line to Heather was down to about three more people, I decided to line up. I did not even say anything yet, when she asked me what was wrong. I said nothing, but Heather did not believe me. She reminded me how long we had known each other and said that she knew something was wrong. She also let me know that she got a very bad vibe from Richard. She was disappointed that we were not going to stay to swim. I did not tell her that Richard was making us leave, but I think she figured it out. She told me that she was always there if I needed her and even though she lived in a small house, I was always welcome to come stay with her as long as I needed. Richard was already getting some of the kids in the car, so she gave me and the kids that were standing with me tight lengthy hugs.

Chapter Eighteen

Later that month, Richard was very angry. I did not know what about, and neither did the kids so we were trying to keep our distance from him. Once he got me into our bedroom, he held me down on the bed. I kept telling him no, that I did not want to have sex. He was so angry, it seemed to be making him stronger than usual, and I was not able to fight him off. He got my pants down to my knees. I was just repeating the word "no" over and over while crying and trying to push him off. Once he finished and let go of me, I just laid there for a minute crying. As he zipped his jeans, he looked at me, saying something about how stupid it was that I was "bawling" and left the room, closing the door behind him. I prayed, asking the Lord to please give me a way out or take me home because I could not keep living this way. I also asked why me, not necessarily to God, and actually thinking that I would do anything to be with Dave again dealing with all of his mistresses rather than what I was dealing with now.

All summer long, Brandon was using my computer to look for houses for rent. He was mostly looking in the suburbs of the big city. Even though he was seventeen and should have understood, he did not seem to understand that without a job or money for rent and deposit, it was not realistic to look into those houses. Once in a house, if the landlord permitted me to, I could start day care back up and make enough to pay for rent and utilities, but I had to get into the house first, which was the main issue. The kids were allowed to get Facebook accounts with the requirement that Richard had to know all usernames and passwords, so he had complete access at any time. I did not have the kids' passwords. Richard said that I had no need to know them. Richard was always checking the history on the computer and accused me of looking at houses for rent. That also caused some very intense arguments.

With our insurance carrier, if we went a whole year without a claim or a late payment, we would receive an incentive check. It averaged about ten percent of our yearly total. I always paid that bill; it was direct withdrawal out of my bank account. It combined our home, auto and my business insurance coverages. Each year that I would get that incentive check, I would just deposit it into my account so it could cover the next premium. Since I had been making less money this year, I was really counting on it to help me with bills. Well this year, somehow Richard found the check before I even knew that it came. He cashed it at his bank and went shopping with the money. I was so upset, but he kept saying that it was our money so he should be able to spend it however he wanted. When I argued that I paid the bill, not him, so technically it should be mine to spend how I wanted, he argued saying that we are married so there was not a mine or his just ours, which was not his usual argument.

I started getting the feeling that Richard was somehow recording me, tracking me, or something similar. He knew who I texted each day, before he even came home and checked my phone. He knew that Elizabeth had sent me a picture of a bare-chested muscular man. It was not someone we knew and there was nothing bare below the belt. I would assume to most people it would not be inappropriate, but Richard was livid and wanted to know why I received that picture. He was not home when I received it, nor was he home before he called me to argue about it. There was no reasonable way he could have known about it unless he had cameras watching me. He also knew about conversations that I had with my kids or had on the phone. Even when no one was around to hear the conversations on the phones, he still seemed to know literally everything.

Even though I really liked the current school the kids had been attending for the past six years, a couple of the kids wanted to be homeschooled. I was okay with homeschooling them; the current school was okay with me homeschooling with their help. Since we were open enrolled though, for some reason it was a rule that I had to get permission from our resident district. The resident district would not agree to it, they wanted me to put my kids back in their schools instead. I tried talking to Richard about it, but he was not wanting to support me. We got into a huge fight one August afternoon. I usually kept our arguments somewhat quiet and away from the kids. I would usually talk to him in our bedroom so that the kids did not witness any of it. This particular argument started out that way, but quickly became loud and not contained to our bedroom. Usually when he was done with the discussion or argument, he would leave the room and I would just completely drop the discussion. This time I followed him out of the bedroom to continue the discussions.

The argument scared the kids, so they decided to leave. Joanna, Ashlee, and Renee went to one of my former day care family's homes. Joanna had taken over babysitting for that family when I retired so she felt comfortable there. Brandon took Sabastian downstairs to his room; I believe to listen to music to help drown us out, which I did not know until later. Cole went outside to ride her bike. I brought up Richard's past behaviors that were continuously getting worse, brought up the nonconsensual incident in our room the month before, asked him about cameras, and explained to him that we needed to separate because I could not live like this anymore. He told me that I needed to quit bringing up the past, told me that it was impossible for a man to rape his wife, told me that there were not cameras but he "has his ways" of finding things out, and told me he did not believe in separations. He did not have a comment when I said that none of this was in the past, it was all happening now on a daily basis. I also explained that I did not use the word rape, nor have I ever used that word when referring to the incidents with him. He made it very clear that this was his home, not mine, and he would not leave. I had asked him what happened to nothing is his or mine, that it is ours. His response was what is his is his and what is mine is ours. He said if I wanted to leave to go right ahead and not to forget to take my brats with me. He said if I left, though, it was definitely over because he did not believe in separation so he would not allow me to come back. I said fine, as soon as I found a job, the kids and I would be gone. I believe these were just threats because he did not believe that I would really leave.

I was shaking really bad. I needed to get away from him for a bit. I had never just taken off from my kids before, but I did not want them to see me this upset either. I left in the car, without my cell phone, not sure where I was going at first. I felt like I had nowhere to really go. I found myself on the street where my great uncle lived and when I passed the house, I saw that my cousin Matt's truck was in the driveway. I decided to stop and say hello. Matt already had his reservations about Richard. He never felt comfortable around Richard. So, I spilled most everything to Matt. My uncle asked me to stay and eat dinner with them, so I did. Matt listened more than giving any kind of advice, but that still helped. I thanked Matt for listening, I thanked my uncle for the meal, and decided I needed to get home to check on my kiddos.

The kids were worried sick. I had never done anything like this before and they had no clue where I might have gone. Most of my kids had my friends on their Facebooks, so they had messaged Aimee, Heather, Charlie, Belle, and a few others. None of them had seen or heard from me which also worried them. Aimee and two of her sisters drove all the way to my house, so they got there about the time I came back home. They did not feel comfortable going into the house with Richard there, so we stayed outside in the yard talking about what had happened. Aimee was no longer working or living in that apartment complex anymore. She had actually moved in with Charlie. She was also in the process of finding a new job and a place of her own to live. We talked about possibly renting a house big enough for her and the boys, and my kids and me to all live in once we both found jobs. Someone, I believe it was Richard, even called my sister Tracy. Tracy called scolding me for what I did and how wrong it was to take off like that without telling Richard or the kids. She did not sound concerned with my safety or why I left, but she seemed more concerned with it being inappropriate behavior. For most of the past year, I had been sleeping in either my office/shop or the living room, but after this argument I never slept in his bedroom again.

In the beginning of September, I had a few more interviews. Three were in the town fifteen minutes away, another one was about a thirty-minute drive southeast, and another one in the same suburb as my interview in May. I did not receive any call backs from any of them either. About three weeks after the interviews, I called some of them to check in on the status of my application. Every single one of them told me that after the interviews, they got a call from a male stating he was a previous employer and they would not want to hire me because I was unreliable. Other than the places I interviewed at, the only other people who knew that I had interviews were the kids and Richard. Richard of course denies calling these places, but I still think it was him. He would be the only one who would not want me to find a job and move out.

Belle's husband had left her and their autistic son about a year earlier. I was her shoulder to lean on since before he left. Over the summer, my kids and I helped her move into a two-bedroom apartment in a small town twenty minutes south of the big city, which made it about an hour and fifteen-minute drive from my house. She was having a real hard time towards the end of September so I told her that I would come down for a few hours to hang out. The last Saturday of September, after everyone ate breakfast and I listed what was available for lunch, I left to head to Belle's place. I did not take any of the kids with me this time. My plan was to be back around dinner time. I took with me a bunch of my old 80s movies; like *Howard the Duck*, *Hiding Out*, *Gleaming the Cube*, etc. Belle had several back surgeries since giving birth to her son. Kellan was four years old, almost a year younger than Sabastian. Belle seemed alright when I first got there. She had put a pizza in the oven for us to eat for lunch and we spent the first hour talking about both of our men issues.

After we ate pizza, I put in *Howard the Duck* for us to watch. Kellan was playing in his room. Belle had fallen asleep in her recliner. I thought she just needed some sleep, so I was going to stay until she woke up since Kellan was awake and I did not want to leave him unattended. When I was ready to go, I could not get her to wake up. I called Richard to let him know that I would be late coming home since I was not going to leave Kellan. I even took a picture of Kellan and me standing next to Belle in the chair to send to Richard because he did not believe me. After I put Kellan to bed, I called Richard again to update him, and then I fell asleep on Belle's couch. When I awoke Sunday morning, Belle was in the kitchen getting Kellan breakfast. She apologized telling me that she was in so much pain before I arrived that she took some of her pain medications that always knocked her out. She told me that the kids and I were welcome to move in with her because she felt like she needed help especially when she was always in pain. Even though her apartment was small, she said we could make it work until I found a job and then we could get a bigger place together. While we were talking, I got a call from Joanna. All she said was "Mom hurry home," and she hung up. So, I left immediately.

    When I arrived home, I could hear yelling before I even got up to the front door. When I opened the screen door, Renee opened the main door. I still had one foot on the outside step while one foot was just inside the door, when I had both Renee and Sabastian crying and hanging onto my legs. They were twelve and five years old. The yelling was coming from downstairs. I inched my way into the house, gave Renee and Sabastian hugs since they were telling me that they were scared, and sat them down so I could check on the yelling. All the other kids were in their rooms, the arguing between Richard and Ashlee quickly stopped when I walked down the stairs. When I asked what was going on, Richard told me that it was none of my business and that he had it taken care of. As I walked to each of the kid's rooms, Richard followed me. When I would ask questions, either Richard would answer, or the kids would just look at him and not reply. For the rest of the day, all the kids stayed in their rooms and Richard did not let me out of his sight.

The next day, Richard called in sick to work. He volunteered to take the younger kids to school and Joanna to her college classes at the community college fifteen minutes away. I had still been unable to find out what happened while I was at Belle's. When Richard arrived, I tried to talk to him about what happened. He continued to tell me that I should drop it because it was none of my business. I tried to tell him that no matter what, it was still my business because even the kids were all acting strange. I knew something was not right and I told him that it was not right, that obviously he had not taken care of it. He continued to ignore me and play his video games. When it was time, he again picked Joanna up from the college and then the younger kids from their school. When the kids came home, they all went to their rooms and again, Richard did not leave my side.

Tuesday morning, I was relieved to hear Richard leave for work. As soon as he had pulled out of the driveway, I had five of the kids standing in front of me, all talking at once. It was like we were all frantically waiting for him to leave. We were also all paranoid and kept checking the windows to make sure that he had not returned to the house. Once I got them all to calm down and talk one at a time, I was able to finally find out what had happened. The kids had been doing their daily chores so that they were done when I got home. Richard took it upon himself to check to make sure they were done to his satisfaction. He apparently did not think that Ashlee had cleaned the shower properly and took a swing at her face, stopping just before making contact. This was normal for him, this was not the first time he had done this, but the kids were done, they had enough. They were trying to stand up for themselves since I was not home, and Richard threatened them if they told me.

Since they had not been able to tell me anything and they did not know what else to do, at school the day before, they had talked to several of their friends and their parents. Joanna, now nineteen, had contacted her boyfriend and his mom who said that she would be able to move in with them if need be. They lived in the town where she was going to college. Brandon, now seventeen, had talked to one of his best friends and his mother. Again, they said that Brandon was welcome to live with them. The mother of one of Ashlee's friends had said the same. She just wanted a notarized letter from me giving her temporary guardianship of Ashlee, almost sixteen, so that she would not get into any legal trouble. Since they had made these other plans, the kids gave me an ultimatum of either leaving Richard right now, or they were going to move in with their friends. I tried to explain to them that I needed to get a job to show consistent income before anyone would let me rent a place. They did not want to hear my excuses or reasoning, so they contacted a few of my friends. They managed to do a 'tele-intervention'. The kids had Heather and Mandi calling me, Charlie and Elizabeth were messaging me on Facebook, Aimee and Belle both called me, and a few others made their concerns known. We tried to be careful since we knew that there was some way that Richard knew all my conversations and text messages. Everyone was letting me know that the kids had told them some of what was going on and that I needed to get out of there as soon as possible. I had five different friends letting me know that their homes were available for the kids and me to move into right now. So, the kids gave me two weeks to figure it out.

One morning on the way to take Joanna to her classes, I decided to stop at an office for domestic violence victims. I had Joanna and Ashlee with me. I had already dropped the other kiddos off at school. I wanted to know exactly what the best way to do this was. After the three of us told the legal advocate a quick story of our lives, she gave us a packet. The advocate was in fear for us due to his threats and him possessing many firearms. Her suggestion was for us to try to move out of the residence while he was away. Her suggestion was also not to allow him to know where we were living, until I was able to get a restraining order in place. She told us to have law enforcement there to remove his firearms and to make sure to let them know that he always carried so they could try to get that from him once he did arrive home. The packet was for us to fill out and give back to her once we got out so she could help us afterwards.

I talked to the kids about each friend that had offered us a place to stay. I wanted them to choose so that we were in a place they felt the most comfortable. Heather lived in a small two-bedroom house in a small town between our town and the big city with her husband and five-year-old daughter. Belle lived in the two-bedroom apartment in a small town south of the big city with her four-year-old autistic son. Annie lived in a two-bedroom mobile home with her husband in a small trailer court in the country between the town Belle lived in and the big city. Mandi lived in a two-bedroom house with a full unfinished basement in the big city with her husband and autistic teenage son. Charlie lived in a three-bedroom duplex, with three floors including a walk out basement in the big city, he lived within walking distance from a large mall and other shopping. Aimee and her two boys were also staying there. Brandon chose Charlie's house. He had several reasons but the main one being it was close to shopping so that he, Joanna, and Ashlee could all get jobs to help me pay bills. The rest of the kids agreed, so that was the plan.

Brandon kept having severe chest pains and felt like Richard was the one causing them. He asked to move in with Charlie early to get away from Richard and to help Charlie make room in the duplex. Brandon moved in with Charlie on Thursday, October 10, 2013. We told Richard that Brandon was staying with a friend because his stress levels were high. I just did not say that the friend was mine instead of one of Brandon's. Brandon helped Charlie paint and move furniture to prepare for a houseful. Brandon, Charlie and Heather were the ones who scheduled the U-Haul. Heather's brother worked for one of the U-Haul places and could get us a discount on renting a truck.

The rest of us tried to lay low and keep from upsetting Richard over the weekend. I had filled most of the packet out and hid it inside Ashlee's trapper keeper full of homework. I also called the police stating that I would need their assistance on the morning of Tuesday October 15 and why. They informed me that they did not make 'reservations' so that I would have to call back that morning to request their assistance.

On the morning of Monday, October 14, the day before our scheduled move, Richard did not leave for work. He got up at his usual time and sort of hung around, creepily watching all of us. He took the kids to school. When he came back home, he informed me that he knew of my plans. He said he wanted to work things out. As I was trying to talk to him about what we needed to work on, he started unbuttoning and unzipping my jeans. I pushed him away telling him that does not fix anything. That he either talked to me or nothing would ever change. He knelt down in front of me like he was going to propose, but before I could fix my pants, he yanked them to my ankles. He tried touching my vagina, but I kept blocking him and trying to fight him off while I got my pants back up. I was finally able to get them back up, buttoned and zipped. Usually when I would fight him off, he would get angry and more violent. He was smiling this entire time, even after I was able to button my jeans. He was not wanting to talk, I was not willing to have sex, so I admitted that the kids and I were moving out the next day. I continued trying to figure out what belongings were going with me and what was not. He again picked the kids up from school and it was an eerily quiet evening.

Chapter Nineteen

That Tuesday morning, October 15, Richard left for work. The gun safe was locked and I did not know how to get into it, so I did not call the police. About an hour later, Charlie and Brandon showed up in the U-Haul with two vehicles behind them. One vehicle was Aimee and her two boys, the other vehicle was Heather, her husband and daughter. Shortly after that, two more vehicles showed up. One was my friend Stacia, who I had become friends with in the past few years, and her sister, who brought a car full of boxes. Stacia's sister stayed for a little bit helping pack and then she left. Stacia stayed filling up her own vehicle with our belongings to haul to Charlie's house with us. I had called my dad to come get Brutus because we could not have him in Charlie's duplex. We did load up the cats, though. We were going to try to hide them from the landlord. When my dad came out to the house, he said "It's about time you leave that asshole. Good luck." I gave him a hug and said, "thank you, I will update you when I can."

I left Richard the 2010 Traverse that seated eight. We had just bought it the year before and we still owed money on it. I took the 2001 Chevrolet Impala that I had bought from a friend for $300 with my day care money. Since the car only held four kids plus me, Brandon rode back in the U-Haul with Charlie, Cole rode with Stacia, and the rest rode with me. Anything that I had bought with Richard, I left behind. I took most everything that I needed to continue my jewelry and accessory businesses. I took most, but not all, of my clothes. I had not gone grocery shopping for a few days knowing that I was leaving. We did take a few food items, but we left him more than half of what was on the shelves. I left most of my dishes which I either had before I met him, or I got in a tradeoff of services...they would do a Premier Designs jewelry party for me and I would do a Pampered Chef party for them. All of my dressers were either ones I bought with Dave, belonged to Dave's family or were Aimee's so I did take all of those. The sectional was actually Aimee's. Instead of her putting certain pieces of her furniture in storage, she said that I could use it until she needed it again. I left all the televisions and his computer, but I took my computer because it stored all my business information, and I left the DVD players. I took the two beds that my parents gave me, Sabastian's toddler bed, and I let the kids pick what toys and clothes of their own they wanted to take. We left more there than we took. The U-Haul was not even filled. Neither were any of the vehicles.

In Charlie's duplex, there were two bedrooms and a bathroom on the second floor. The kitchen, dining room that had sliders to a deck, living room and second bathroom were on the main floor. The basement had the third bedroom, computer area, storage area, laundry room, and extra living area with a walkout. The back yard went downhill into some timber and a creek. We put Aimee's two boys, Brandon and Sabastian in one of the bedrooms on the second floor, the second bedroom up there was for my four girls and me. Aimee slept in the bedroom in the basement and Charlie slept on the couch in the living room. He was the bodyguard, no one was coming into the house without Charlie hearing them.

My first priority was getting the kids back in school. I did not want them missing more than they needed to. They started school October 18th in their new suburban schools. The plan for Joanna was that she was going to stay at her boyfriend's parent's house during the week so she could attend her college classes and then stay with us on the weekends. At least until the end of the semester and then maybe transfer to the college closer to us which is the one Daniel had attended. I called the legal advocate lady to let her know we had gotten out and to get her mailing address for this packet. She informed me that since I had left the county she worked in, that I was going to need to find resources in my new county, which was very disappointing. My next priorities were finding a job and a lawyer. I went job hunting online first, applying for as many jobs as I thought I qualified for. I also applied for food stamps, but not the state cash benefits. Then I called legal aid and another local non-profit legal business that was similar to legal aid. Legal aid told me that they only handled so many divorce cases a year and they had already reached their limit. I would either have to wait until after the first of the year or contact the other organization. I contacted the other one and they said something similar. Again, I was told they were not taking on any new cases until after the first of the year. They suggested that I contact legal aid, and when I said that I already had, she apologized to me for not being able to help.

I was hired on rather quickly with Bath and Body Works as a part-time seasonal sales associate. It was minimum wage and mostly evenings and weekends. I took it though because I figured something was better than nothing. When something else came along then I would take it. I talked to the kids about it and they said they understood, and they were fine. I left them the food stamp card so that while I was working, they could go to the store and get snacks. I would also make dinner before going to work. A time or two, Aimee and I made dinner together before I would leave. Within a couple weeks, Aimee and the boys ended up moving out. I was usually only working one or two evenings a week since I worked full days both Saturday and Sundays. On those nights, besides Charlie being in the house, I also had three teenagers to watch the two youngest kiddos plus Joanna was also there on the weekends. I had stocked the house with groceries, but I still left the food stamp card with the kids. I felt bad that I was gone, and they were left in unfamiliar surroundings. I kept telling them and myself that this was temporary. Once I found a better job we could move into our own place.

We brought the two emergency phones with us and I continued to have my cell phone since they were in my name. Richard was not paying for them anyway. They had the same phone numbers as they always had. I did not keep the kids from calling or texting Richard. I just told them not to give him our exact address due to the suggestion of the legal advocate. To my knowledge, Richard never tried to contact the kids on those phones. He did however call me on a regular basis. He was constantly telling me to come back home, but he was not wanting to talk about anything in depth. He also said on many occasions that he would go to extreme measures to take my kids away from me so that I had no choice but to come back to him because he knew that I could not live without my kids. We did not yet have a court order, but I also did not want to keep his kids from him. I had to work a lot of hours over Thanksgiving weekend since it also contained Black Friday. I did not feel that it was fair to the kiddos, so after talking to the kids about what they wanted to do, I asked my parents if the older kids could stay with them. They did not want to stay with Richard. So, I took the older kids to my parents, and then dropped the younger three off at Richard's with the agreement that I would pick them all back up that Sunday when I got off work. We also made a verbal agreement that he could have the kids every other weekend. Just the kids that wanted to go to his house, I was not going to force the older kids.

 Charlie had been dating since his breakup back in the spring. Our agreement was that if he was going to date, I did not want him bringing the girls back to the duplex while my kids were present. He respected my wishes. He did go on a few dates, but he did not bring them back to the house. Richard must have been 'stalking' Charlie's Facebook, though, because he told the kids and convinced the kids that Charlie was cheating on me after he found a picture of Charlie out to dinner with a woman. That Thanksgiving weekend, Charlie did not have any dates and with the kids gone, we had some alone time to talk uncensored. We talked about everything like we used to, we talked about his women issues, my new issues, the kids, our feelings, if we thought there was a possible future for us in more than just friends. We agreed to talk to the kids before we made any long-term decisions. I was still planning on getting an apartment for just the kids and me as soon as I possibly could no matter what happened with Charlie and me.

We knew it was probably too soon to talk about a new relationship when I had not even filed for divorce yet, but it was like having an elephant in the room. We both needed to know the expectations of the other. He knew that I was his soulmate and did not want to lose the chance if there was one. He also did not want to wait around for something that would never happen if I was not interested. I did not know when I would be ready, but I also did not feel it fair to him to have to wait for me when I had no idea how long it would take. After being married to Dave and Richard, I had little faith in any man. I had grown a hatred for men. I knew that was not fair, but I really had no intentions of ever being in another relationship again. I had lost so many people in my lifetime though. I was afraid I would never know true love or know what a real relationship felt like and if given that possibility, should I give it a chance or protect myself? Angie and her four-year-old son were killed by her husband over a year after Joanna was born, Shay passed away from her kidney disease a year after Sabastian was born, my neighbor, who was a few years younger than me, was killed in a car accident a few months before I left Richard, one of Tracy's high school boyfriends, that my brother and I were close with, shot himself in the month before I left Richard, Dave's stepsister, that I had been close to at one time, was killed in a motorcycle accident the year before, and the list continues.

We did not talk to the kids right away after bringing them back home. I was actually shocked and relieved that Richard did not fight me on picking the kids back up from him that Sunday after Thanksgiving. Cole was causing some issues at the house as well as at school. I told her that she needed to treat others with respect and follow rules if she was going to live with me. She was being disrespectful to her teachers, being rude and not doing her homework. She was disrespectful to her siblings, Charlie and me. This was not new behavior with her. We had this same problem before we left Richard. It just seemed worse now. Well, she decided to call Richard and tell him that I kicked her out, so he needed to come get her. I told him and her that I did not kick her out, I just told her that if she was going to live there then she had to follow rules and be respectful of others. I did not think that was too much to ask for. So, Cole moved back to Richard's house in the second week of December.

It was the second weekend of December that Charlie and I sat all the kids down in one of the bedrooms to tell the kids about our past history, our feelings then and now, and that someday we would like to start a relationship but wanted their opinions. Joanna was present for this little family meeting, but Cole and Daniel were not. Daniel was still living north of my hometown, which was a good two hours away. I made sure to let them know that if they were not comfortable with it then we would not be anything more than platonic friends. The kids said that they were fine with it, because they liked Charlie and I had been the happiest that they had seen me in many years. Because of weather issues and travel, this was the last weekend that Joanna ended up staying. I wish that I would have known that because I would have made it more special.

There was a family worker with the school. I do not recall her official title, but she was like a social worker that worked closely with the school district on helping families in need, but she was not really with a state agency either. Anyway, this worker gave me a name of a lawyer that she recommended. She also donated gifts so that the kids and I could have a small Christmas because I could not afford anything. I called this lawyer's office, but he was out of the office until after Christmas, so I left a message for him to call me. I called other law offices, but everyone wanted a retainer of over five thousand dollars. I did not have that just laying around. Three days before Christmas, I was served with divorce papers. Richard filed for divorce in his county. Our first hearing was scheduled for February 10, 2014. I did not have a lawyer, I had no money, and not much time to figure it out. Everyone kept telling me not to worry because Iowa is a mother state and as long as I have never broken the law, they would not take my kids from me.

Christmas was a Wednesday in 2013 so the kids, Charlie and I had a very small Christmas at the duplex. Then the kids and I went to Dave's family's Christmas get together. The whole time I was there, Richard kept calling me and texting me. He kept telling me that he would drop the divorce if I just came home. When I would tell him that it was too late, that I was not taking him back, he would start threatening me with doing whatever it took to take all the kids away from me. He would hang up angry and then call back or text a few minutes later to apologize and then the whole conversation would repeat. I kept telling him that I was trying to enjoy family time. He reminded me that Dave's family was not my family and I had no right to be there. That following weekend was an agreed weekend for the kids to go to Richard's. Again, I took the older kids to my parents because they were going to have Christmas that weekend and I had to work.

Brandon was a senior, and I had just paid the minimum possible for his cap, gown and five invitations. I took his senior pictures and made wallets at Walmart. I also needed to buy some of the kids' winter gear and when I asked Richard to help with the expenses, he refused. I also tried to get him to help out a little with the cell phone bill, which again, he refused. The bill was late. I only had part of the payment, so they agreed to keep two of the phones on with the money I had, only because I had been a valued customer for over eleven years and had never been late. So, they shut off Richard's line and one of the emergency lines. The agreement was to come back in a couple weeks with another payment. Richard called me from his work phone yelling and complaining that I had his personal line shut off out of hatred. I tried to explain my circumstance, but he did not care.

That lawyer finally called me back after New Year's. He told me that he would need a five-thousand-dollar retainer before he would even look at my case, but he was willing to talk to me on the phone for a few minutes as part of his free consultation. He told me that I needed to force the older kids to go to Richard's on the agreed weekends otherwise he could use that against me in court. He suggested I start recording any interactions that I had with Richard because I told him about the phone calls and harassing me while at a family Christmas. He said if Richard was really talking to me like that then it showed abuse and intent. He also gave me the number to a young new lawyer that would have a smaller retainer. He said she had experience with cases of domestic violence, and he thought she would be a better fit than him anyway. Since I did not have any money, I chose to try to call back the other two non-profit organizations before calling this other young new lawyer. Legal Aid told me to fill out the online application and someone would contact me if and when they decided to take the case. There were certain criteria in order for them to decide which cases they would accept. I could not get anyone to answer at the other organization. When I called this young new lawyer, her retainer was one thousand, and she would need at least half before she would look at anything and she would take payments for the remaining. I had about a month before we had to be in court which did not give me much time to get her paid so she could have time to look at the case.

The second weekend of January was another agreed weekend for the kids to go to Richard's. I fought with the older kids to go; they did not want to go. I explained to them what the lawyer told me. Brandon finally agreed and got ready; Ashlee waited until about five minutes before I was supposed to meet Richard for the switch. I felt bad. I felt like I was being a bad parent, but I also did not want Richard to have anything to use against me in court either. I started a new job as a front desk associate at a massage business. It paid a few cents more an hour and I got a few more hours than I had with Bath and Body Works. The season was now over so they were not needing me anymore anyway. When the kids came back from Richard's, I found out that Tracy got married that weekend. I was not invited, but Richard and the kids were. They were also acting different towards me and being somewhat aggressive. They told me that Richard changed, that he apologized to them and promised things would be better. They told me that they decided they were moving back in with him and if I cared about them that I would move back to his house too. The kids also accused me of being mean to him by shutting his phone off on purpose. I felt defeated. I felt like my whole world was falling apart. I prayed asking for guidance on what I was supposed to do now.

Two days later, in the middle of the week, Brandon and Ashlee packed up their belongings and told me that I was supposed to meet Richard at the mall to pick them up. Brandon would not even look at me. He did not give me a hug or say goodbye. He just got out of my car and into Richard's. Ashlee looked sad and said "Mom, all you have to do is move back home and we can all be a family again." She got out of my car and into his as he started walking towards me. I was behind him in a position that once they were in his vehicle, I could not see them. I was being torn to pieces inside trying to figure out what just happened. A week ago, they did not want anything to do with him and were angry with me for making them go to his house for a weekend visit. Three months ago, these same two children were begging me to leave him and giving me ultimatums. Now, they were wanting me to go back to him. What? I was so confused.

Richard sat in my front passenger seat with one leg still outside of the car. He told me that this would all be over if I just came back home. I reminded him that he did not believe in separations. I told him that we had not worked out any of our issues, and I told him that his house was not my home. He started to reach over towards my leg, but I pushed his hand back to his side of the car. He laughed and said that I should let him touch my pussy because she probably was not getting the attention that she needed. I told him not to touch me and to get out of my car. As he climbed out of my car, he said, "well if you change your mind, you know where to find me." I told Charlie about this, so he got me a recorder immediately. We both wished that I had gotten it sooner. A few months later, I found out that he had told the kids that I let him touch me, that it was my idea, to get him all excited and to try to get what I wanted from him. Not sure what that was supposed to be, but I have since realized that is part of his manipulation tactics.

I was trying to borrow money from anyone that I could. I had helped many people out financially over the years when I had enough, but now that I needed help, I was having no luck. I did not like to borrow money, but I felt like I was losing everything, and I was not sure how or why. I also found out that instead of putting the kids back into the school that they were in when I left him, he put them back into the resident district that I fought to get them out of over six years earlier. Besides needing money to pay a lawyer, I had the cell phone company threatening to shut off the two remaining lines. Belle was having her own issues with her phone service so she offered to pay the minimum amount they would accept to keep the lines open if she could get a line added for herself. I agreed. She paid whatever the minimum amount was, and they added her line. What I did not realize is that she told them to turn off the only emergency phone that I had left, and I still had Renee and Sabastian living with me. They needed a cell phone.

The last weekend of January was another agreed weekend for the kids to go to Richard's. I had tried to discuss switching the kids for the weekend; the younger ones go with him while the older ones go with me. He claimed they did not want to see me. According to the lawyer, I was not allowed to deny him visits so why could he deny me? That Sunday, I had my recorder on and recording. I met him at the gas station to get the kids back from him, once I pulled up, he got out and into my car without the kids. He asked me if I got his message about meeting him early to talk and so I could be nice to him.

Defending myself, I said that "I am always nice to you and you are accusing me of stuff that isn't even true."

He said, "Even if I wasn't accusing and you wouldn't let me go play with your pussy over there, so whatever."

I asked, "So who isn't being nice? It isn't me."

He replied with "You! We could go talk for a couple minutes."

My reply was "I am not being nice because I won't let you touch me?" My voice was slightly raised because I was in shock at how he justified me being mean to him.

He said "whatever" and got out of the car. The kids are already getting into the backseat of my car. He told me to have a bad week and told the two kids to each have a good week before slamming my car door shut.

I did not hear from Legal Aid after filling out the online application, so Charlie and I were able to scrounge up the five hundred dollars to pay the young new lawyer. I took the money and all the paperwork I had on the divorce issue to her office a week and a half before court. The secretary said that she would give everything to the young new lawyer and that she would contact me soon. I called leaving messages almost every day the week before with no answer. Finally, the Friday before court, which was on Monday, she called wanting me to come into her office so we could go over what was to happen on Monday. I was at work and had to try to get someone to cover me so I could go meet with her. I had not met her in person prior to this. I had talked to her on the phone a month ago, about her fee and if she was willing to take the case. Otherwise this was literally the first time. Before I arrived at her office, she was trying to get a continuance due to the fact that I had just hired her, and she had not been given enough time to prepare. They obviously denied her request so to court we went.

Chapter Twenty

Court was on Brandon's eighteenth birthday. I had not seen Brandon or Ashlee since I let them move back almost a month ago. Even though I was still giving Richard weekend visits with Renee and Sabastian, he was not returning the courtesy with the other kids. I had not seen Cole or Joanna since December. Joanna was a little bit different; I had talked to her on the phone, but she was also acting funny with me and I was not sure what was going on.

Richard was present with his lawyer and I was present with mine. He had affidavits from my mother and Tracy. I did not have any due to the fact that I did not know that I needed them. My lawyer did tell me to start thinking of people that would write affidavits for me because I would need them at the next trial. Even standing there in front of the judge my lawyer tried to get a continuance since she did not have time to prepare. It was denied. I did not get to talk, but I did whisper to my lawyer corrections in anything that was being said. Nothing Richard or his lawyer said was true and the affidavits from my mother and Tracy were filled with incorrect information as well. They claimed that I had an affair and ran off with another man. That Richard had no idea that anything was wrong, so he was shocked to come home to an empty house. They claimed that I took everything, leaving him with nothing, not even food. They claimed that I would not allow him to contact the kids, that he had no way to contact them, and he had not been allowed to see them until he filed for divorce.

After hearing all the things that I was accused of, I talked to my lawyer about them. I asked if she thought it would be better if I moved in with one of my female friends. Charlie and I had not really been able to start or have a relationship anyway with the constant roller coaster that Richard had me on. My lawyer did not think that it was a good idea to move in with a different friend. She thought it would look worse on me to not have a stable place to live if I kept moving between friends rather than staying with Charlie.

Almost three weeks later on Friday, February 28, 2014, I received the court order giving Richard temporary custody of ALL five of my minor children. It stated that his custody would start on March 1, and I was ordered to pay child support with us splitting costs of the children's expenses. The child support amount confused me because even though I had turned in my pay stubs to prove my employment and income, they did not report it correctly. They listed my employer as still being with Bath and Body Works, they listed my income being three times MORE than it actually was and listed Richard's income at about fifteen thousand dollars LESS than his actually was. It stated that I was to give him all birth certificates and social security cards for ALL the children. It gave me visitations on every Wednesday evening from 5:00 to 8:00 pm, and every other weekend starting the second weekend of March. We had been doing the switching of children at a gas station that was somewhat between his house and Charlie's most of the time.

The court order stated we could continue meeting at the halfway point. Once in a while it would be at the mall near Charlie's house, just because Richard was already going to be in town for something. The reasons the court order gave were that I left the family home, taking the kids away from their home, school, and church, that I took them away from family and friends. It stated that my income was not adequate enough to care for the children, and that my living quarters were inadequate. I had never lived without my kids before; I was shocked and devastated, but I knew I had to fight. That was just the temporary custody hearing. I needed to be ready for the next hearing.

Richard called me to inform me that he got his copy of the order and that I could bring the kids and ALL of their belongings to the church where Joanna was getting married at such and such time. He was probably the most excited that I had ever known for him to get. I felt numb. Married? No one had told me that she was getting married. Tomorrow? Was it a rush wedding? I was not going to ask him these questions. I tried to hide the shock, surprise, hurt, and all the above feelings that were overwhelming me at the moment. I did not want him to know that I did not know about the wedding. I tried to get ahold of Joanna to find out, but she did not answer my calls.

I loaded as much of Renee's and Sabastian's belongings as I could into my car. I had picked up Daniel on the way to the wedding because he was now living in my hometown where the wedding was taking place. None of us were dressed for a wedding but I was not sure what to expect either. When we arrived at the church, I was told that we were late, that they had taken family pictures an hour ago. I looked at the clock on my phone and said "no, I am actually five minutes earlier than the time I was told to be here." The ladies continued to whisper and quickly move me and the three kids to the sanctuary. Everyone was already seated, and the ceremony was about to start. They seated me about halfway in the back on the bride's side. Tracy motioned for the kids to all move up front where she was sitting. My parents, my children, Tracy and her new husband, and Richard's dad and stepmom were all in the front two rows. I was seated about three rows behind all of them like I was not family, let alone her mother. It was very hard for me. I had always imagined that I would be a part of all my children's weddings, and then to be separated from my kids was just more than I could handle. I had a knot in my throat, one in my chest and one in my stomach. It took everything I had to keep it together.

    The kids eventually told me that Richard had told Joanna he would only help with her wedding if she did not invite me. Since he had Ashlee living with him, and she liked to bake, that included him allowing Ashlee to help bake the cake IF they kept me in the dark about the whole event. His original plan was for me not to be invited at all and find out after the fact that she even had a wedding. When the court order stated that he gained custody of the kids ON her wedding day, he took great pride in humiliating me in front of EVERYONE by having me hand over custody of the kids to him with an audience. Joanna also told me that Richard asked her to go see a movie at the theatre with him. She had told him no because she felt it was creepy. Then he asked her to "hook him up" with some of her college friends, which she also said was gross because he said he liked them young when she mentioned their ages.

My cell phone was disconnected due to not being able to pay the bill and Belle had not helped with it since the middle of January. She was mad at me and quit talking to me. Charlie felt that I needed a phone for safety among other reasons, so he added a line to his account for me. I felt bad, but I was in no condition to complain or refuse. I continued to record all my interactions with Richard as he was consistently inappropriate. He offered several times that this whole thing would go away if I would just come home. Sometimes he even claimed that things would be better than they were before, but his nice behaviors were not consistent. Joanna's husband was in the Marines, so they were stationed in South Carolina starting in May 2014.

The next hearing was scheduled for the last Monday in August. My lawyer told me to get her as many affidavits as possible. Most of them emailed their affidavits straight to my lawyer, with some cc'ing me, so she had them immediately. The friends of mine that the kids had contacted the fall that we moved were completely shocked. Heather and Aimee could not figure out why the kids went back after everything they had said about Richard. They both wrote affidavits since they were there when we moved and knew the truth. I had affidavits from Dave's aunt stating she had witnessed some of Richard's abuse and also mentioned that the dressers that I removed from Richard's home were family heirlooms for my older four kids. She also said that she told me not to leave them with Richard. I received affidavits from Stacia, Cathy, Mandi, and several other friends from every stage of my life. Daniel and Joanna even wrote affidavits, but my lawyer said she could not use anything from the children. Elizabeth was torn because she had witnessed Richard's abuse firsthand and did not think he should have any type of custody of the kids. She did not write one, though, since she was actually Richard's sister and thought it would be unethical to go against 'blood family' in court. She was also very surprised that the courts were in favor of Richard. I had never done anything legally wrong and was a good mom.

On most of my visitations I would only have two or three of the kids. Richard was not forcing them to come on my visitations, but I forced the kids to go see him when they did not want to before there was a court order. Brandon turned eighteen the day we had court. He graduated in May and moved out of Richard's house immediately thereafter. He said Richard had not changed and he could not handle it anymore. He moved in with me for about three weeks, then moved out and in with friends who lived in the same small town as Richard. He told Daniel that he wanted to stay close to the younger kids just in case they needed him. He told others that he moved out of my house because I was going to charge him rent. That was not true. I was not charging Daniel rent and Daniel was also living with us at the time. I continued to pay child support for Brandon for three months after he moved out of Richard's, even while he was living with me and other people.

During one of my phone calls with Joanna, she brought up some memories from when we were all still living with Richard. She was having nightmares which triggered these memories. She told me that sometimes after I would go to bed, Richard would wake her up and sometimes Daniel. He would force them to drink some of his hard liquor; Jack Daniels, peppermint Schnapps, etc. She did not like it and was always begging him to let her go back to bed. She said he would usually send Daniel back to bed first and make her keep drinking until she felt like she was going to vomit. She said there were many times that she did not even remember getting back to bed, but some of her nightmares were pointing to possible sexual abuse. We also talked about Richard's real reason for taking the lock off her bedroom door when she was sixteen. I told her then that she needed to get therapy to dig deeper into those dreams and her memories.

Daniel was living with me so when I realized he too was having nightmares I asked him if he wanted to talk about them. A few of his girlfriends had told me that they were scared to sleep next to him because he would sometimes choke them in his sleep. He said whenever he did that, he was dreaming that Richard was sitting on him and choking him so he was trying to choke Richard back so he could get away. He always felt really bad for hurting the girls. He also brought up times where Richard would wake him and Joanna to drink the hard liquor. His story was very similar to Joanna's with slight variations. I did not tell him until a few months later when Joanna came home for a visit, that she had those same memories. The three of us talked a little about it. Daniel became upset because his memory of Richard coming out of Cole's room years earlier made him realize that there was possible sexual abuse to his sisters. He felt somewhat responsible since he was the oldest and should have protected his siblings. I understood because I felt the same.

    My child support was so high that my employer was garnishing the maximum allowed by law and it was still not covering it. When I talked to Child Support Recovery Unit about it, they said that there was nothing that they could do, that was the amount that was ordered by the courts. Since it was still an open case, I had to wait until the courts changed the order to reflect my correct income. Once I cashed each of my paychecks, I would march straight up the CSRU to give them most if not all of my remaining check just to stay current. Since we were meeting at the halfway point, on Wednesday evenings, the kids and I would hang out at Charlie's house or across the street at the park. During these months, I was having a really hard time connecting with my lawyer. She was never available when I called, and she never returned my calls. I did not start to get worried though until about a week before we were to be in court again.

Just like last time, she finally scheduled a time for me to come into talk to her about the hearing the Friday before court. I was working, but I was able to get my manager to agree to cover for me for an hour and a half so I could go meet with my lawyer. I told the lawyer that the kids said Richard had witnesses and that some of the kids were going to testify. She told me that they must be misunderstanding because we just need the affidavits now, no witnesses. She also said that in divorce cases, children who are in the middle of the custody case are not allowed to testify. That was her reason for not allowing Daniel and Joanna's affidavits to be considered. Even though they were adults and not in the middle of the custody, she said they would not be allowed.

I lost my job the day of court because we were short-handed and there was no one to cover me that day so I just did not go into work. This hearing was more important to me than a job. Aimee went with me for support. My lawyer showed up late and was dressed to go out on the town rather than a morning in court. Aimee and I were dressed more like lawyers in our pant suits and blouses buttoned up to our necks, and conservative dress shoes. My lawyer came in a sleeveless blouse that showed all of her cleavage, barely holding in her breasts, and extremely high heeled stiletto heels. Richard brought three of the kids with him, my mother and Tracy. The first five to ten minutes was my lawyer trying to give the judge copies of documents that she brought for the hearing, including all my affidavits. It turned into a bit of an argument between them because he told her that the deadline to have those submitted online was the Thursday before court. She claimed to not have had enough time to do so and was wanting them to be submitted as evidence at that moment. The Judge refused. She then asked again for a continuance, so she had time to prepare. He denied that motion as well. He then asked how many witnesses we had brought for today; I looked at my lawyer in surprise. She told the Judge that she was unaware that we were to have witnesses. She stated that she brought affidavits, in which he stated that we were supposed to have the affidavits for the past February hearing not this hearing. I felt every chance at getting my kids back slipping away from me as she was unprepared even though she had the last six months with me constantly turning in every piece of documentations that I thought would help me. I decided to fire her at that moment. I do not know if that was a mistake on my part or not, but I thought that I could not do any worse for myself than what she was doing.

 The judge gave me a few minutes to compose myself and asked me if Aimee was a witness. When I agreed that she would now be a witness, because I felt that was my only choice, he had her exit the room until she was called to the stand to testify. I had brought my own copies of documents, and was thankful since I unexpectedly was going to be doing this hearing pro se. I did not have all of the affidavits, but I did have some of them just in case the judge did let me submit them. Even though I was told that I could not use any of my children, Richard had three of the kids testify against me. When I counter witnessed them, they would not look at me and when I would mention a true fact that contradicted what they said, they could not answer. Ashlee ended up in tears because I was bringing up true facts. I felt bad, but I had to keep my emotions in check while acting as a lawyer. Tracy and my mother also lied in court. When I tried to ask Tracy if she had ever witnessed me doing what she was claiming, she changed the subject and started arguing with me, enough that the judge excused her from the bench. With my mother, she started bringing up her being abused by my father which was also a bunch of bull, but I ignored that part since it had nothing to do with this hearing.

One of the documents that I had brought was a letter of discharge of services from the counselor the kids went to in 2007. It stated there was abuse in the home and that she suggested Richard get help or I get the kids away from him until he did. It also stated that she did not think she could help them as long as he was still in the home. When Aimee testified, she mentioned witnessing abuse and hearing it over the phone when she would call me. She mentioned different things that she heard the kids say, including the intervention the kids asked of all my friends prior to moving out. She was also able to testify to when we moved because Richard and his witnesses were all stating that we left him a completely empty house.

Again, I was accused of having an affair and leaving him for another man. I was accused of taking everything from the house, not leaving him furniture or food. They said that I kept the kids from him, that he had no way to contact them. They claimed that he did not know that we were moving out, that he came home surprised to see an empty house. He also claimed that I did not work, that I slept most days away because I was depressed and talked about suicide. Tracy claimed that I was having inappropriate conversations with the kids about the sizes of penises, when I never had a conversation like that with any of my adult friends, let alone my children. I was accused of having all of his utilities shut off when I moved out and accused of changing my address at the car lot where I had recently gotten the oil changed in the Traverse, which is the vehicle that I left him.

The judge gave us joint custody with Richard getting full physical care. The court order also gave him the right to claim all the children on his taxes every year. I could not claim any of the kids and I had childcare expenses that I had paid earlier that year. Physical care meant they lived with him full time while I was given visitations, but joint custody meant that we were to make decisions about the kids jointly. That was an issue for us while we were married. He was not about to allow me to have any say so on anything now that we were divorced. My visitations again were every other weekend. They set specific holidays that we each were to get the kids. My first holiday weekend was Labor Day weekend, but since I did not even get the court order until after that weekend, I lost out on having the kids. I also continued to get every Wednesday evening, but they changed it from 5:00 to 7:00 pm. I lost an hour with the kiddos on Wednesdays, but it also stated that I was now required to do ALL the transporting. I now had to drive all the way to his house every Wednesday and find something to do with the kids for two hours. He lived in a small town in the middle of nowhere. The weather was only going to be nice for a short time longer. For the first month or so, I would buy food from a grocery store and we would have picnic-like dinners at the park.

When it started getting too cold, I started taking the kids to the McDonald's in the town fifteen minutes from his house. Most Wednesday night visits were less than an hour by the time I found the kids, drove to McDonald's and then had to leave there early enough to get back to his house by 7:00. Most of the time I had to hunt for the kids because no one would be home for me to pick them up at my scheduled time. I had to do both the pickup and drop off on every other weekend. Again, I would have to find the kids in order to pick them up, and again, I still did not get all of them on my visits. This order did remove Brandon from child support, but it did not lower it by much. They still had my income listed as over twice my actual income and listed his income about $15,000 lower than his W2's actually showed.

Since I was not working for that first month after court, Charlie had to help me pay child support, put gas in my car, and give me money so I could feed the kids. It was probably a good thing that I was not working because I went into severe depression having suicidal ideations on a regular basis. I could not handle being away from my kids, especially not knowing if they were safe with him. People kept acting like I must have done something wrong because they still argued that Iowa is a mother state. The only thing I did wrong was marry and have children with an abusive narcissist that took control over me and my kids from day one. I should not have to stay married to an abusive man, live in misery, just to keep my kids. I did not want to live anymore. I felt like there was no reason for me to live. Charlie became very concerned with my mental health and did talk me into seeking therapy. Between Charlie and my therapist, they helped me to realize that I needed to live for my children, because some day they were going to need me. They helped me to realize that I needed to use this time to take care of myself so that I was strong enough to be there for the kids when they needed me and to fight for the truth.

About two months after court, I was able to get a new job, making a couple of dollars more an hour than I had been but still nowhere near the total amount the court orders claimed my income to be. I continued to record all interactions with Richard as well as most interactions with my kids. I did this because in court I was accused of saying and doing things that I had not done or said so I was now needing to protect myself pretty much at all times. I was not upset with the kids. I did not blame the kids, but I did believe that Richard was either brainwashing the kids or bribing/threatening them to say things that were untrue. I had on recording some of their comments that backed up my suspicions that he was bribing and threatening them to stay in alliance with him.

Chapter Twenty-One

The first few months, Richard was constantly coming out to my car to talk to me before letting the kids come out if they were even home. Sometimes he would come out and talk to me for a bit before letting me know that the kids were not there for me to pick up. I also would pull into his driveway to pick up or drop off the kids. Just in the first month we had several conversations that seemed to hit my emotional state pretty hard. It is a wonder that I did not completely break. I just cannot express enough how grateful I am to my therapist and Charlie. As I am listening to these recordings so I can accurately document them, I am still shocked at how well I handled his behaviors. These are the same behaviors I dealt with while we were married so this was not something new just because we were divorced. He just had limited time to try his same manipulation tactics. There are times I wish I would have either stayed quiet so he could ramble, or I would have said something different than I did, but that is what happens when you are in the moment.

About two weeks after court, Richard stated with a condescending tone, "How am I supposed to, ok here's the deal, first of all it doesn't matter if I am nice or an asshole to you, One, it don't get me anywhere, Two, you don't give a shit, and Three, it's not like I can ever do anything to to change your mind or make you realize anything or to get you to come back. So, it doesn't matter if I'm an asshole or if I am nice to you."

Trying to stay strong and seem unaffected, I replied to him with, "Every time I see you, you do something to prove to me that you are still the same."

He became agitated and said, "It doesn't matter though because it's not like you'd ever come back. Cuz you are in love with fuck face."

Still trying to remain strong, I calmly stated, "Ok, good people don't call other people names."

Now he was very frustrated and defensive, so he told me, "Yeah go fuck yourself."

About a week later was another awful conversation with him. He was always accusing me of giving him attitude when I would pick up or drop off the kids. I think what he was feeling was not attitude but rather a wall that I had learned to put up to protect myself from emotional suicide. I pulled up in front of his house instead of the driveway. I got out to open the trunk for the kids' belongings. He was yelling from the middle of his yard as he walked up to my car, something about me having an attitude. So, I said, "I didn't have attitude before you came up here."

He walked up to my car with Brutus. Apparently, my parents could not take care of him anymore and Richard did not want him either. Richard's response to me was, "You know what? I was bringing you your fucking dog. So why don't you go fuck yourself. Stupid Cunt anyway. You got attitude."

Still trying to figure out why he thought that I had an attitude, I tried to defend myself in a calm voice, "I don't have attitude...."

He cut me off before I could finish, "You do, you have no reason to fricking hate me like you do whenever I have done nothing but try to kiss your ass and and and and earn you back and . ." When we were married, he would act like he did not do anything and made me feel like I was crazy or confused, but here he was still trying to manipulate me into believing I was in the wrong.

Hoping he would enlighten me, I asked, "Kiss my butt? You have never kissed my butt."

Richard ignored my question, which was normal, and proceeded with saying, "Your dress is coming up; I can almost see your underpants. Yeah that would be bad if I saw that. You never know what's in there now."

Earlier this particular day, I had a job interview and did not have time to change my clothes prior to picking up the kids. From the time I was a little girl up through even today, I have ALWAYS worn shorts under my dresses or skirts. He should have known this fact. The kids were putting their bags in the car at this point, so I am pretty sure they heard what he said. The kids were hanging out outside the car and in the yard while they waited for me to be ready.

Standing on the driver's side of the car he continued, "I don't know why I even try to be nice to ya or anything else. You damn sure don't deserve my love, except for some reason I still have for ya. I don't know why. You know what? You can think what you want, you can think that I don't love you, you can do whatever the fuck you want, I don't care."

Still remaining calm and defending myself, I said, "A man who really loves a woman doesn't treat her the way that you have treated me."

He retaliated with, "You know what, in the last year, you've deserved everything you got. That's what happens when you go fuck someone else."

Knowing that I did not have an affair so that was not his real reason, I stated, "You would have pulled something no matter who I moved in with. If I would have moved in with one of my female friends, you would have probably brought up in court that I was having a lesbian affair."

I believe he was flustered with not getting the reaction he wanted from me, so he said, "You know what? It doesn't fucking matter, I'm happy with the outcome that I got. The only thing that I'm not happy with is not having your ass for some reason. I still can't figure why in the hell I can't get over you. Cuz you ain't all that and a bag of chips but for some reason I think you are, and I don't know why. And for some reason I can't get over your ass. Hopefully one of these days I move on."

I am still trying hard not to let him intimidate me, I added, "You know what? I'm not the cunt and the bitch that you keep saying I am."

His reply was "Really? Really? Really? I'm not the fucking prick that you think I am. You chose to go fuck someone else, you chose to go live with someone else, you chose to still be with that fucking person. You could have came home, we could have tried to make it work, we could of tried to have

Mom & Dad around both of our kids, but it didn't fucking happen. Yeah you know what, I might of..."

Still defending myself I said, "I'd liked to have Mom & Dad around..."

He interrupted, "You know what? I might've been an asshole in the past and I might still be an asshole to ya but you know I can't uh I can't do anything to change your mind ever so it doesn't matter if I'm nice to ya or if I am a prick to ya because you're still going to hate me regardless so and it's not like I'm ever going to hook back up with your ass so it don't really matter if I'm a prick or not. I might as well be a prick and enjoy myself."

Watching the kids run around the yard, I decided to remind him by saying, "It's unhealthy for the kids."

His reply was more stabs at me, "Really? Yeah it is unhealthy because (he changes to a *whisper*) they don't want you around."

In a normal volume I calmly said, "They haven't said that to me!"

Still whispering, he took another jab, "Well they are happier since you're not. So why don't you just go fuck yourself and get the fuck off my property, you stupid bitch."

I replied, "I'm not on your property; I'm in the middle of the street. And I'm tired of you telling me to go fuck myself."

As I am trying to open my car door, he said, "All you are doing is fuckin irritating me and you're upsetting me."

Again, defending myself I said, "I'm not doing anything. You're the one that's calling me names and saying all kinds of bad stuff."

As the kids started to get into the car, he said, "I hate you and love you at the same time. And you don't give a shit, you know what?" He turned to the kids and said, "She's not worth it because she's fucking stupid." The three girls were in the car. We were still waiting on Sabastian to get in. Richard took this opportunity to continue his argument, "Maybe from now on you should have your fucking retard boyfriend come get the kids or something. Cuz I cannot deal with you."

Still trying to get into the car, I replied to him, "I didn't even do anything; I don't know why you're so frickin angry."

He quickly said, "I can't deal with you. I can't deal with your attitude. I can't deal with anything."

Still confused about his anger, I stated, "I have no attitude. You are the one with an attitude."

He proceeded with saying, "No. I try to kiss your ass, I try to be nice to you, I try to work things out, and you still shit on me, because you do not care. Because I'm never going to be Dave and I'm never gonna be Charlie, I'm never gonna be good enough for you. It doesn't matter how I could be; it doesn't matter anything; my kids see how that I am, but you don't *(voice changes to rage)* because you don't want to. You know what, you don't give me a chance, you don't fucking try to hang out with me, you don't try to talk to me like I'm a person, you talk to me like I'm some piece of shit ex-husband and that I'm some fucking nothing."

The girls finally got Sabastian in the car and told him to get his seatbelt on. I looked at Richard, and said, "I do not talk to you that way."

Richard continued, "If you would of came around, and you wouldn't of hooked up with your boyfriend, maybe if you would have fuckin been by yourself, you could of fucking, you could of saw, you could of tried, but you didn't even give it a fucking chance. You..."

I interrupted with a fact, "I did give it a chance for 15 yrs."

Richard seemed to ignore me and continued, "You left with full fucking intentions of never coming back."

Again, reminding him of the facts, I said, "Yeah because you told me in August (2013), once I left there, it was over."

He still seemed to be ignoring my statements, and continued, "You know what? You didn't fucking care, you had to go out and hook up with your God damn boyfriend that you had been in love with for 17 fucking years. I hope he is your best fucking friend; I hope he is your God damn soulmate."

Confused with his dates, I asked, "17 years?"

He heard the question but still continued, "I don't give a fuck. You fucking left with full intentions on never coming back. You didn't want to come back; it wouldn't have mattered if I was the best fucking guy in the world."

Defending myself I commented, "If you were the best guy in the world, I never would of left." I got into my car and closed the door. Richard opened my car door back up, so I stated, "You don't want to talk to me so and you told me to go fuck myself so can you please shut the door so I can go."

Still not finished ranting he continued, "You know what? I've been wanting to fucking talk to you. But you won't talk to me like I am a God damn human. You talk to me like I'm some fucking loser."

Obviously, he was not going to let me leave yet so I said, "How am I supposed to talk to you when you are constantly calling me names and telling me to go fuck myself?"

He said, "Oh I told you to go fuck yourself twice. It doesn't do any good because it's not like you're ever gonna fuckin see me in anything other than what you see me as because your boyfriend is way better than I am, so is your ex-husband. Your ex-husband, the asshole that walked out on you & your kids is still better than I am in your eyes. Your boyfriend who never had anything to do with his kids is still better than me in your eyes. Yeah, I know that he didn't want nothing to do with his kids."

He had his facts incorrect, so I started to say, "Yeah he did..."

Richard interrupted again, "Really? That's why he signed his rights away?"

Again, Richard had incorrect information, so I stated, "He didn't sign his rights away! His kids come over. He didn't sign away his rights, he's still paying child support. You don't know. You don't even know him."

Before I even left Richard, I tried to get him to be friends with Charlie, but he refused. Richard continued, "I don't want to know him. Because if it wasn't for him, your ass probably wouldn't of left."

I jumped in, "Yeah I would have."

Richard still trying to convince me otherwise, "No, I doubt it. Him and that fucking stupid bitch Aimee. You know what, next time you come over here, I won't come outside."

I said, "You know, it doesn't matter what I say, it doesn't matter what the truth is, because you believe what you want."

Richard got defensive, "Neither do you. You see what your boyfriend has fucking put in your head for the past 11 months. I'm sure he has just like the comments about hiring a hitman and fucking curb-stomping me and everything else." This is something that Cole had said that her and her dad were going to do to Charlie.

In trying to correct his false statement, "He has never said any of that. That is what we were told that you had said."

He replied with, "No I had never said that. I sure as hell wouldn't hire a hitman if I wanted him taken out."

This unproductive conversation had gone on long enough so I asked, "Can I go please?"

He replied, "So I don't know what I even fucking waste my time talking to you for because..."

In frustration, I commented, "I don't know, because I don't deserve the abuse that I still get from you."

With his voice raised, "No because oh really? I don't deserve not getting fucking talked to like I'm human and you you doing this shit. I'm sure you're happy that you're fucking divorced. You could have chose 100 times, I left that fucking door open for you all the time and you fucking chose not to because I'm not good enough."

I replied, "No, I chose not to because of your behavior."

Richard, apparently not understanding a friendship, said, "I hope he is all that you hope he is. And in 5 years whenever he's not, I'm gonna fucking laugh at you. I will."

Still waiting to leave his house, I stated, "Well I'm ready to go. I can't leave because somebody won't let go of my door."

He justified, "Because for some reason, I just I can't figure out why in the hell I just can't fucking move on."

Over the next few months, there were several comments that Richard made out of the blue that were inappropriate and immature. One of which was near the end of September. He stated, "And I know you're not gonna come over here and have sex ever because you're getting your good stuff at home and you hate me. I hope he is the best you ever had. I damn sure wasn't good enough to give you what you needed." In October, he offered for me to stay for dinner and I politely declined. His response was, "Plenty of chili, you could of ate chili in there. I don't think the kids would have minded and it wouldn't have confused them or anything like that." He then turned to the kids, "I invited your Mom in for chili... That's what I asked her. I think that was just a polite way of saying she doesn't want to eat with us. Or she doesn't want to go inside. Yeah cuz she don't want to be a Mom."

For fall conferences, I attended at the same times as Richard. While we were married, he never attended any of the kids' conferences. I went to all of them by myself and talked to teachers. This evening, they were starting at the high school.

He did all the talking, including flirting with the female teachers, and I felt like he was purposely ignoring me and leaving me out. I would go to ask a question and he would interrupt. He would sit between me and the kids to where I sat furthest away from everyone. When we went to leave the high school to drive over to the elementary, Sabastian asked to ride with me. Richard told him no because it was not my scheduled visitation. I explained that he was not wanting to go to my house for the night, he was just wanting to ride with me a few blocks to his school. Then I explained that we had joint custody and the court order stated that my visitations were not limited to what was listed, that it was up to our discretion on allowing me more time with my kids. He agreed to the court order stating that fact, but reminded me that it was ultimately his decision, his discretion and he was not going to allow me to have more time with my kids.

In December we had a really disturbing conversation. It gives me chills listening to it. The kids had just gotten out of the car, when Richard knocked on my window, "Can you roll your window down? You could have came in."

I rolled down the window about three inches, "I need to go, I have low fuel, I don't know if I am going to make it home."

He repeated himself in a calm whisper, "You could have came in." *I shook my head no.* "Why? I miss you. I do. Can I ask a favor?"

Not sure what to expect, I said, "Maybe."

Still in a calm whisper, "I know you hate me, Sorry. Ah never mind, you'll say no. I just wanted one last kiss." I shook my head no again. "Why? It's just a kiss."

I replied with, "And we're divorced."

His voice changed into a low growl, "Not by choice. I didn't want that."

I stated a fact calmly, "You filed. I got to go; I am not runnin out of gas sitting in front of your house."

Still in a low growl but with a bit of frustration, "Can't you do one last kiss."

Quickly I said, "No."

He said, "Yeah, Fuck you."

In disbelief I asked, "Really?"

He said, "Yeah... Somethin simple." Back to a whisper, "It's not that you give me hope."

He intimidated me so I asked, "Can I go please?"

His voice changed again into a really creepy dangerous growl, "I hope you fucking die. I hope you get Ebola and just fucking keel over. I hope so. You fuckin bitch."

I am really getting tired of the name calling, "Why am I a bitch? Because I won't give you a kiss? You had 15 years of getting kisses."

His voice raised, but was still a creepy growl, "Yeah fuck you, I hope you die, you fucking cunt."

He finally moved away from my car and as I rolled up my window, "Yeah that's why I know you never loved me."

About a year later, we ended up in court again. I retained a new lawyer, a seasoned male lawyer who had been practicing for over thirty years. He listened to the above recording as well as many others. With this one even the lawyer was creeped out with the changes in Richard's voice, almost like he had gotten possessed. That lawyer asked me why I did not just run Richard over. I said because I would get into trouble. The lawyer told me that I would not have gotten into trouble because I asked him to let me leave multiple times. He was keeping me there against my will. This lawyer also told me that he saw very few actually good people and that I was one of them.

In February 2015, we were sitting in a doctor's office with Ashlee. While in the waiting room, Richard whispers, "All I wouldn't mind doing is fucking you once."

Thinking of how he lied in court, I said, "You did."

He continued, "That's all I want from you."

I said, "And you still are."

After a long pause he said, "I try to be a team player."

With a nervous chuckle, I said, "No you don't. No."

After another long pause, he continued, "I ain't gonna give you what you want ever. I'm not gonna give you what you want, when you want, ever."

He confused me, but I shook it off and remembered that I had received paperwork from this doctor in the mail that needed our signatures, "You have to sign it."

He replied with irritation, "I don't have to sign this. I don't have to sign this; they didn't give me anything to sign down there. Where did this come from?"

I answered, "It came in the mail the other day."

His frustration got more intense, "Why did it go to you? And why do I have to sign it?"

Again, I answered, "Because it says both parents have to sign it."

He mumbled, "It ain't very legal. It ain't very legal, I didn't get all these. Why did you not put my cell phone number? You know my cell phone number."

Nervously I replied, "Because I forgot to look it up."

There was a long pause while he was reading what the papers stated. He angrily whispered, "God no, I didn't give you permission. I don't know if I give permission."

Confused I asked, "What for them to call you?"

He says, "No, for you." They had found a brain tumor in Ashlee's pituitary glands. She was going to have several more appointments to monitor its growth. It was in a position that was too dangerous to do surgery to remove it. Richard was not wanting me or my contact information to be on any doctor forms. He had already removed me from the kids' other doctors and their school records. I had to keep fighting for my parental rights to see or know crucial information on my kids. I had to keep sending copies of the court orders stating that we had joint custody, so I WAS supposed to be on all records.

We had spring conferences at the end of February. Charlie went with me so he could help with the kid's academics when needed since he was around my kids as much as I was. A couple weeks later, Richard was annoyed, lecturing me loudly, "These fucking children of of ours are not numb nuts kids either, So he doesn't need to go to parent teacher conferences or anything else because he's not their parent, he's not their step dad, he has no right to be there. Ok? None... I didn't decide, I didn't agree. We have legal custody; I need to agree for his ass to be around OUR children."

Changing conversation directions, but still lecturing me, he stated, "The only one that's pissy around here ever, pretty much, I mean Ashlee & Cole go back & forth, but the more time that Cole spends around you the shittier she gets."

Cole was fifteen and piped into the conversation, "Really? Really."

Richard looked at Cole, "Yeah cause the more time you spend around her," pointing at me, "the shittier you get around here. You act just like her."

Cole sighed in frustration and shook her head no. Richard continues, "You do." He turns back to me, "Yeah, she does. She says the same shit you say, she acts the same way."

 I was finally able to say, "Ok, You used to tell the kids all the time that they needed to pop my titty out of their mouth ...... so that is what you said to to one of the kids for coming down and spending Christmas with me."

Richard laughed, "Oh Brandon?"

Obviously, it was true since I did not mention which child said something, but I still asked, "So the kids are lying about that?"

Richard's admittance, "You know what? Here, I'm a tell ya somethin and you're not gonna believe me, you know why I made fun of the kids? Or said little comments to the kids about going to spend time with you? Because for some reason um, I'm jealous that they get to spend time with your ass. Ok.... Fuckin believe it or not. Now get the fuck out of my house."

As I got ready to leave, he continued, "You know what? I wasn't good with emotions ... Fuckin sue me......So when I do tell you something, you have to fuckin belittle it. Oh, you're full of shit, you're just trying to get into my pants. You're just doing this."

I replied, "Because that's what you've done for 16 years. You said stuff to me just to get in my pants."

He justified, "We were married."

Being a little concerned about his reason for making fun of the kids, "Why should I believe you? You've never told me the truth."

His response, "Why should I try to be nice to your ass then?....... For our kids? You know what fuckin marriage is, marriage is a business commitment is what it is.... With some emotion. That's what marriage is.... there's no fuckin soulmates."

Cole and I went on a prom dress shopping trip one Saturday in March. I start a conversation, "None of you guys tell me that you love me if he's around, is it because he says something?"

Cole agreed, "Yeah, whenever I go with you out to places or give you a hug, he'll... Well when I go up to him, he goes (*kissing noises*) 'Kiss butt kiss butt.' Yeah, he got mad at me one time because he was like 'now you're on your mom's side instead of on mine, you were always on mine.' And I'm like

I'm not on anybody's side; I just want to live my life and not always have to worry about what you or Mom is doing all the time. Then he's like 'no, you're on her side.' Uh no it's called I want to be myself. And I have already yelled at him and told him that I don't need to know anything that happens between you two, he was like 'fine I will treat you like a child now.'" After a long pause she continued, "I still don't like to be home when he's there. Yeah, I don't like to be alone with him."

Now that I am more educated, I would have handled this differently, but this was my response, "He took Joanna's lock off her bedroom door, because he would walk in while she was getting dressed."

Cole continued, "Yeah he walked in... Ok he doesn't knock on my door. He'll just walk in and I don't sleep with pants on and sometimes I sleep in a sports bra and no sweatpants on because I get too hot. Like I don't, I have to sleep with a blanket and shorts and a tank top. It still gets too hot. And one time I get out of bed, because I was going to brush my hair right before I went to bed, well he walks in, and I cover and go behind the door, and he goes 'What?' and I'm like I'm in a t-shirt and underwear, you can at least knock. He goes 'well I walked in on Joanna one time and she had no shirt on and so I saw her boobs,' ok that's different."

I got a knot in my stomach and said, "That's disgusting... that's wrong! And it was more than one time that he walked in on Joanna. Maybe one time that he actually saw her boobs, if she didn't have a bra on but..."

Cole continued, "I'm like, you are a male, you need to knock before you go into a female's room or the bathroom. Everybody else knocks." I agreed with her. Cole ended the conversation with, "I don't like to be home alone, that's why I shower before he gets home. If I know I have to be home alone with him and then I sit in my room. Cuz I don't want to shower while he is there cuz what if he is the only one and he just walks in."

Around this same time, Cole was begging me to let her come live with me. I explained to her that I would have to get Richard to okay it. I also told her that the judge would have to change the court order in order for her to live with me. She got upset with me saying that her dad was right, I did not care about them and did not want them to live with me. I explained to her that I would call my lawyer as soon as possible. I had hired that older male lawyer for more than just things that Cole had been telling me, mostly about the continued abuse from Richard. I also had him on several counts of contempt especially with the lack of cooperation during my scheduled visits and him denying me access to school and doctor records.

Chapter Twenty-Two

About a month later, when picking up the kids, they mentioned that Sabastian had a spring concert that I knew nothing about. When I asked why no one told me about it, because I would have been there, Sabastian now seven, replied that he wanted me to come but his dad did not want Charlie there, so they were not supposed to tell me. This was not the first one that I was left out of. Sabastian also had a winter concert a few months earlier where the girls sent me a picture of him wearing a suit and tie. They did not send me the picture until the next day though, so I was still not able to attend. They also said at that time that their dad did not want me there, so he did not want me to know about it.

Three weeks later, I got a call from Ashlee. She was very upset and told me to come get her. She said she was feeling suicidal. She had an argument with Richard where he told her that he did not care if she killed herself, to go ahead and do it because no one would care. In my opinion, more went on than what I was told. She also screen shot her text messages with him and sent them to me. He had already threatened to kick her out a few days earlier, but now he was really wanting her to move out of his house. I told her that I needed an email from him giving me permission to come get her so that I did not get into legal trouble. I did finally get an email, but it was not giving me permission for her to live with me. He told her that he did, but I showed her the email where he was just trying to get me to agree with him. I did pick her up from his house, but we just sat in the car talking for a few hours.

A few days later, when I was there for a visitation. Richard came out to talk to me. He started out bringing up the fact that I left him. I commented, "But after you threatened Ashlee, I didn't have much of a choice, I had to hurry up and find somewhere."

Richard retaliated, "It's not like I would ever do anything to her .... but like I said you peeled with no intentions of working shit out and nuttin else. And that was big mistake fuckin running off."

I explained, "But... I didn't think me & the kids deserved to be treated like you treated us."

Ignoring my statement, "But when you peeled, you peeled with no intentions of comin back. Well you know you fucked with me so......you fuck with me and I fuck back twice as hard, you know that."

With a sigh of distress, "Yeah I know that."

Richard threatened, "People ought not fuck with me."

I tried to turn the conversation back to Ashlee wanting to move out of his house because she had already made plans to go live with Joanna in South Carolina for a couple of months. I would have to drive her there. I thought I could do the trip in a weekend, my visitation weekend. Richard started off, "Yeah you haven't fuckin convinced me any, you haven't convinced me why I should let them go witcha other than 'I'm their

Mom'.......You know you say you go by the papers, the papers say 5 to 5 so."

I corrected him, "I didn't say by the papers, I said by the book."

He stated, "Well that's by the book, 5 to 5."

I said, "No because if you read it, it says..."

He interrupted, "I know what it says, I've read the mother fucker."

I continued, "Yeah I read it all the time .... We can make adjustments if we discuss it and agree."

He played his power, "We can, It's just a general guideline."

I reminded him, "Your actions are louder than your words."

Defensively, Richard said, "Yeah well it doesn't mean you know how I feel. .... I feel one way and act somethin totally different all the time."

I explained the obvious, "Well then I don't know how that's my fault.... I don't read minds."

In a tone of blame, "It is your fault. If you wouldn't of left, everythin wouldn't of came crashing down around me.... Of course, then I wouldn't of saw a lot of shit, but still point being shit wouldn't came crashing down....... I wouldn't of lost my wife. You wouldn't of lost seeing your kids every day."

A little further into our conversation he said, "What the fuck am I gonna gain from blowin smoke up your ass, not a God damn thing............ It's not like it's gonna get me anymore time talkin with ya, it's not like it's gonna get me any fuckin sex."

In frustration I said, "You've already had over an hour."

Ignoring my comment, "It's not gonna get me jack shit blowin smoke up your ass. Is it...? If you were gonna have sex with me ever, you'd already done it by now. And ya ain't so......."

I said a bold, "Nope."

Richard continued, "Then I'll just keep doin what I'm doin...... Told ya, there before, if I'm not gonna get something tangible outta something then it's not worth my fuckin time, my effort, or my tryin. So... I sure as hell ain't gonna blow smoke up your ass cause you ain't gonna give me no pussy so it don't matter. You know what, it's amazing how much more pleasant people are whenever they get, when they feel like they're .... Someone's bein nice to them like that."

I asked, "Bein nice to them like what?"

He explained, "Guys like that kind of stuff."

Still trying to clarify, "Guys like attention?"

He scoffed, "Uh, yeah, it's not like I would of told anyone."

I agreed, "I know guys like attention but..."

He interrupted, "It's not like I woulda told anyone if something woulda happened."

Realizing what he was stuttering about, "I would know, God would know." Getting us back on the reason for this conversation, I said, "We might have been able to get her to wait til June if you could do something about Cole or if you didn't laugh at Cole when Cole tells her to kill herself. Or tell her that she's crazy and and that you want her to move out."

He justified his behaviors, "Ok, with the movin out thing um, she was standin over there basically by that fuckin tree sayin you're the worst dad ever, I'm gonna move out, I said fine, move out, I don't care, I said move in with your bitchy ass mother, I said that.... I said you wanna move out, move out, I said I begged your fuckin mother not to move out err to come back whatever, I said I'm not beggin your ass. That's what I told her, if she wants to say stupid ass comments, I'm gonna say stupid ass comments back to her."

Continuing on in a conversation that felt endless and unproductive, "Just because we would not be getting back together, just because I am not gonna give you some attention, doesn't mean it's no good, if we can talk things out and and figure out how to be friends for the kids then it would make the next twelve years ..."

Richard interrupted, "That'll never happen, you even said that'll never happen, I can't be friends with exes."

I corrected him, "You're the one who said that... if you have changed and you have been trying, well if you have changed then we should be able to be friends for the kids so the next twelve years isn't hell for all of us."

Richard continued to argue, "Ok we can't be friends because when guys & girls are friends eventually somebody wants to have sex with another one. Ok? And it's the honest to God's truth, guys & girls are incapable of ever bein friends because eventually one of them is gonna wanna have sex with the other one and then eventually a lot of times it happens and then if it doesn't happen then it just sucks. So, it's impossible for men & women to be friends and never want to sleep with that person."

Confused again with his logic, "Then why do you keep blaming me that we can't be friends?"

He claimed, "Because you're snotty and you make me feel like shit. Most of the time."

Not really believing that I had ever been snotty, "When you say something that..."

Again, Richard interrupted, "I'm never not gonna wanna sleep with ya."

Defending myself, "Well that's not my fault that we can't be friends then."

He burped and with a mischievous grin, "Well there's easy solution to it, we can start havin sex once in a while."

I sighed in frustration, "No, I'm not gonna..."

With his usual interruption, "Then it won't work......I'm just bein honest with ya."

My frustration was high, "Well then don't tell me that it's my fault and don't blame me for this, that, and the other."

He continued to blame, "It's all your fault."

Again, clarifying his claim I asked, "The next twelve years for our kids is gonna be hell because I won't sleep with my ex-husband?"

He said, "And other things."

Richard finally agreed that I could pick the kids up on Thursday evening even though my visitations usually went from Friday at 5:00 pm to Sunday at 5:00 pm. It was a twenty-hour drive one way to Joanna's house for Ashlee to stay there. He did not want her staying with me, but whatever was going on between him and Ashlee, there was no way she was going to continue to live with him. When I got there at 6:00 pm, Ashlee, Renee, and Sabastian were all sitting on the front steps with their bags, pillows and blankets. They did not hesitate on piling in my car, they were all ready for our long road trip, Ashlee was ready to just get away from Richard. Cole was back to not talking to me and not coming on my visits because I would not let her move in when she wanted to a month earlier. I paid for her prom dress, shoes, hair, and for her dress to be altered just before she stopped talking to me. Their prom was on my weekend, so I helped them get ready for prom, drove them up to their school which was an hour away and then went back to get them at four in the morning. So, I spent a total of four hours in the car getting Ashlee and Cole to and from prom.

    I drove for about six hours. Charlie got a hotel for us in a town that he estimated we would be in at about midnight. By the time we got into the room, I only slept for about five hours before getting up to shower. I showered to help wake me up to finish our drive. We were back on the road by 6:00 am, the kids continued to sleep while I drove. We would only stop for food, potty breaks, and gas. We got to Joanna's about 7:30 Friday night. Joanna made us dinner, we played frisbee outside for a while and then I went to get some sleep while they played, talked and enjoyed each other's company. The next morning, we had breakfast, went for a walk around the base that they lived on, and went to the barracks to visit Joanna's husband. Richard wanted the younger kids back to his house by 5:00 pm Sunday, so we went back to Joanna's so I could take a short nap before driving straight through back to Iowa. Renee, Sabastian and I left Joanna's about 10:30 Saturday night after giving hugs to Joanna and Ashlee. The kids slept and again, we only stopped for food, potty breaks and gas. Renee kept Richard updated on our whereabouts throughout the drive.

    I pulled into Richard's driveway about 6:00 pm. He came out of the house, I thought to help the kids carry in their bags, pillows and blankets. Instead he had his chest puffed out, his arms crossed, he glared at me and followed me around my car as I unloaded the kids' stuff. I was setting some of it on the driveway next to my car, the rest I was setting up on the front steps. The kids were hauling their things in the house while Richard was still following me. He again asked me to stay for dinner, but I had to work the next morning and was very tired. I wanted to get home. As I got into my driver's seat, I said, "Your glares aren't gonna intimidate me anymore."

    Still standing next to me in his intimidation stance, "I ain't tryin to intimidate your dumb ass."

    Confused I asked, "That's why you keep standing near me just glaring at me... and watching me walk by."

    His excuse, "You know what, I can look at you any fuckin way I want."

    I said, "You can't look at me however you want to."

He again repeated, "I can look at you any fuckin way I want."

I replied, "That's rude to glare at somebody."

He angrily said, "You know what, I don't give a shit if I'm rude or not."

I said, "I know you don't care."

His comeback, "You're fuckin rude."

I replied, "I am not rude. I politely told you I did not want to stay for dinner. You're the one who gets all upset."

With an angry tone, "I offer, I cook supper and offer to feed you a good meal .... Go home and not fuckin eat nothin... whatever.... I took time to cook a fuckin decent meal."

With logic I said, "Uh, because you have children."

Richard said, "Um, no cuz... that was part of it but I was kinda hopin you'd eat dinner with us but .... but once again, whatever I try to do is not good enough......... whatever, go fuck yourself. Go home to your stupid boyfriend......... I don't know why the fuck I even bother tryin with you."

Confused, "You don't try with me."

His defense, "I do. Yeah, I cooked a dinner hopin that you would eat dinner with us."

Still confused, "And why would I do that? I haven't gone over to anybody else's house to have dinner."

He said, "I made a proper meal hopin that you would have dinner with us .... Wishful thinkin that doesn't get me fuckin nowhere."

My reasoning, "I left for a reason, why would I go in there and put myself right back in it."

He said, "I don't know Jorgie .... guess I was just hopin."

Wanting clarification, "Hopin for what? You don't try for 15 years and as soon as you file for divorce for some reason it's my fault you didn't try, and I'm supposed to try."

His defense, "You know what, whatever, I can't help I love ya............. Doesn't do me any good .... Can't change the past... doesn't do me any good to try to do anything."

Reminded of his current behavior, "No you can't change the past but the .... the past is still continuing into present."

Almost like he does not hear what I said, "You ain't interested in friendship or anything .... You want civility."

I said, "I would of done friendship but Tuesday you made it very clear that the only way there's any friendship is if you get sex."

He repeated, "You want civility."

I replied, "I would be your friend if I knew it wouldn't..."

He interrupted, "No you wouldn't, you want civility, you want fake ass bullshit... I want more than that."

I replied, "You could've had more than that, but you chose not to."

Ignoring me, "And if I don't get more than that, I ain't gonna have nothing............. I want way more than that."

Using logic, "That's not how you treat people that you supposedly love."

In his frustration, "Well I do love you……. You know what? Go fuck yourself, you can think I don't love you or not …………. Stay with your stupid ass boyfriend, I don't give a fuck."

Curious, "Why do you keep bringin him up?"

He replied, "Because I fucking hate him."

I replied, "You don't even know him."

Richard said, "I don't care."

I said, "Well maybe Dave hates you, you took his family."

Grumbling he said, "I don't really give a fuck about that, I don't care about that either."

Knowing him the way I do, "I know you don't. You don't care about anybody."

As he got increasingly angry, "So go fuck yourself. You stupid fucking bitch."

I defended myself, "I'm not a stupid fucking bitch."

He said, "Yeah, fuck you."

I continued, "That is rude to call me names just because I won't have sex with you."

Angrily, "Shut up…I didn't say we needed to have sex."

With my logic, "If you can glare at me then I don't have to shut up."

He grumbled, "Fuck you ………… Don't ask for nothing else… extra."

Confused again, "What do you mean, anything else? I haven't asked for anything."

He gloated, "I gave you the kids Thurs …"

Confirming, "Uh, that was not for me, that was Ashlee. I would've left Friday morning."

Richard said, "You fuckin should've but see I was being nice."

I felt like he was more concerned with controlling me than the actual safety of the kids. He was giving me a short amount of time to drive a forty hour round trip drive. If the roles had been reversed, I would want him to have as much time as possible to safely transport my children. I continued, "It took 20 hours to get there and 19 to get back."

He said, "You know what, I don't give a fuck how long it took for you to get there."

Irritated, "I know you don't care. You don't care about anything except for you."

Threatening, "I don't get what I want, you don't get what you want. You stupid fucking cunt. Goodbye. You fucking bitch."

Relieved, "Thank you."

His threats continued, "You will get nothing, you fucking bitch."

Confused at what he thinks I am getting, "I haven't gotten anything."

He fired back, "You know what, you definitely won't get anything."

Still confused, "Anything like what? What are you talking about?"

Richard exploded, "Shut up and go fuckin home to your stupid faggot boyfriend, you stupid cunt. Get the fuck off my property."

Growing really concerned with his mental health, "You need to go take some medicine."

He fired back, "You need to go fuck yourself you stupid bitch."

As I backed out of his drive, "Something is seriously wrong with you."

When I was about two blocks from home, Renee's cell phone was calling me. I always answer for my kids, so I answered the phone. Hello? "Hello............. how come you're not responding?" Richard had apparently been messaging me while I was driving.

Realizing that it was Richard instead of my kids, "Cuz I don't have to."

He continued, "Are you home yet? Why don't you turn around?"

I replied, "Um cuz I'm almost home and I need to go to bed."

Richard claimed, "Well we need to talk."

Tired and already irritated with him, "Um, so you can continue to call me names?"

He continued, "No .... you need to turn around so we can talk."

Shocked at his demands, "I'm about to pull into my driveway."

Disbelieving me, "Yeah whatever."

With seriousness, "I am."

With anger, "Yeah fine, whatever, fuck you." He hung up and I was so glad that I still had the recorder on to get that conversation. I was not understanding his behaviors, they were not that different than when I lived with him, but living with him, he had more control over me when I could not escape him. Now that I was away from him, I noticed how extreme his inappropriate behaviors really were.

He allowed the girls to take on babysitting jobs and signed Sabastian up for baseball that interfered with my scheduled visitations. Since Cole was not talking to me and refusing my visitations, he would allow her to have her boyfriend over instead of hanging out with me. When I tried to talk to him about the interference issues, he made it sound like he kept bending over backwards for me and that I was not cooperating. I was willing to switch my visitation days, but he would wait until last minute to tell me which days that I could use. I have emails with these conversations, he had changed his email signature to "tangible benefits" after making that statement last month. He would not tell me where Sabastian's games were, just what nights they were so I could not use my visitations. In one email, he stated that I could use my visitation after one of the games, but that he did not want Charlie there so I would have to come alone. There was no way that I was going to go to a baseball game without a bodyguard, so he never told me where the game was, but he did try to use it against me stating that I never supported the kids' activities.

For Mother's Day weekend, I was supposed to get the kids from Friday at 5:00 until Sunday at 5:00. Renee had to babysit until 8:00 pm that Friday. Richard argued with me saying that he was not getting anything out of this so why should he help me see my kids on my scheduled visitation. He finally agreed that I could pick the kids up at 8:00 that night and he would pick them up from me at 8:00 Sunday night. Then Sunday morning he changed his mind saying that he will pick them up at 5:00 Sunday and if I refused to give him the kids then he would call the sheriff. He was in contempt since he was making obstacles for me to use my visitations. He was also refusing to force the kids on my visitations. I gave my new lawyer all the emails and recordings and he was just blown away by Richard's behavior. Joanna and her husband were coming back for a visit over the July Fourth holiday, so they brought Ashlee back. I had finally gotten written permission from Richard for her to live with me even though I was still paying him child support for her, plus the three younger children. I was still working at the place I started almost a year ago, but I also decided to take on a full-time college load in August.

Renee also wanted me to fight for custody. She said that Richard lectured them constantly about what I did or said while they were with me. She said that if she refused to give him a play by play of what went on at my house, he would get angry with her and threaten to take her to get a shot (she had been deathly scared of shots since she was a young toddler), or to take something else away from her. She also said that he was constantly making the comments that they are either with him or against him. Anytime they were nice to me or enjoyed their time with me he would take that as an act against him. I could not stress enough to her that she was allowed to enjoy time with, and love, both parents.

In September 2015, I had four subjects that Richard and I needed to discuss. I wrote them down to help me stay on task because he had a habit of going way off subject and then I would forget. The four things were Ashlee's medical bills, homecoming, insurance cards, and why the kids were never ready on time for my visitations. When he first came out of his house, he was acting smitten about how good Cole looked in her school pictures. He said that she woke up late, so she did not have time to do her hair or make up, but she looked "pretty damn good" was his words. Then saying that fortunately she looked like me and not him. I made the comment that she was not even smiling. He quickly showed me Renee's and Sabastian's pictures, but did not comment on them. Then he went back to saying how good Cole looked. She was sixteen now and these comments sounded very creepy to me. He then proceeded to tell me how much he paid for the pictures and offered me half of them if I paid him half of what he paid. I told him that the website said a lower amount than what he was telling me. He said he would show me his check proving how much he paid, but he did not go get it. Instead, when I tried to talk about the four things on my list, he kept changing the subject or calling me names.

I first brought up homecoming because it was Renee's first time to get to go and she wanted to go with a male friend of hers that she went to elementary school with. They had been friends at the school that I had open enrolled them in before leaving Richard. She asked me because she could not get Richard to answer her. Homecoming fell on his weekend, so I felt it was his responsibility to figure out how she and her date were going to make it to the dance. Her male friend had moved to the town I lived in and Richard did not want to drive back and forth. He kept making the issue about the divorce, not something for one of the children. Since he refused to help out, I did end up having to drive to his house to pick up Renee, back down to my town to pick up her friend and then back up to her school so they could attend the dance. Then I went back up to pick them up from the dance, took her to his house, and then took her friend back home before I went home.

 In this conversation, every time I would bring up my list, he would ask a personal question about me. He said that he would not discuss the subjects pertaining to the children unless I answered the personal questions. He continued to tell me to shut up. He also kept calling me names, but he also made fun of me for going to college with my boyfriend. When he would say boyfriend, he would say it with a snotty tone. When I corrected him, he called me a liar and then tried to get me to call Brandon a liar because supposedly Brandon was the one telling him that Charlie was also in school with me. I could feel that it was some sort of trap, so I refused to say that Brandon was lying. I just continued to say that his information was incorrect. With the doctor bills that he just gave me a week earlier, he insisted that I was supposed to pay him for my portion of the bills. My lawyer said that was incorrect. When he gave me the bills, I was supposed to pay directly to the billing department. Any money that I give directly to Richard was counted as a gift, not part of my responsibility. I tried to explain to him that I tried to call and pay my portion, but that I was not on the accounts so they would not let me pay. He insisted that he had already paid them and that I was supposed to pay him. A couple weeks after this conversation, I did finally get some of these billing departments to talk to me. I found out that these bills had not been paid so they went into collections. These bills were from the beginning of the year and he did not give them to me until the first of September. Like usual, he ended up telling me to get off his property in a very rude tone and wording, so I ended up leaving without being able to discuss these four subjects.

Chapter Twenty-Three

Charlie and I decided to rent a three-bedroom, two bath, split foyer home with attached garage and a large yard in October 2015. We were ready to get out of the duplex anyway, but my lawyer suggested getting a more family friendly residence before our hearing in November. Since Ashlee was living with us, she helped us move and clean the duplex. She was also now a senior at the local high school. We moved from being in the city to the suburb where I was attending college. We did not transfer Ashlee; we would just transport her to and from school. She was doing well enough to graduate mid-term anyway. She had been living with Joanna or me for the past six months, but I was still paying child support to Richard for her as well as the younger three kiddos.

A couple of weeks before we were due in court, Ashlee and I were headed up for my Wednesday night visitation. Before we got there, Renee texted Ashlee stating that I needed to pick her up from a friend's house because Cole had slapped her across the face, so she left taking Sabastian with her. I picked up the two kids and then we headed over to Richard's house because Cole texted Ashlee stating she took a bunch of pills. So, we headed over to check on her. I stayed in the car since Richard was home. He did not know anything that had happened so as soon as Ashlee went into the house, he decided he would take care of Cole. Ashlee, Renee, Sabastian and I all headed to town to get something to eat, when Renee got a message that Richard was taking Cole to the hospital. We decided to go to the hospital also. Richard was not happy that I was there, but she was my child too and I wanted to make sure that she was going to be okay. I did leave to take the younger kids back to Richard's and Ashlee home so they could get some sleep for school the next day. I then grabbed some essentials and headed back to the hospital.

The hospital social worker came in to talk to us, appointing a staff psychologist and recommending individual and family therapy after release. The hospital psychologist spoke with Richard first and then both of us. He then said that he understood "after what I did to the family" that it was hard for Richard to sit in the same room as me, but it was essential in the healing of Cole. I asked the psychologist to elaborate on what he meant. He looked at Richard nervously and said, "well it is my understanding that you abandoned the family for another man." I nervously laughed, but I informed him that he was given incorrect information and that was not what happened. Back in Cole's hospital room, the social worker brought a phone in, stating it was the counseling office that she was referring Cole to and that the lady needed to talk to both of us. She handed the phone to Richard because he was the closest to her and was reaching for the phone. Richard was obviously answering questions with "Yes's" and "No's." There were a few "I'm not sure's" and then he said "oh, no ma'am, the mother is not involved." I said, "excuse me!" He glared at me and shook his head and then he said goodbye and hung up. The next time I saw the social worker, I pulled her aside and told her what had happened. She apologized stating she noticed that this was not a good situation between him and me. She said she would get the office back on the phone. After speaking to the counseling office, I learned that they gave him a first appointment time which he was not including me in. I also gave her my information and told her what the real situation was. She then told me to bring the custody order with me to the first appointment. This was the same counseling office that I had taken the kids to back in 2007.

At the first counseling appointment, Richard was very shocked to see me there and wanted to know why I was there. The secretary actually overheard and told him that whenever possible they encouraged both parents to be involved with therapy. I showed her the current court order and told her we would be going to court soon. She made copies of it and then asked for my information because Richard did not list me on any of the paperwork that he had already filled out. She then asked me if the emergency contacts he listed were people that I agreed with. He had listed my mother as an emergency contact and someone that was allowed to bring Cole to her therapy appointments. I told the lady that I did not agree and wanted her removed. She said that if it was his mother, which is how he listed her, she could not take her off. Once I said she was my mother, the lady looked confused, looked at Richard, and then said she was immediately removing my mother from the file. I also made it known that Cole had been in this same office a few years earlier, but she had seen another therapist, in case they were allowed to share information. This time she was getting a male therapist.

Cole told her sisters and me that after she slapped Renee, she was afraid that she was going to get into huge trouble for slapping Renee so she decided to take a bunch of pills so she would get sympathy instead of punishment. Richard told everyone, including the courts, that Cole attempted suicide because she was upset about our upcoming hearing. Tracy again involved herself saying that I needed to stop the court stuff because I was upsetting my children. She did not believe me when I told her that the court stuff was for the children, the children were the ones who told me that they wanted to live with me, besides all the contempt. Tracy also accused me of playing games, stating that she did not understand why I was playing these immature games. I again told her that I was not the one playing games. I felt like it was Richard who was playing games to punish me for leaving him.

On November 13, we ended up having mediation instead of an actual hearing. The mediator was a lawyer from a county between his and mine. Richard and his lawyer were in one room, while Charlie, my lawyer and I were in another and the mediator went back and forth. Richard was refusing to compromise on anything. The mediator listened to some of the recordings, including the one from the previous winter where he said he hoped I "get Ebola and keel over" when I refused to give him a kiss. The mediator said that one creeped him out. The mediator told us that he lectured Richard in front of his lawyer on the inappropriate ways he interacted with me. I believe the mediator and both lawyers went into a third room away from Richard, Charlie and me because they mentioned letting Richard's lawyer listen to a few of the recordings.

When they came back, the offer from Richard and his lawyer was that we switch to fifty/fifty custody (one week on, one week off, switching the kids on Mondays), he would now pay me child support, Ashlee would get dropped completely from the order, and he had until April 1, 2016 to move to the county I lived in or my address became their primary address. With my address becoming their primary meant that they would start attending school in my resident district as of April 1, 2016 if he did not move. The reasoning for this was he worked in my county, I worked here, went to school here, and lived here. The only thing in his county was his residence. His residence was an hour from his employer and a forty-five-minute drive from my new residence. It made no sense to anyone, including the lawyers, to keep the kids in a town and school that was so far away from both parents during work hours. My lawyer and the mediator also recommended that I keep interactions with Richard to emails only and only about the kids. They said that if he emailed me about something that did not pertain to the kids then I should ignore the message. They still based child support on incorrect income, so for the three kiddos he was only ordered to pay a total of forty-three dollars a week, but I was now able to claim Renee on my taxes and every other year I was to claim Sabastian. I agreed with the offer because I was not trying to take the kids from him. I just wanted my fair share of time with my kiddos without having to get permission from him. Shortly after this hearing, Richard's lawyer resigned as his representative due to Richard breaking his contract of honesty.

Since they changed our custody, I had to drive twenty hours a week on my weeks to get the kids to and from the school in Richard's resident school. I ended up losing my job because they could not justify keeping me with changing my hours to part-time. I did continue my college classes though. Charlie would have to get Ashlee to and from school though since it was in the opposite direction as the younger kids' school and she had to be at her school about the same time the younger kiddos did. I was also able to take Cole to some of her therapy appointments even though she was still refusing to come on my weeks. A couple of her sessions, her therapist had Richard and me join in. I also got the younger children into counseling at the office that I went to. I had all the children in therapy until each of them came of age.

After one of her final appointments, the therapist asked to see me without Cole or Richard. He told me that he had talked with the previous counselor to get more of her background. He also stated that he could tell that it was very hard for me to sit in with Richard there because of his constant belittling. He went onto explain that he was concerned with the family dynamics. How he explained it to me was that in a normal healthy family, the husband is the king, the wife is the queen, and the kids are in the next level of importance. He said in our family, Richard is the king, but Cole is the queen, and the rest of us seem to be treated like hired help. His belief was that Richard instilled this order into Cole from the get-go. I was completely agreeing with everything he said, and I did not have to say too much to him. He also said that this would be a tough case for him unless something changed. He did not specify, but I understood. I do not know if Richard knew about this meeting or not, but he started canceling Cole's appointments with this therapist. Richard stated that she did not need therapy, that it was a waste of time. I was then able to get Cole into a counselor at my counseling office also. Richard was not happy about any of the kids seeing a counselor but with the joint custody I no longer needed his approval.

About the middle of March, Richard was again trying to intimidate me into taking blame for the upcoming hearing. "If we have to go to court, Cole and Renee's gonna have to be in there, they are gonna testify," he threatened. "I don't want them back in there, I don't want them in court, Cole's already been in court once."

I replied, "They don't need to be, they shouldn't have been in court then, they shouldn't be in court now."

Talking over me, he repeated, "They will be, they will be. If I have to be at court, they will be."

I asked, "Well if you cared about the kids, why would you make them go through that?"

His justification, "Well if I have to go to court for contempt on them not going to your house, then they will go in and testify and explain to the judge why they didn't go to your house. I never forced them not to go to your house."

I explained, "No you tell them that I am forcing them to move so they get upset with me."

With intimidation, "Well you think about it for a day or two, if we go to court, we go to court, it's gonna suck but."

I again explained, "Yeah I can agree to work on stuff with you and get my lawyer to cancel the hearing, and then we will be right back where we are because you'll say, ha-ha I got her to back down."

He said matter of fact, "You have my word. Don't agree with me then, whatever. I will get them to go to your house, but you drop this bullshit and get this legal shit handled."

When it came closer to April, though, and Richard had not moved, I did enroll the kids in my school district after verifying with my lawyer that I was indeed to do so. My lawyer said that if I did not get them enrolled by April 1, that I could be in contempt. April 1 landed on a Friday and on Richard's week. I did not think he would cooperate on making the kids start the new school on his week. Since my week would not start until the afternoon of Monday, April 4, I told the schools that the kids' first day would be Tuesday, April 5. The morning of Monday, April 4, we had court in my hometown. It was scheduled during our mediation because of the contempt that we had on Richard. My lawyer said he would cancel this hearing if Richard finally started to follow the orders. He doubted we would need to cancel though since in the last two years, Richard had not been following any of the court orders. I was still not getting Cole on my weeks, and sometimes Renee would refuse to come. They were angry with me about making them switch schools. They would not believe me that it was not my idea, it was the offer I received from Richard and his lawyer, that I just accepted. I usually would not discuss the court details with the kids, but they had been given incorrect information, so I chose to correct them since they kept hounding me.

Instead of sending the kids to school for their last day, he brought them to court. The judge lectured him about bringing the kids, he was lectured on not having representation, and a few other things that he was supposed to have done but did not. Apparently when you are going to court for contempt, you have to have representation. The judge rescheduled this hearing, giving Richard time to do as he was required. After court, Charlie and I had a brief meeting with my lawyer and stopped at a gas station for something to drink and fill up the car. I emailed Richard asking if I could get the kids now instead of making another trip back down here to get them in about three and a half hours.

We picked up all three kids just before noon. After dropping Charlie off at work, I went straight to Sabastian's new elementary school. We took a tour around the school and they allowed him to stay the next two hours to meet his teacher and new classmates. Then the girls and I went to Renee's new middle school to do the same. We met with her guidance counselor and set her up ready to start the next morning. The girls were giving me attitude and being disrespectful to me and the school staff. They kept whispering to each other and giggling, then glaring at me. We then finished up at the high school counseling office where Cole was going to start school. Cole's attitude there was so bad that her guidance counselor sternly got onto her about being inappropriate and disrespectful. She then sent Cole out of her office for her and me to finish getting Cole set up to start school the next day.

Once we picked up Sabastian and went home, the attitudes of the girls continued and escalated. Ashlee had moved in with friends once she was finished with high school, so she was not there. Joanna had called me from South Carolina which was almost a daily ritual. She overheard Cole screaming, yelling and calling me names. Joanna was upset about the behavior, but also that she could not be here to help me. I told her I needed to hang up to deal with the girls. When we hung up, she called Ashlee and Daniel to tell them to come help me. Daniel was working so he sent his girlfriend over to the house. I had not asked for help, but I was not complaining when Ashlee and the girlfriend showed up. Cole kept belittling me about calling in reinforcements. Ashlee took Renee aside to talk to her away from Cole because this was not normal behavior for Renee, and they had been close sisters. Daniel's girlfriend went up to talk to Cole. The girlfriend came down to tell me that Cole called Richard, said it was time, and hung up but refused to explain to the girlfriend what that was about.

Almost immediately the doorbell rang, an ambulance with its lights on was in my driveway and a paramedic was at the door at 9:30 at night. The paramedic said that they got a call that a fourteen-year-old overdosed and the mother was refusing to call 911. I stated that I was the mother, but that I had no knowledge of anyone overdosing. She was rude with me and asked to speak with the fourteen-year-old. Renee came to the door. Ashlee stated that they had been talking for half an hour or so and she did not take any pills in front of her. The paramedic asked Renee what she took, how many and when. With hesitation, Renee said she did not know what it was. It had an M on it and her boyfriend gave them to her, and that she took about six of them. With a few more questions, the paramedic determined that it was probably Melatonin. Still with hesitation, when asked multiple times about when she took it, Renee finally answered saying it was around 11:00 am while she was still at her dad's house. The paramedics tone with me changed, almost to an apologetic softness, told me that Renee looked fine, no need for her to further examine Renee, but did suggest I take her into the hospital for a mental evaluation.

Realizing Richard's new plan of action, I decided to take Renee to the local children's hospital. Ashlee went with us. By the time we got to the hospital, it was about 10:30 at night. After examining her and asking the same questions as the paramedic, as well as many more, the doctor pulled me into a conference room down the hall. He informed me that he did not think she took the number of pills she claimed, if she took any at all. He said that her behaviors throughout that day would have been different; she would have been groggy, wanting to nap, etc., and that it would have been more apparent earlier in the day. He did want to keep her for a mental evaluation. He did not feel that she was suicidal. He felt like she was following instructions from someone else. She ended up being put in a locked inpatient behavioral health ward for three days. I was the only one who went to visit her and participated in the family therapy which was required for her release. Richard did not visit her or attend the therapy, instead he was upset that she was even there. A few months later, the girls did slip up stating that "Dad's plan backfired," referring to this incident.

Over the next few months, Cole's behaviors became a roller coaster of extremes. Somedays we would get along great, she would talk to me like a normal mother-daughter relationship and confide in me about personal worries. Then there would be days, which were more than the good days, where she would treat me like Richard did, but felt extremely worse. She would scream at me calling me a cunt, a whore, a stupid bitch, a fucking bitch, tell me and Charlie that our "mothers clearly missed with the coat hanger." She told Charlie that he "should blow his face off with a shot gun cuz he was ugly." She told him that he looked like a clown or a penis with ears, she threw things, she broke something around my house at least once per week when she was there, she threatened to stab or kill us, she would get violent and physically abusive towards Renee and Sabastian, etc. During one outburst, she made a comment about a beer bottle in my vagina. She would not repeat it and I could not make it out on the recording, so I did not know what the reference actually was. Again, I have this all on recording because I needed to protect myself. I found out a couple years later, that Cole made a similar beer bottle reference to Joanna, but more referring to something happening with Richard and Joanna. Joanna had no idea what Cole was referring to but made me think that Richard may have used a beer bottle on each of us at some point while we had been unconscious.

That first week, though, Cole and I were sitting at the dining room table. I was working on my homework while Cole was eating a snack and on her cell phone. Renee and Sabastian were in the living room watching television. Out of the blue, Cole said, "What the heck? Dad texted me saying, aren't you special, adding new kids from that S-H-I-T hole school."

I asked, "How does he know that?"

"Cuz I have him on Facebook," she answered. She tried to call him to find out what his problem was, but he refused to answer.

A couple weeks after this incident, Cole was skipping school and being aggressive, so I grounded her from prom. She was upset in her room, so I went to talk with her. "Oh, I understand being irritated and I understand being disappointed cuz you have been planning on it, but your behaviors Cole," I said softly.

"Yeah I know," Cole softly replied, after a long pause, "it doesn't help that some people keep telling me to be mean to you."

With concern, "Who keeps telling you to be mean to me?"

She whispered, "I don't wanna say."

Not quite understanding exactly what she had said I repeated what I thought she said, "You're not allowed to say who is telling you to be mean to me?"

Cole raised her voice a little in order to correct me, "No, I can say but I just don't want to."

May was a busy month. We had Ashlee's graduation party at our house. Most of my kiddos were there, including my granddaughter, Daniel's daughter. Joanna was the only one who could not make it, but they were supposed to be moving back to Iowa soon. Cole did take off with some friends the day of the party. A couple weeks later, Ashlee's graduation ceremony was at a huge auditorium in the city. Joanna had moved back so she was able to go along with Renee, Sabastian, and me but, Cole did not go. Dave's parents were at both the party and the ceremony.

We ended up going to court three more times for this same hearing because Richard was still refusing to follow the orders given to him. The hearings kept landing on his weeks with the kids and he kept bringing the kids to court which frustrated the judge since the courts kept reminding Richard not to do that. Then one of the hearings in August, Richard did not show up, but he did call into court stating that he could not be there since Cole had run away in the middle of the night. Cole was now seventeen and the judge did not think her running away from his house in the middle of the night was a valid reason to miss court. Cole told Richard's stepmom and sister that she ran away because he was going to make her testify in court and she did not want to. They scheduled another hearing for the following week since Richard did not attend. Since the kids were with me, I sent them to school instead of taking them to court. I did not even talk to them about when the hearing was, so they did not have to stress about it. At the hearing, he still came without representation. The judge again lectured him on the contempt, explained to him that he was the parent and he needed to enforce the visitations. He also lectured about the fact that we should be co-parenting and that the court orders were mandatory, not optional. It was basically a slap on the wrist for Richard instead of the usual fines that people normally get for contempt.

Renee turned fifteen about a week later. She asked me about getting her belly button pierced. I told her no. I felt that she was only fifteen and did not need one right now. I told her when she turned seventeen, we could discuss it again if she was still wanting one. I even told Richard that I was against it. That was probably a mistake, though, because he used it to his advantage. He told Renee if she was mean to me, then he would let her get her belly button pierced. He did the same thing for her fourteenth birthday, but it was a nose piercing. That proved to the kids that I had no authority and it made it very hard for me to discipline or be a proper parent.

Chapter Twenty-Four

About three weeks later, Cole spent a Saturday night with a friend. Sunday afternoon the friend and her group of friends were going to go to the lake. They brought Cole home sooner than I expected. When Cole came in the house, she asked why I wanted her home. I was not sure what she was talking about, but her friend motioned me to come outside so she could talk to me. The friend told me that Cole was flirting with the boys and causing arguments between some of the kids in the group. This group had been friends for a long time and realized that Cole was trying to cause rifts, so they decided they did not want Cole hanging out with them at the lake. They told Cole that I wanted her home. After they left, I went to try to talk to her, but I think she knew that there was more to her coming home than me asking. I did get her to come eat some cereal. She was not one to eat what I made for dinner. About an hour later, Sabastian told me that Cole was in the bathroom throwing up. She was laying on the floor in the bathroom, partially eaten cereal in the toilet, and she was somewhat out of it. Since I knew that she had been using marijuana in the last couple of years, I wondered if this was a side effect of that. I had never taken drugs before and knew nothing about any of it, including marijuana. I called the friend who had dropped her off to see if she knew anything. Initially she said no, so I just tried to comfort Cole thinking that she may have just gotten the stomach bug.

After attending to the other two kiddos and getting them settled into bed, Cole's friend called me back saying that I needed to take her to the emergency room. Apparently, Cole had texted her ex-boyfriend telling him that she took a bunch of her anti-depressants, so he contacted the female friend. Charlie said he would take care of the younger two while I took Cole to the children's hospital emergency room. I did email Richard to let him know what had happened. We stayed overnight in a suicide watch wing. The next day was the Monday that started Richard's week. He did come up to the hospital when he got off work, but he was mad when the doctor advised against him taking her home. To the doctor, Richard asked, "Is she getting out or what is she...?"

The doctor stated, "I think they need to look for a bed for her."

Richard grunted, "Well I don't agree but okay."

The doctor continued, "You can take her out against medical advice, you are always welcome to do that."

Giving my opinion, "I think she needs to stay, because we need to figure this out, you take her and its gonna start all over again, we are going to do this every few months."

With much irritation in his voice, "Whatever, my opinion, eh never mind, I'm just not even going to say it. Actually, why don't you ask her," (pointing to Cole). "Let's give the decision to HER."

Remembering the lecture from the judge three weeks ago, I stated, "But we are not supposed to."

Richard said, "Why? She is almost an adult."

I replied, "Did you not listen to the judge the last time we were in court?"

Richard sighed, "Oh my God."

I continued in frustration, "If we give her the decision, she didn't even, she took pills, she..."

Richard said, "People make mistakes." Turning back to Cole, he said, "Do you think you need to be in here for a couple nights away from your mom and I or do you wanna come home?"

Cole whispered, "I don't know."

Richard demanded, "No I'm asking you; we don't want an I don't know."

She again said, "I don't know."

The doctor stated, "I think that is a lot of pressure to put on her especially with being presented with going home."

Agreeing with the doctor and growing irritated with him, I said, "I think you and I need to discuss this and probably not in here."

Doctor said, "Alright, I am going to go let the residents know what my recommendations are."

The doctor left the room and I continued talking to Richard, "You obviously don't see the same thing that I see, you don't see the same thing that some other people see..."

Richard interrupted with a gravelly tone, "You don't see the same thing that the children have told you for months so..."

I continued, "No you don't, you get a different, you don't get the same story that everybody else gets, you don't get the truth."

Cole said, "Mom, let's not..."

Richard interrupted, ignoring me, "So do you think that you need a couple of nights in here or what do you need?"

I continued, "Do I have to prove to you what I go through?"

Still ignoring me, Richard asked Cole, "What?"

She explained to him, "I don't think that I am in the right state to make a decision. Cuz my head's still foggy."

He makes a grunt like he does not believe what Cole just said, so I tried to continue, "We aren't supposed to be discussing this stuff with the children."

I finally got him to leave her room to try to discuss things. First thing he brought up was my psychology classes. Telling me that "psychology is a joke, that it is a dying trade, and that it does not work." Then he told me that he was not happy that I left and was still not happy that I left him. We were here to talk about our daughter, and he was bringing up issues that did not pertain to why we were here. I reminded him that we had three children that we needed to get along for and his response was "well then you need to get them to where they don't want us together because that bothers the kids." I had talked to the kids about this, telling them that it was okay to feel like they wanted us back together, that it was normal, but all the kids told me that they did not want us back together because things were better with us not being together. I did not ask for details on what they meant, but it did tell me that he was trying to be manipulative. He then told me that he did not like talking to me because I recorded everything. I explained that I recorded to protect myself because I had been accused of things that I had not done. I also mentioned that if he was not saying or doing anything wrong then the recording should not bother him. Then he accused me of twisting the recording to make them sound worse than they were. He said, "If I have to have you record shit for the next twelve years, nah, I won't deal with that, cuz it's irritating, and stupid and annoying, and I don't like it."

While I was trying to talk to him, I started getting text messages from three of Cole's friends, asking how she was doing, and wanting to know if they could come visit her. I let Richard know that her friends were texting me. His response, "She doesn't have any friends, she's got little twats that she hangs out with. Half these idiots she hangs around with are worthless fucks. I try to put a little trust and faith in her that she is gonna make proper mistakes and she is gonna fuck up, I don't lock her down and ground her a bunch, they're not gonna learn nothing. They're gonna go through life not knowing that..."

Irritated with his tone I stated, "None of them are grounded right now, and it has been more than two weeks that she has been skipping school so I do not know what you are trying to put on me and I wish you thought that years ago. Maybe things would have been a little bit better, but you grounded the boys for six months for you don't even remember what for. Two weeks is not a massive grounding for a seventeen-year-old, two weeks for an eight-year-old, yeah, not for a seventeen-year-old."

His excuse, "Our parenting skills are always gonna be different, like I told ya, because I don't know."

I explained, "How we raised kids together was wrong, how we have been raising the kids apart is wrong, and if we don't figure something out then I don't think either one of us need to have those three kids cuz we're screwing all of them up."

He got defensive, "No one's gonna take my kids, someone ever tries to take my kids fully from me and it'll be hell on earth."

Getting a knot in my throat, "That's what I thought too, because they were my life, and you did it with lies. I did not leave you for another man, I did not cheat on you…"

He interrupted, "Yeah well, you did, you did…that's not what I was told."

I continued, "But when Cole calls me a whore because her dad told her that I've cheated on him, she wants to go get a blood test because you've told her that I cheated on you and you don't even know if you are her dad."

He said, "She also told you that I supposedly said she could go set shit on fire on your boyfriend's house, but I never told her she could set shit on fire."

I reminded him that I was not the only one she told this to. She told my landlord, his stepmom, his sister, and the officer who came over after she set a tampon on fire. Richard started laughing and said, "I do think it is kinda funny, but I didn't tell her to do it."

I explained, "It's not funny. She could have hurt herself, she could have hurt Renee, Sabastian, and she thinks it's funny." In frustration I continued to explain, "I'm trying to work with you, and you keep saying that you can't work with me because we have different opinions and different parenting styles. Well that's why we need to take our two parenting styles and find what the middle ground is and..."

He interrupted, "I don't know how to make the kids not hurt because mom and dad are not together, ok, I don't fucking know. I don't have a clue. And that's a lot of their fucking problem."

I said, "Ok IF that has been Cole's problem for the past three years, what was it before that, Richard?"

He grumbled, "I don't know, Jorgie."

I continued, "Was it because we were together and now it's because we're apart? Does she need to get away from both of us?"

He got defensive, "No, she ain't goin to my stepmom's or my sister's."

I continued, "Since she has had this problem (for several years), and you and I are the only common denominators, maybe she needs to get away from us."

Cole went to the same inpatient behavioral health ward for a few days that Renee was in a few months earlier. She came back home, but not much changed. She was still skipping school and calling me names, being disrespectful most of the time. About a week later, Cole was confiding in me about Richard. She said, "After I threw a fit because there was one-time Renee was full of attitude and I was like ok, you'll take my phone, but you'll never take hers and he quit taking my phone." After a long pause, "What he had said is he told me that it was stupid for me to try and kill myself because he doesn't have enough money to bury my butt."

Three weeks later, I picked the kids up from school and we were headed home. Cole calmly said, "If it's true mom, I'm gonna be getting into fights." Cole was upset about some girl at school and turned to Renee who was sitting in the backseat.

Renee said, "She didn't say anyone would, she said that there might be people who might want to."

Cole raised her voice, "No one even likes Hannah in the first place and that would be petty bullshit if she would have someone fight me because she can't keep her legs closed. I'm serious like keep yer frickin legs closed and you won't have this problem."

Renee said, "Well Cloe says it wasn't true because that girl has a boyfriend."

Cole continues, "There's a video, Kyle showed me the video. Yeah, she has a boyfriend, but she's been giving Kyle blowjobs. Still there's a video and it was dated like the fourth day of school. When I hung out with Kyle, and then there was another one I got showed about four weeks ago that was dated four-five weeks ago. Just cuz someone has a boyfriend don't mean that they're not gonna cheat. And I can't wait til Preston finds out, I can't wait til someone tries to fight me because then

I can beat the shit outta someone finally cuz you won't let me fight you."

Renee said, "No."

Cole continued, "Dude, I just really wanna beat the shit outta someone." I finally piped in asking why because I did not understand the reason for violence. Cole continued, "I don't know. I also wanna slit someone's throat and watch them bleed out. It would be fun; it would be like ha I'm taking a mother fuckin life."

Getting very concerned, I cleared my throat and said, "No, that that's not fun, that's psychotic."

She continued calmly, not angrily, "Their life is in your hands, their life is literally bleeding out and you're watching someone die. Yes, it would be terrifying but like the power to it. That's funny I might get into fights."

Two weeks later was another very memorable day. Cole was still skipping school on a daily basis. This particular day she was pushing really hard to get to go out with her friends after I told her no. I told her that if she would stay at school for a full day every day for a week, then she could go out with her friends. She did not want to follow rules, so I was not giving in to the hanging with friends. I was not getting any help from Richard, so it was a parental fight all my own. It started out normal and calm. She said she understood, but if I let her go out this one time, then she will not skip school the following week. She had already played this card, and she did not keep her end of the deal. Then she tried to throw Renee under the bus. She told me that Renee got her belly button pierced. I was upset about it, but that was another discussion for Renee and me, not Cole. Her agitation continued to grow, and she started to get a little more aggressive. She started getting in my face, puffing up her chest like her dad did. At one point I was sitting on the couch, she put one foot on the coffee table and leaned over me. In a threatening tone, she told me that I had two choices, either I let her go out with her friends or she would break something or hurt someone.

Joanna and her husband came over to watch the baseball game. He was a fan, but they did not have cable. By this time, Cole had gotten loud and very aggressive. She was calling me names, Renee names, she was threatening physical harm to both Renee and me, she was again telling me that my mother missed with the coat hanger. She broke one of my ceramic wax warmers. Then she went outside and threw her cell phone, which bounced off the concrete driveway and hit the side of my car, leaving a clear rectangle shape dent in the passenger side door. About six hours of her throwing her fit, screaming, yelling, calling names, threatening physical harm, she had changed her clothes, and put a bag by the front door. She told me that she was going out with her friends. Joanna stood up to tell her that she was being very disrespectful to her mother and that was not the way to speak to her mother. Cole lunged at Joanna, hitting her and pulling her hair. Since Joanna was over eighteen and Cole was not, she thought she would get into trouble, so she just tried to block the punches instead of fighting back. Cole got Joanna to the ground and they were rolling around. Joanna's husband acted as a referee because he too did not want to get into trouble for touching Cole. Sabastian was scared so I was holding him in the kitchen so he could not see the girls. I tried to somewhat watch, but I too was very scared. I thought Renee was sitting on the stairs watching, but later she said that she did not see any of it because she was in her room. I could not see the stairs from where I was in the kitchen, but I do know that she was sitting on the stairs when the altercation first started. Renee was sitting on the stairs when I picked Sabastian up and went to the kitchen. It seemed like forever, even though I think it was actually ten-fifteen minutes. Then Cole jumped up, grabbed the bag she had by the front door and left.

Joanna had scratches on her arms and was already starting to bruise in spots. She had chunks of her hair pulled out and was very shaky. I called the police for a few obvious reasons. When the officer arrived, he took pictures of Joanna's injuries. He filed a runaway report so that they would be out looking for Cole. He suggested that Joanna press assault charges against Cole. He also suggested I go to the juvenile courts and ask for assistance for a teenager with behavior issues. I expressed concern for not only my own safety but the safety of the younger two kiddos. Not that I wanted anyone hurt, but I was thankful that Joanna was here. I wondered who Cole would have attacked if it were only Renee, Sabastian and me at home. Joanna had been athletic most of her life and was definitely stronger than I was.

The next morning, Cole showed up at the house while we were all getting ready for the day. She took a shower and changed her clothes to get ready for school. I did not say anything to her. I did not even ask where she stayed. I was trying to keep things peaceful at least for the moment. I dropped all three kids off at school and picked up Joanna. She and I went straight to the city's downtown. We found the juvenile courts. There was paperwork for us to fill out and then we waited to see a judge. I explained to the judge all the behaviors that I had seen in the past few months with Cole and the judge saw the marks on Joanna. The judge determined that Cole was a danger to others and possibly herself. The judge filed an order to have Cole picked up from the school at the end of the school day and transported to a juvenile facility by an appointed figure until a further hearing could be set. As Joanna and I left the courthouse, Cole's high school guidance counselor called me stating that Cole was claiming that I punched her and broke her nose so under law they had to call and report it to DHS. I completely understood and was somewhat relieved. Cole also claimed that she bled all over the sweatshirt she was wearing the night before, so I went home to take pictures of it to show that there was no blood on it. The guidance counselor also told me that she let DHS know that they had Cole's sister at the school to talk to as well as Cole. The DHS investigative worker did show up to the school, talked to both Cole and Renee separately, and then came to me. I gave her Joanna's phone number in case she needed more information. She said that Cole's story alone was inconsistent and questionable before she even spoke with Renee. My story closely matched

Renee's so the worker said she was going to file the report as unfounded.

Cole was placed back in that same inpatient behavioral health ward that she had been in a little over a month earlier. I did email Richard. He was livid and blamed Joanna and me for everything. There were three court appointed lawyers; one for Cole, one for me and one for Richard. We had two court hearings while she was in the inpatient behavioral health ward, then they moved her to a Youth Emergency Services and Shelter. DHS was required to be involved, but it was a family social worker instead of the investigative worker that did the last report. The judge ordered a specific extensive evaluation to be done on Cole in order to get a proper placement. I gave my juvenile lawyer many of the recordings of both Richard's behaviors and of Cole's violence towards her siblings and me. The judge also listened to these recordings and felt that Cole needed to be in a structured group home, but she could not place her there without the evaluation. The family social worker became too friendly with Cole. She treated me like I was a criminal. She kept putting into the paperwork that Cole was in "placement due to abuse from mother" and she was refusing to get the evaluation that the judge had ordered. We had two more court hearings while she was in the shelter.

Every time we went to court, the judge would lecture the social worker on not doing what was mandatory. Besides getting the evaluation, there was supposed to be both individual therapy for Cole plus family therapy with Cole, Richard and me. I also asked for supervised visitations for the younger kids and me because I did not feel safe around Cole. The judge agreed with my request given the evidence and also made it mandatory for Richard to have supervised visits since the judge felt like Richard was instigating Cole's behaviors. The judge also made it clear that the social worker was to go through me for any decisions made for Cole while in the shelter. Since the social worker refused to do what the judge ordered, Cole did get her individual therapy, but there was no family therapy set up. The social worker did make sure that all my visitations were supervised, but Richard was allowed to visit unsupervised. The worker also allowed Cole to go on some weekend furloughs with Tracy, without my consent. These were all things that the judge lectured the social worker about at almost every hearing. After four months of the social worker still not getting the required evaluation, the judge had no choice but to pick an alternative placement. The shelter was a temporary placement and Cole had already been there longer than kids usually stayed there. The judge asked if there was a family member that I approved of for Cole to live with and the judge also asked Richard. I chose Richard's stepmom and Richard chose Tracy. Since Tracy had sent a letter to DHS and the courts that was mostly bashing me and I was able to prove that most of the letter contained false information, the judge ordered that Cole be sent to live with Richard's stepmom with all the same orders. While Cole was at her grandparents, my child support changed again. Richard was now ordered to pay his stepmom eleven dollars per week for Cole and I received thirty-two dollars per week for Renee and Sabastian even though I was currently not working. I was a full-time student.

Our final juvenile hearing was just before Cole's eighteenth birthday. Not much had changed other than Richard's stepmom was trying to follow what she was told. Richard was still supposed to have supervised visits, but the social worker said that as long as his stepmom was there, she could supervise the visits, but they would not allow the same for me. There was also supposed to be family therapy which never did happen, and her new therapist refused to communicate with me like he was supposed to. Shortly after this, that social worker was fired. The judge apologized to me for not being able to properly help my family. The judge also recommended to my juvenile lawyer to talk to me about filing a modification for custody of the remaining minor children. It was the judge's belief that Richard was causing a toxic environment for the kids and with his refusal to coparent with me showed that a fifty-fifty custody would not work. The judge also recommended that we get the case moved to my county since everything was here and the juvenile judge would be able to continue to help.

Chapter Twenty-Five

We filed a modification in August of 2017. My juvenile attorney also filed to switch the case from Richard's county to mine stating the reasons why. This attorney also advised me to send a letter to a state senator/lawyer who was already in the process of suing the Iowa DHS office due to negligence in other cases. I never did hear back from the senator/lawyer. Richard's county denied the motion to switch counties. My juvenile attorney and the juvenile judge were shocked by this. They both said that counties usually have no qualms about moving a case. This attorney also told me that she did not get a lot of honest clients in her line of work and that it was refreshing. She made this comment because I had evidence to back up everything that I claimed.

Mediation was ordered to be completed by the end of January 2018, with a mediator appointed from a small town north of the town my parents lived in. The order also stated that if mediation was not completed by the deadline that whoever was noncompliant would be in contempt. My attorney was in contact with the mediator, but the mediator was having trouble getting Richard to answer her calls and he was not returning them either. At the beginning of February, my lawyer filed a motion that Richard be in contempt of court for not complying with mediation. I joined a meeting at the State Capitol building with the head of Judiciary and two other senators along with a few other people from a Parental Alienation group. In this meeting, since there were not very many of us, we were all given ample time to talk about our cases. We were given copies of the Iowa Codes pertaining to family courts. The senators went through it with me and we highlighted the codes that were not complied with in my case. The head of Judiciary told me that since I was currently in the middle of an ongoing case, he could not help me until it was over. He did tell me to let my lawyer know that I met with him and show her the highlighted Iowa Codes.

Since nothing was happening with the motion, my lawyer contacted the Chief District Judge about the failure of this county. He then filed a new deadline of April 30 for the completion of mediation with the same consequence that was stated previously. After several attempts to contact Richard to schedule mediation, he finally responded to the mediator at the end of April. We finally had mediation on April 30, 2018. It was a waste of time and money though. Richard attended by himself, without a lawyer, and refused to discuss or agree to anything. He told the mediator that the only thing that he would agree to was if he was to get complete and full custody of all remaining minor children. There was no way that I would agree to that. The hearing for modification was scheduled for October 2-4, 2018. Apparently, they thought it would take multiple days. They demanded that we not use any evidence that was prior to our November 2015 hearing which was completely fine because I had tons more recordings and emails proving his unwillingness to coparent and that showed continued abuse. We also were going to provide the documents pertaining to the juvenile court hearings.

I had graduated with my AA and was now working full-time, not in the area of my degree though, so I was not making more money than I had been before taking classes. My plan was to go on to get my BA, but Charlie's health was not getting better, so I needed to try to become the main breadwinner. The kids were still attending school in my district. A few of the current issues were mostly lack of coparenting and his lack of communication with me. He refused to email me about important issues. Sabastian was getting into some trouble at school with exhibiting inappropriate behavior which seemed to be on his dad's weeks. The school called me telling me that Sabastian had sent a picture of my neighbor girl via snapchat to a few of his friends with the caption, "Alice likes to suck dick." Sabastian did not have a cell phone at my house, nor did I approve of him having a snapchat account. The school tried to talk to Richard about the incident, but he was not cooperative with them. When I emailed him about it, he brushed it off as normal behavior for kiddos, but Sabastian was only in fourth grade. When I talked about Sabastian needing to be grounded from electronics, Richard disagreed and refused to help with discipline. A few days later, I had a parent of a different child at my door. She was livid and extremely upset. She explained that her son had been playing with Sabastian on the game systems, when she told her son that it was time to get off the games. She heard Sabastian tell her son over the headset that he did not have to listen to the dumb bitch. The conversation between the boys went on long enough that she took a screenshot of the messages after the boys were no longer on their headsets. They showed that Sabastian continued to use inappropriate language towards his friend's mother. Again, Sabastian was at Richard's house during this incident also. These boys had been friends and playing together for the two years since we had moved to this neighborhood. The boy's mother was very shocked with Sabastian's behavior because she had never witnessed this type of behavior from him before. This was not behavior or language that was used in my home, but I had heard these same things from Richard. On my weeks, Sabastian remained grounded. I also made him write apology letters to both the neighbor girl and the mother of his friend. I made him hand deliver them along with verbal apologies. Again, I tried to email Richard on this new behavior of Sabastian's and what consequences that he was willing to enforce. Richard again thought there was no need for disciplinary actions. The kids told me that Richard laughed about it, high fived Sabastian, and told them that he thought it was stupid that I grounded Sabastian plus making him do the apologies.

Most of our emails showed lack of coparenting. One email was him stating that he bought Renee a new winter coat and he wanted me to pay him for half of it. I had replied stating that she had five winter coats at my house and that I wish he would have checked with me prior to spending the money. About a week later, Richard had taken the kids to the eye doctor. The kids were on Medicaid through me and it only covered certain frames. Apparently, Renee did not like any of the approved frames, so Richard paid over four hundred dollars on a pair and then wanted me to pay him for half of those also. I refused stating that expense was not part of the court order. Another email was about prom dresses. The kids commented on numerous occasions that Richard did not have much money and could not afford this or that. When Renee wanted to look at dresses, I gave her a price maximum and then emailed Richard about the maximum limit that I gave her. I thought neither of us could afford an expensive dress, so I was trying to keep the dress cost down since we also had the expenses of shoes, hair, and nails. She found one that she liked, and I scheduled a time to go look at it, but before we could look at it, Richard took her out to buy a dress that was more than twice the limit that I gave her. Then he sent me an email telling me what my half would be. I could not afford it. He then made it sound like I was unwilling to cooperate with him and that I made him pay for everything. I even had Renee mad at me for not helping her Dad pay for the dress or her glasses. I did however pay for the shoes, hair and nails without asking him for half.

There were many times that I bought something and never even mentioned to him about paying his half because I was trying to avoid any possible arguments from him. I bought Sabastian's winter wear for three different winters; that included coat, snow pants, boots, gloves, hat, and scarf. I never once asked him for half. Every year that I had the kids on the tax-free weekend for school supplies, I bought all their supplies without asking him for half. I did however keep the receipts to prove that I bought them. On the years he would buy the school supplies, he would send me an email asking me to pay him for half. Then he told me and everyone else, including the kids, that I never paid for anything. Even though the kids were there when I paid for things they needed, for some reason they still believed him that I was not paying.

In our October 2018 hearing, the judge was very snippy and rude with both my lawyer and me. He spoke to Richard all nice and sympathetic, almost as if he thought Richard was the victim and I was the evil witch. Richard continued to lie on the stand. When my lawyer would bring up the facts about something he just lied about, he would nervously back pedal. Richard still did not have a lawyer representing him. My lawyer did not submit anything prior to our 2015 mediation but the judge did. He made his decision on the hearsay of Richard and his witnesses from the August 2014 hearing, none of which were factual statements, there was no proof of anything that he claimed. We believe he had made his decision before we even started the hearing; he clearly went over the transcripts from the August 2014 hearing. The judge re-victimized me by using all the lies Richard told, which caused me great anxiety and he refused to acknowledge any of the hard evidence that I did have. This hearing cost me a lot of time and money. The only thing that did change was they increased the child support, but they gave him all rights to claim both kids on his taxes again, which again, I had childcare expenses that I would not be able to use as deductions.

I wrote letters to Senators and the Iowa Bar Association. I did not hear back from the Iowa Bar Association, but I did hear back from a few Senators who were very concerned with the way that county handled my case. I also had a second meeting at the State Capitol in February 2019. The State officials who attended were disgusted with the actions of that county, but since there were several of us victims in attendance, they did not give anyone priority attention. They did tell me to continue to fight for justice and to send them as much information as I could. I got busy with work and writing this book, so I have not continued my fight.

With all the stress that this divorce and custody battle caused me, my health had some consequences. After seeing an audiologist for the first time in decades, she fitted me with hearing aids in May 2014. The hearing aids only amplified what was already in my hearing range, so if it was not in my hearing range without them than I still would not be able to hear it with the hearing aids. I also still could not tell what direction a sound was coming from. She diagnosed me as being legally deaf. She had gotten my old childhood records that showed my hearing loss had been between 40-60% in each ear. Now her tests were showing me with a 70-75% hearing loss in each ear. I finally went to see a neurotologist, which is a specialist of the inner ear. This is the kind of doctor that I should have seen as a child, but my mother refused. This doctor was an older fellow that had been a neurotologist for almost forty years. He told me that he knew of my childhood ENT doctor, and thought highly of him, but that the surgeries he performed were not the proper procedures for the issues I suffered from. He ended up doing an extensive surgery on my right ear in August 2016. I continued to have problems with my ears, continued to have constant ear infections, and my hearing continued to deteriorate so my audiologist referred me to a different neurotologist. The new neurotologist was a little younger but more modern and proactive. He had been practicing in the area for over twenty-five years. By the time I saw him, my hearing loss had gotten to between 75-80% in each ear. He was very concerned with the condition of my right ear. It was in worse condition than my left. I had never had any surgery to the left ear, but I did have three to the right ear, so he did not want to add more trauma to my right ear unless it was absolutely necessary. He monitored it every six months. He did eventually have to do a fourth emergency surgery in January 2020.

Over these first few years after the divorce, I experienced many symptoms that caused me to seek medical care on multiple occasions. I had MRIs, ultrasounds, physical therapy, sent to a cardiologist for testing, Cat Scans, EKGs, and had a lot of blood work analyzed. The physical therapist and the doctor said I had all the symptoms of Postural Orthostatic Tachycardia Syndrome or P.O.T.S. so I was sent to see a cardiologist, who said that my heart was fine, so they ruled out the possibility of P.O.T.S. With all these scans, they did find two separate lumps about two years apart. They removed them and biopsied them. Thankfully they were both benign. One of the doctors believed that my symptoms, including the lumps, were induced by severe stress and anxiety.

My mother also told my kids that I suffered from bipolar disorder and schizophrenia, but that I refused to take my medicine. I talked to two separate doctors and my therapist about this, wanting to get tested. None of them believed I had anything close to either of these disorders nor could they test me without having sufficient documentation giving good reasons. One of the doctors told me that he would assume that my mother was the crazy one and that I should not listen to anything that she said about me. My mother likes to gossip so recently she has been calling Daniel's ex-girlfriend, who was abusing him and his daughter. My mother was bad-mouthing Daniel to her. She was also telling this ex that I had warrants out for my arrest for dealing drugs in several different towns, including out of state. I have never even tried drugs, let alone gotten into trouble with them. I have never been in trouble with the law. I have never done anything illegal to warrant any trouble. I have not spoken to this woman since 2013 and she still finds ways to get to me. This is what narcissists do, even though I have cut her off, I still seem to be her target.

As well as seeing my new neurotologist, I was also referred to another ENT doctor to look at the reasons that my breathing had gotten worse over the years. After getting my history, he wanted to know what medicines I was on as a child. I said that I was a very sick child, but that I outgrew it as I came into my teens. He thought that finding out what medicines I was on would help determine what I was diagnosed with in my childhood, but I could not give him that information. This doctor also told me that the deformity of my ears is very rare and linked to drug use during pregnancy. Even with our strained relationship, I defended my mother telling the doctor that she did not use illegal drugs. He then told me that drug use just means using any type of drug, including over the counter, that women should not be taking during pregnancy. He said that with given my childhood history his guess was that my mother took some over the counter drug in excess while pregnant with me. After reviewing my MRI, he told me that he noticed an old nose fracture that was probably an incident from before the age of ten. He asked if I remembered breaking my nose and if I knew why it had never been fixed. I again had no answers for him. I had no knowledge of ever breaking my nose. His recommendation was surgery on my nose to re-enforce the fractured area because with my age it was causing a shift in my cartilage and that was why I was having trouble breathing through the left side of my nose. Charlie did not feel good about the surgery, so I did refuse it. I did not return to this ENT doctor, but it did pique my curiosity to order my childhood medical records.

It took me a couple days to go over all my records and research certain words or names that I did not know. It was a mixture of many emotions. I cannot quite describe how I felt. I was shocked, confused, not really sad or upset, just kind of lost. There was nothing in my records to back up all the stories I had always known about my childhood. It stated that I was a healthy baby. It did not list medicines that I was supposed to be on regularly. It did not list any kind of diagnosis of why I had been sick. So, I contacted both of my sisters to find out if they knew what medicines I was taking as a child. Sue's response was that she knew that I was sick a lot, that we all had a shitty childhood, we were all abused by our mother, and that we need to leave the past in the past to move on with our lives. She has not talked to me since. Tracy said that I was a spoiled rotten brat and that I was so sick that all the family money was spent on my medicines and special foods. That they went without so I could have what I needed. When I tried to explain some of what was in my medical records, she blocked me. I then contacted some of the family members of the family that lived in the country with horses and cats. They also could not tell me what medicines that I was on as a kiddo. They did say that they had always had suspicions of my mother having Munchhausen by Proxy though.

    These records stated that there was a flat spot on the side of my head due to "the way the child lies." With many years of childcare, I had seen the 'flat head' of infants from either laying in the same position all the time or the most common cause was being in a car seat too often. It also stated that I had muscle spasms in my neck that caused my head to tilt slightly to the right, but stated it was "still within normal limits." There was nothing about a brain issue or deformity, there was nothing about me not being able to crawl or walk. There was nothing anywhere stating that I was not supposed to live.

There were no records of any allergies or allergy tests. It did state that I was breastfed only until six months of age, then switched to a mixture of breastmilk and whole milk until ten months of age, and then switched to whole milk only feedings. It stated that at seven weeks old, I was treated for a rash, caused from being fed baby food to early. Again, with being in the childcare field for thirty years, I knew that feeding baby food before four months of age can develop into possible allergies. Why my mother was feeding me baby food before I was even two months old is beyond me.

The records also stated that I had low iron levels causing anemic deposits. At about a year old, the doctors placed me on over the counter iron drops and iron fortified formula. It showed that four years later, doctors were surprised that I was still on the iron drops and the formula. Since my iron levels seemed to be at normal levels, the doctors told my mother to keep me on the iron drops, but to discontinue the formula. I was five years old when my records stated that the doctors said to discontinue my "special milk." Until I got these records, I did not know that my "special milk" was actually formula. I had suspicions when feeding babies, my own and others, formula because the smell was familiar. My mother kept me on that formula until I was twelve years old and in sixth grade. Being a mother, I know that formula is very expensive, and most parents cannot wait until their child is old enough to switch to regular milk.

The only mention of me being colicky is an entry when I was just under three weeks old that stated, "mother called in reporting colicky type pains." Instead of making an appointment they called in a prescription for an anti-diarrhea medicine. At six months old, there is an entry that stated I was brought in because I fell off a bed, but there was "no evidence of injury." At three and a half years old, an entry stated "mother reports child wears off the toe of her right shoe faster than the left. When examined, her feet appear perfectly normal, and her gait was normal." At age four, I had stitches in my chin. It does not state what happened, but I have always had a scar on my chin. At age six, I was seen for contusions of left knee and left hand, but again does not state reasons. There were a lot of test results for various things throughout all these records and all seem to say negative or within normal range. Usually anytime there was a positive result, it was for ear infection or tonsillitis.

The first time that I remember having a fainting spell was in second grade two months after Great-grandma Ivy passed away. I was on the twisting bars at school during recess. I was wearing a salmon colored corduroy skirt with an off-white, button-up blouse. I remember swinging my legs to spin, then everything started to get dim and dark, I had ringing in my ears, and I saw sparkles. The next thing I knew, I was being picked up off the ground with a bloody nose and lip. My blouse was covered in blood. My mother was there at the school for some reason, so she was in the nurse's office with me. This incident was listed in my medical records. It stated that I had abrasions over the upper lip with some swelling, bleeding from the nose, abrasions over the knees, but no evidence of a fracture of the nose.

The second time I remember having a fainting spell was when I was in fourth grade. I was standing at the back of the classroom with a few other kids getting ready to use the paper cutter. Again, the room started to go dim, my ears started ringing and I saw sparkles. I do remember turning to look out the window, once the dimness started, wondering if it was getting dark outside. The next thing I knew I was waking up on the floor with several of my classmates surrounding me. They said I just fell straight backwards hitting a desk on my way to the floor. I believe this was listed in the medical records as "mother reported child was observed to have a mild grand mal seizure at school, so they were scheduling a neurological evaluation." My mother had no medical education so not sure why they took her word for it.

I was sent to four different hospitals for the testing of possible seizures. One was in my hometown, one was a specialty hospital in another town in Iowa, the other two were in Omaha, Nebraska and Rochester, Minnesota. They all showed no abnormality. No epileptiform activity, therefore, all of my tests results from all the hospitals were inconsistent with seizures. I call them fainting spells because I do not know what else to call them. I did have two more of these while I was a minor.

The third one was that time that I was babysitting for Susan. When I came back from the town loop, I was talking to her about what happened with Dave while she finished getting ready for her date. I remember sitting on her bed, talking, and then the next thing I knew she was standing in front of me with a peanut butter and jelly sandwich and I was laying on her bed. As I sat up, I asked her when and why she made me a sandwich. She said that I was just talking away, then said I was hungry, so she asked if a sandwich was ok. She left to make the sandwich and she said when she came back in the room, I looked like I was sleeping. She said she was probably out of the room for ten minutes or so and I had no recollection of it.

The fourth one was while I was in the group home. It was while Heather was my roommate. We were talking and doing homework in our room. I was sitting on my bed and she was at her desk. I remember talking, then the room got dark, the usual ringing of my ears, and then she was standing over me with a staff member. Heather said that I was talking and just stopped mid-sentence and fell backwards on my bed. I was not responding to her, so she went to get a staff member to help wake me up. They took my temp and then scheduled a doctor's appointment. Nothing ever came about from the doctor's appointment and this was the last time that I am aware that I had a fainting spell. I have had many close encounters, but I have learned to steer them away and I have stayed conscious. I have wondered if they were effects of whatever medications my mother had me on.

Chapter Twenty-Six

Charlie and I bought a three-bedroom, three-bathroom house together before Renee's eighteenth birthday. We are still best friends, soul mates, and life partners. He is still the only man that I feel completely safe with. We do occasionally get on each other's nerves which is completely normal and healthy. This has been the only real intimate relationship that I have ever been in. It feels meant to be and completely natural. For the first time, I feel truly loved. I now know that what I dreamt was love, is what true unconditional love feels like. I still have my women's accessories business, I keep my inventory in the house, and Charlie helped me get a website up and running. It is currently an online store so most of my customers are still from other states.

With my healing, I have also begun repairing relationships with my kiddos and talk to all seven of them on a regular basis. Some of the kids still keep our contact secret because even though six of them are adults, Richard still gets upset with them for talking to me. When he has found out that they talk to me, he has taken them off his health insurance, car insurance (even though they pay him their portion each month), changed his Netflix passwords so they cannot use it, and any other threats that he can make. By Cole getting away from the toxicity of the divorce, she has become the wonderful person that I knew she could be. The last two winter holidays, I had six of my seven kids plus Charlie's son and their families gathered here at our home. Progress is slow, but rewarding, and I am proud of all my kiddos. I enjoy the hugs and kisses from each of them. Tracy has family holiday gatherings at her home. She invites most, but not all, of my kids. I am not welcome there, but Richard attends. After all the grumbling I got from him over the years for attending Dave's family gatherings, I do not understand how he justifies him attending my blood family's gatherings. Dave now attends his family gatherings, so I no longer go, but some of my kids are still invited. They have all tried to start relationships with Dave, but he has no interest apparently and treats my kids like they are not his relation. I have been told that Dave tells people that he has no biological children.

Since I took several psychology and sociology classes, I learned a lot and wished that I had taken these classes years ago. It may have saved me from a lot of heartache. Much of what we went over in my classes, I could relate to in my own personal life. It also opened my eyes to things that I had either not noticed or was trying to avoid. I started noticing patterns in my life and my personal history. Most of my essay papers were based on my real-life events and issues. After reading my papers, many of my professors suggested I write a book about my life. My counselor agreed, stating that it would be a great healing tool. I do believe that in writing this book it has helped with my healing, but I am also hoping to help at least one person out there that can relate to my experiences.

My dad always felt like his mother abandoned him and that his stepmom and stepsister hated him. When his memories became clearer after his accident, he realized the memories of brushing his mother's hair were good memories. Being locked in a closet were apparently his stepmom. He dropped out of high school and joined the Navy to get away from his family problems. What he seemed to unknowingly do is marry someone just like his stepmom or his dad, there was definitely abuse there whether intentional or not. I tried very hard not to be like my mother. I wanted to be the best mother that I could possibly be, but I unknowingly married someone just like my mother. Most of my kiddos are more like me, but they have unknowingly found themselves in the same toxic relationships. The cycle will continue unless I can help my kids realize the possible outcomes.

My mother is not unique, there are many more out there like her. There is actually a name for parents like her... An unloving narcissistic parent is one who is emotionally distant, withholding, inconsistent, or even hypercritical or cruel. This is actually so common that you can find books, YouTube videos and other types of support groups about, and for, this exact issue. I did not know any of this until after I left Richard and started educating myself. My mother acted as though she could do no wrong, but everyone else could not do anything right. I spent over forty years trying to win my mother's approval and love. Learning about an unloving narcissistic mother, helped me to understand that I was not the problem. She does not have the capacity to love or accept me for who I am. I learned that I will never be good enough in her eyes, but that I only need to be good enough in my own eyes. I will be good enough for anyone who truly loves me. With having an unloving narcissistic parent, comes low self-esteem and toxic relationships. Another typical sign is scapegoating. A narcissistic parent always blames one child. It does not always have to be the same child. If you have siblings, sometimes you may be the scapegoat and sometimes one of your siblings is the scapegoat. I do believe each of my siblings was a scapegoat at one time or another, but I believe I was the main scapegoat. My sisters have resentment towards me because I was sick, and they were told they had to do without so I could get my medicines and special foods. When I asked Tracy why she lied in court to help Richard take away my kids, her answer was that I was a spoiled rotten brat and I thought I was a princess. I feel like my mother made me the scapegoat for everything that was wrong in all of our childhoods. Sue is withdrawn and mainly keeps to herself, living in Minnesota. I believe she has a good relationship with her son. Tracy is still very social, usually the "life of the party" and from what I have heard, her relationship with her son is strained. We all have been married and divorced at least twice. All four of us have relationship issues, which is expected after having a toxic mother. I was married twice with no proposals, no engagements, no bridal showers, and no honeymoons. I gave birth to seven children and never had a baby shower. I chalk this up to being a side effect of being a scapegoat child.

I stayed close with my aunt Lorraine up until she passed away at the end of 2017. I have been somewhat close with my mother's brother, who is just older than her, for most of my adult years. My uncle Arthur and I still talk regularly. Aunt Lorraine did not know why my mother acted the way she did, and she thought of my grandma Berta as her best friend until she passed. Aunt Lorraine never mentioned their father. I always assumed she may not have really remembered him. My uncle Arthur also does not know why my mother acts the way she does. He does not believe that she was ever abused, and he too speaks highly of Grandma Berta. Aunt Lorraine was his favorite sister. Uncle Arthur says their dad was a great man, a deacon in their church, and very strong but easy going. It was Grandma Berta that was the disciplinarian and Sunday school teacher. He is proud of both of his parents and became a parent himself to mirror what he learned from his parents.

In the last couple years of living with Richard, he bought both Joanna and me a couple pairs of thong undies. I was not interested in them; they did not look comfortable to me. He would get upset with me for not wearing them. He got upset with Joanna for not wearing hers. At the time, I thought he was just trying to irritate me. After our divorce, I learned from the younger girls' that he continued to buy thong undies for them even if they were not at the store with him. I found that quite disturbing. I also learned that Richard had a sexual affair with my son's live-in girlfriend. It did not surprise me since that fits his behaviors. I felt horrible for my son, but it is something that I have stayed out of until my son needs me. I did not blame the girlfriend either because I knew how good Richard was with his threats and manipulations. No matter what Tracy believed, leaving Richard was the right thing to do. A toxic relationship is never a good thing to stay in, especially when children are involved.

There are many different forms of abuse. The main one is physical abuse. It is easier to determine and prove. Most children do not report physical abuse inflicted by a parent, though, because they know that their consequence would be way worse if authorities do not remove them from the situation. Often times, like in my case, kiddos do not realize that they are being abused until someone sees it or talks about it. Many women have the same fear of their consequence if they turn in their intimate partners for abuse. A majority of the time, they are blamed for staying and putting up with it. People who do not have experience with abuse, usually make the comments that "it must not be too bad" if the victim stays. There are resources out there, but not as many or as easily accessible as they should be. Richard would grab my kids by the throats and hold them up off the floor. He would sit on them and hold them down, laughing at them as they struggled to get free. Richard was very careful about the physical abuse. He knew not to leave a mark and he made sure that I knew that he was aware of that fact. I think he knew this information because his dad and stepmom were volunteer first responders.

The other forms of abuse are mental, verbal, emotional, sexual, financial, and psychological. Examples and meanings of each of these will blur together. They are all harder to prove so it is less likely to be reported. I have experienced all of these, but I did not know it until I went to therapy after my divorce to Richard. What I did not learn from therapy, I definitely learned from my college classes. I would usually verify with my therapist to make sure that I was understanding it correctly or labeling my experiences correctly. There is a Power and Control Wheel that really opened my eyes to what my kids and I experienced. On this wheel it talks about intimidation, coercion and threats, emotional abuse, isolation, economic abuse, male privilege, using children, and minimizing, denying and blaming. With intimidation, Richard would give me dirty looks, puff up his chest and back me into corners. He would throw things at me or the kids, barely missing us on purpose. If he had us up against a wall, he would punch the wall right next to our heads. He would also talk about his guns and how many he had along with how much ammo he possessed.

With coercion and threats, Richard threatened to turn me in for neglect to DHS if I tried to leave him. He threatened to kill me and/or my kids if I tried to leave. I picked up the phone to call 911 to report him while he was abusing my kids, but he threatened to take me down with him for being an accessory or an enabler. That is why I felt it easier to sacrifice myself so he would let loose of my kiddos. With emotional abuse, Richard was always calling the kids and me names, telling us that we would never amount to anything, that we were not smart enough for college. He was constantly calling the kids stupid or, when referring to my older kiddos, he would say "stupid people shouldn't breed." Isolation was Richard's way to control us, keeping track of us at all times. He did not like me going anywhere, talking to anyone, not even family members. He always kept our vehicles where they would barely make it to the store and back, he monitored my cell phones and emails. He would monitor everything the kids did; he did not want them in sports or any other extracurricular activity unless it benefitted him.

The one that really shocked me was the financial or economic abuse. I did not know that was a form of abuse, but it completely made sense once I did realize it. I never had access to his money, even when we had a joint account. He would spend all of his and some of my money to the point where I could not pay our bills on time. Then with the separate accounts, I was still paying for everything, including his needs and wants, instead of him using his own money. At the end of our marriage he was keeping me from getting a job. He never wanted me to have a job outside of the home, that is why he was supportive of me being self-employed as long as I was making good money. I never spent money on myself. My money went to pay bills, get the kids their necessities and whatever Richard said he needed or wanted. He usually came before the kids too. I blame myself for allowing that to happen. The male privileged also shocked me. I just thought he was a male chauvinistic pig, which he is, but it is also a form of abuse. He said many times that the household chores were the woman's job, taking care of the kids was the woman's job. He never got up at night when the kids were babies, he did not do dishes, did not change diapers, etc. He told me that my job was to take care of the kids, clean the house, have dinner ready for him when he got home from work, and to tend to his manly needs. He made the comment that I was just a sex object, nothing more. The mowing and shoveling he would have the boys or me do because he would have some excuse to why he could not.

Using the children against me is something that he did before, during and after our marriage. If I refused sex, he would hurt one of my kids until I would agree. He threatened to take them away from me from the first couple months after I met him. After I left him, his exact words were that he "would take all my kids away from me because he knew that I could not live without them and he knew I would have no choice but to come back to him." He did take them away with lies and the divorce. He was always minimizing, denying and blaming. He would either tell me that it was not abuse because he was not leaving marks, or he referred to it as disciplining. Many times, he would tell me that such and such did not happen. When he would force himself on me for sex, he would say that a man cannot rape his wife because it is her biblical duty to please him. He always blamed me for him abusing the kids, telling me that if I would not argue with him or reject him then he would not have to go after the kids. Even after the divorce he says everything is my fault. He says that I would not have lost the kids if I would have stayed home where I belonged. That everything going on with the kids is my fault, their attempted suicides were all my fault.

Another term that I became very familiar with is Parental Alienation. It is a form of abuse by proxy. Parental Alienation is when psychological manipulation caused by one parent results in the child being estranged from the other parent. Parental Alienation causes rifts between a parent and child that at one time had a good healthy relationship. Some of my kids were struggling with cognitive dissonance at first. They remembered the abuse and would say that I made Richard abuse them, but then turn around and say there was never any abuse. Richard manipulated them into believing that I made up all the abuse, that it did not really happen. He was able to get them to believe that I did not care about them just because I refused to reconcile our so-called marriage. Making fun of them for wanting to spend time with me or enjoying their time with me is Parental Alienation. Telling the kids that they "are either with him or against him," that "I am the bad side and he is the good side" is Parental Alienation. He told me that if he and I were not together then I needed to sign away my rights. I have heard stories of others who had their exes tell them the same thing, and they signed away their rights thinking that was the better alternative than fighting with the other parent. Family Courts claim that they acknowledge Parental Alienation and that you can sue the alienating parent if you can prove it, but there are millions of people around the world that are fighting this on a daily basis. I had shown proof in court, but the judges here did not care, nor acknowledge it, which is common for courts to ignore. This caused all of my kids to suffer from PTSD, some of them also suffer from Stockholm Syndrome, one was diagnosed with Antisocial Personality Disorder, and one diagnosed with severe Separation Anxiety. They all have high anxiety during certain instances. During the first three years after the divorce, four of my seven kiddos had attempted suicide at least once. Richard had not changed, and I was no longer there to buffer the abuse. Instead of acknowledging the truth, they blamed me for leaving and not being there to protect them from him.

Children will normally align against the good parent and take the side of the angry parent in cases of Parental Alienation Syndrome. This happens because they are not afraid of a loving parent. They do not fear their nurturing parent's disapproval, or rejection, but they fear the abusive parent and will align with them in order to avoid their wrath or rejection. A loving, nurturing parent does not reject their child anyway but in this confusion, the children are in survival mode. If you are a good parent, and your ex is a pathological narcissist, then they can turn your child against you to make your child hate you without real cause. It is a nightmare.

I have been in support groups for Parental Alienation also. One man was alienated from his little boy by his ex-wife. He could not get the courts to help him when she would refuse to let him use his court ordered visitations to see his son. He also had a recording of her threatening to kill their two-year-old son because she wanted him to come back to her. She made good on that threat along with killing herself. Because the courts and law enforcement did not listen to this man, he had to bury his child. One woman had been a stay-at-home mom, being the primary caregiver to her three children. She left her husband after finding out that he was molesting their daughter. She had counseling reports plus other documentation proving sexual abuse and the courts gave her husband full custody of all the children. As of the last I heard, she has not seen her kids since that court hearing. Another lady, was also a stay-at-home mom, had two kiddos, a boy and a girl, and pregnant with twins. While she was attending her own baby shower, her husband packed up his SUV, showed up to the baby shower to get the two kiddos and announced in front of everyone that he was leaving her with the kids in tow. He filed for divorce and got everything, including full custody of the two older kids, while she did not even get visitations. After a few years, he ended up kidnapping the twins. She tried to file a kidnapping report with no luck. By the time they got to court, the twins had been with him for a few months and already in a new school, so the judge again ruled in favor of him. He again received full custody of all four kids, and she did not even get visitation rights. Once in a while the kids would secretly contact her or send her pictures of themselves but that their dad was not allowed to know. Eventually all contact stopped, but she is one of the biggest advocates for Parental Alienation. Another man has joint custody and court ordered visitations, but his ex has refused to let him see his two girls for the past several years. He has taken her to court for contempt and to change the order since he has proof that she deals drugs, but the judges ruled in her favor, telling her that she should allow him to see his girls, but no consequences were given. He still has not seen his children. Almost daily there are parents who are victims of Parental Alienation who commit suicide. These could be lessened if not stopped with more education and acknowledgment.

Again, I noticed a pattern. Whether anyone realized they were doing it or not is not for me to say, but Parental Alienation is nothing new. I believe it has been around for decades. My dad was alienated from his mother. I was alienated from my dad. Richard and my mother alienated me from my kids. I believe Richard and Dave's wife alienated Dave from my kids. Dave's mother has been somewhat alienated from some of her kids and grandkids. Richard's mom was alienated from him. I have tried very hard over the years to keep Dave's and Richard's biological mothers involved with my children. Especially now that I know what it is and how it feels. I fear the same for some of my grandchildren.

All children should be able to freely have healthy relationships with both parents whether they are still married or divorced. As long as the child is safe, not in any imminent danger, then no one should interfere. The children should not be forced to pick between parents. They should be supported to love and care about both parents. Being jealous or just because one parent is not getting what they want from the other, should not determine whether the child gets to see the other parent. In almost all cases of Parental Alienation, the alienated parent is a good, loving parent who has done nothing wrong to lose their kiddos. In many cases, the alienating parent has shown other abusive behavior.

 My goal with getting my psychology degree was to help victims of abuse. The more I learned, I realized that I still want to help victims of abuse but also specialize in Parental Alienation. It is harder said than done though. I was scared for many years, partly because I did not know that there were others in my situation and did not know where to find resources that I could have had access to. Besides writing this book to heal from my own emotional pain, I want others to know that they are not alone and there are places to go and people who will help. I still get severe anxiety and have panic attacks on occasion. I now seem to have a bit of a narcissist and abuser radar, because I get anxiety when I am around people who exhibit those behaviors. Listening to my gut instinct is somewhat hard for me, but I have realized it is in my best interest to do so. If you find yourself in a situation, please reach out safely. If you cannot right away, learn some coping mechanisms to help get you through until such time arises. When I am feeling anxious or needing to calm my mind and body, I have found a few different things that help me. The smell of lilacs or the sound of a waterfall soothes me. I put lilac scented lotion on my hands, cup my hands around my nose, close my eyes and envision being in a field of lilacs with a waterfall in the distance. My counselor also suggested I sometimes use a color to 'shower through me' to wash away the anxiety. I do this by closing my eyes and imagining a shower with my color. Everyone will have their own technique, but it is helpful.

If you are in an abusive situation, call for help, give all details even if you do not think they are important, especially if you are in imminent danger, let them know so they can make the right arrangements or give you the right resources. No matter how scared you are they will understand and help the best way possible. If you get away, do not go back. Abusers and narcissists do not change. A narcissist will manipulate you very well into getting you back into their trap. There is light at the end of the tunnel once you get through your healing process.

Every person in the world knows at least one person who is or has been a victim of abuse whether they know it or not. More than twelve million people a year are victims of abuse. More than 35% of women and more than 28% of men have experienced abuse in their lifetime. These are only statistics for known cases. These numbers do not reflect the victims who stay hidden. In most cases, including rape, the offenders are a family member or intimate partner.

If you need to find resources, please contact:
National Domestic Violence Hotline
1-800-799-SAFE (7233)
Thehotline.org/help

Author Bio

CJ Bralt resides in Iowa with the love of her life. She enjoys family time with her children and grandchildren. She is a mother of seven children, has a degree in Psychology, and survivor of decades of abuse. She is an advocate for Parental Alienation and wants to educate the world. Her writings are mostly non-fiction with some fiction. She writes hoping to help others. www.cjbralt.com

Made in the USA
Middletown, DE
15 April 2022